Stage Left

Stage Left

The Development of the American
Social Drama in the Thirties

by

R. C. Reynolds

The Whitston Publishing Company
Troy, New York
1986

Library of Congress Catalog Card Number 85-52030

ISBN 0-87875-311-7

Printed in the United States of America

CONTENTS

ACKNOWLEDGEMENTS

The completion of this book would not have been possible without the aid and cooperation and support of a great many people, not the least of which have been my family and friends. I am deeply indebted to the University of Tulsa faculty, in particular Professor Daniel Marder, for their active support of this project. I also am grateful to the librarians and staff of the Humanities Research Center of the University of Texas at Austin for their assistance in locating out of print and rare materials. Additionally I would like to thank the faculty and administration of Lamar University for providing two separate grants to assist me in preparing the final manuscript.

A version of the concluding chapter of the manuscript appeared, in slightly altered form, in the *Journal of the American Studies Association of Texas* (1981). I wish to thank the editor, Marvin Harris, for permission to reprint.

Finally: I would like to thank the following publishers, authors, and copyright owners for permission to quote from the sources listed:

Alfred A. Knopf, Inc., for *The Fervent Years: The Story of the Group Theatre and the Thirties* by Harold Clurman, copyright @ 1975, reprinted with permission of Alfred A. Knopf, Inc., copyright @ 1945, 1957, 1973, 1975, by Harold Clurman; Cornell University Press, for *Theatre in America: The Impact of Economic Forces 1870-1967.* by Jack Poggi, cited by permission of the publisher; Crown Publishers, Inc., for *The Theatre in Our Times* by John Gassner, copyright @ 1954 by John Gassner, used by permission of Crown Publishers, Inc.; Edward Arnold, Ltd., for *American Theatre* by John Russell Brown and Bernard Harris, reprinted with permission of the publisher; Elizabeth Dos Passos, for *U.S.A.* by John Dos Passos, cited with permission of Elizabeth Dos Passos; Francis Fergusson, for *The Human Image in Dramatic Literature* by Francis Fergusson, cited by permission of the author; Frederick Ungar Publishing Company, Inc., for Clifford Odets: *The Thirties and After* by Edward

Murray, and for *Lillian Hellman: Playwright* by Doris Falk, both used by permission of Frederick Ungar Publishing Company, Inc.; Gerald Weales, for *Clifford Odets: Playwright* by Gerald Weales, cited by permission of the author; Grove Press, Inc., for *Six Plays by Clifford Odets* by Clifford Odets, including citations from *Waiting For Lefty*, copyright © 1935, renewed by Clifford Odets 1962, *Awake and Sing!*, copyright © 1933, 1935, renewed by Clifford Odets 1961, 1962, *Paradise Lost*, copyright © 1935, renewed by Clifford Odets, 1963, *Golden Boy*, copyright © 1937 by Clifford Odets, copyright © renewed 1965 by Nora Odets and Walt Whitman Odets, *Till the Day I Die*, copyright © 1935, renewed by Clifford Odets 1962, reprinted with permission of Grove Press, Inc.; Harcourt Brace Jovanovich, Inc., for excerpts from "The Philadelphia Story," copyright © 1939, 1940, 1942 by Philip Barry and Ellen S. Barry, copyright © 1939 by Dodd, Mead & Co., Inc., © 1966, 1967, 1969 by Ellen S. Barry, reprinted from *States of Grace: Eight Plays by Philip Barry*, edited by Brendan Gill, by permission of Harcourt Brace Jovanovich, Caution: All rights are strictly reserved, inquiries on all rights should be addressed to Harcourt Brace Jovanovich, Inc., 757 Third Avenue, New York, New York 10017; Indiana University Press, for *Drama and Commitment: Politics in the American Theatre of the Thirties* by Gerald Rabkin, reprinted by permission of Indiana University Press; MacMillan Publishing Company, for *The Splintered Stage: The Decline of the American Theatre* by R. H. Gardner, reprinted with permission of the publisher; Methuen & Co., Ltd.; *Drama and the Dramatic* by S. W. Dawson, cited by permission of the publisher; New York University Press, for *The Complete Plays of William Dean Howells*, edited by Walter J. Meserve, cited with permission of New York University Press; Oxford University Press, for *Contours in Time: The Plays of Eugene O'Neill*, and for *The Political Stage* by Malcolm Goldstein, both cited by permission of Oxford University Press; Random House, Inc.; for *Dead End* by Sidney Kingsley, and for *Federal Theatre Plays*, edited by Pierre De-Rohan, and for *The Little Foxes* by Lillian Hellman, all cited with permission of Random House, Inc.; Richard Moody, for *Lillian Hellman: Playwright* by Richard Moody, reprinted by permission of the author; Russell and Russell, Inc.; for *"Modernism" in Modern Drama: A Definition and an Estimate* by Joseph Wood Krutch, copyright © 1953 by Joseph Wood Krutch, copyright renewed, reprinted with permission of Russell and Russell;

Simon and Schuster, for *American Playwrights, 1918-1938: The Theatre Retreats from Reality* by Eleanor Flexner, cited by permission of Simon and Schuster, a Division of Gulf and Western Corporation; Stanley B. Doyle, Jr., for *Upstage: The American Theatre in Performance* by John Mason Brown, reprinted by permission of the Executor of the Estate of John Mason Brown, Stanley B. Doyle, Jr.; Susan Amanda Lawson, for *Theory and Technique of Playwriting* by John Howard Lawson, and for *Marching Song* by John Howard Lawson, both cited by permission of Susan Amanda Lawson; Twayne Publishers, for *Philip Barry* by Joseph Patrick Roppolo, copyright © 1965, and for *Maxwell Anderson* by Alfred S. Shivers, copyright © 1976, both reprinted with permission of Twayne Publishers, a Division of G. K. Hall & Company, Boston; University of California Press, for *The Anatomy of Drama* by Alan Reynolds Thompson, 2nd edition, cited with permission of the University of California Press; University Microfilms International; The University of Missouri Press, for *The Drama of Attack: Didactic Plays of the American Depression* by Sam Smiley, cited by permission of the University of Missouri Press and the author, copyright © 1972 by Sam Smiley.

INTRODUCTION

In *American Playwrights, 1918-1938: The Theatre Retreats from Reality* Eleanor Flexner argues that Eugene O'Neill, Philip Barry, Maxwell Anderson, among others, had turned away from "reality" and had sought "artistic detachment" by writing fantasy, history, and romance. They were not, in her view, facing the grim verities of their time: the depression, the rise of fascism, and the inequitable distribution of wealth, especially in the United States. She despairs of the "direction" of these writers, accusing them of responding more to newspaper critics and a desire for commercial success than to a sense of social obligation, and she feels they should use their talents to illustrate social ills and call for redress.[1]

American Playwrights generally condemns American playwriting, declaring that "our drama has declined with our theatre, and our favorably received plays have been grossly overestimated."[2] Looking back to the days of the "mature drama" of Clyde Fitch, Flexner lauds such plays as *The Truth* and *The City* as "full fledged examples . . . of the drama of ideas, specifically of social comedy"; and she claims that Fitch set the pattern for American writers to follow, though few have done so.[3] Although she sees the work of Eugene O'Neill as hopeful in the twenties, she decries him in the thirties as a self-indulgent romantic who has turned his back on the "drama of ideas" while contending that others, such as Philip Barry, Thornton Wilder, and William Saroyan, have squandered their talents in Hollywood, a town she names "the graveyard of Broadway."[4]

Lashing out at critics who favorably review plays which "amuse, titillate, excite, mock, and afford vicarious enjoyment of pleasures not always countenanced by society,"[5] she finds the only hope for American drama's future in the Federal Theatre Project's plays. Although they "were not very good plays, not very well acted and produced," she writes, their popularity indicated a strong "hunger for the first rate" in playwriting among theatre-goers. They communicated "an understanding and a

vision of life."[6]   In other words, a bad "drama of ideas" which
addresses social wrongs with an eye toward correcting them is
preferable to a "retreating" drama of romantic pap which ignores unpopular notions and caters to critical approval.   She
fears, however, that the younger playwrights of social dedication
will become trapped by Hollywood's lures, cornered by critical
complaint, or driven into "retreat" by the unpopularity of their
material—vital social issues.   But if they do not, she predicts
that they—Lillian Hellman, Clifford Odets, among a very few
others—might have the potential to bring their early promise
to fruition and reverse the "retreat" of the American drama
in the twentieth century.   However, it was O'Neill, not Hellman
or Odets, who would become *the* American playwright of the
twentieth century who would lend a literary distinction to American drama; but that distinction would not be the result of an
examination of social problems.
    More recent critics have taken a tack opposite from Flex-
ner's.   As "apologists" for the American playwrights of the 1930's
(exclusive of O'Neill), they suggest that if the drama of this period
lacks any lasting significance, it is because it moves too far in the
direction of "reality," focusing too much on the economic,
political, and social issues of the day and becoming more polemic
than literary.   These critics, Gerald Rabkin, Michael J. Mendelsohn, Sam Smiley, and Louis Broussard, for example, divide the
American drama of the thirties into two categories: those plays
written only to entertain, garner favorable notices, and sustain
long runs, and those which are didactic, political, and/or propagandistic.   Although they do not agree on which plays belong
in which categories, these critics suggest that the major contribution of the 1930's drama is in polemical *tours de force*.   Sam
Smiley, for example, sees the plays of the thirties more as road
markers in the progress of the social drama than as models of a
universal pattern for the writing of such plays.   He writes: "A
growing recognition of these didactic playwrights is welcome,
but . . . perspective must be maintained."[7]
    In spite of Moses J. Montrose's 1941 statement that "During
recent decades, there is no gainsaying the fact that the American
drama has vastly improved in its technical expression, in the
quality of whatever thought it might possess," certain critics,
including Morris Freedman, Brooks Atkinson, and George Jean
Nathan, have declared the works of John Howard Lawson, Maxwell Anderson, Sidney Kingsley, Lillian Hellman, and Clifford

Odets to be more historical or literary curiosity than dramatic literature; and while they admit that the playwrights in question took their work seriously, they suggest by implication and through direct condemnation that such plays are hardly worthy of consideration as bona fide, literary endeavor.[8]

John Gassner, writing a preface to Flexner's work, states that her perception of a "retreat" in the theatre in the thirties is accurate, but he claims that a proclivity for "mysticism or romanticism" does not prevent a "new life" from emerging in the American drama; and he tempers Flexner's complaint by stating: "despite serious difficulties, American society has revealed a remarkable capacity for producing important theatre, and the one real quarrel with it is that it has merely scratched the surface."[9]   While agreeing with Flexner's condemnation of much of American playwriting, he suggests that the potential for meaningful drama not only exists but that several writers, especially Odets, Hellman, and Saroyan, have already written plays of high quality and social awareness.

In 1922 Arthur Hobson Quinn wrote: "Beside the intellectual and artistic life of a nation, its commercial and industrial achievements are but incidents, and there is no vehicle so powerful and so competent to carry the meaning of America to our assimilated and our unassimilated population as the drama."[10] And in 1935 he responds to voices of complaint by declaring that the "real hope" of American drama rests in the combined excellence of the playwrights: "Actors come and go, but the playwright is a constant factor." He applauds Barry's romantic comedy and the use Maxwell Anderson makes of historical figures and poetic drama, and he despairs of those who join in calling for more "reality" on stage, branding such complaint the "heresy of little souls. . . . According to this theory it makes no difference what one writes about, provided it is an accurate photography of something."[11]   He concludes that the major problems of American drama are clearly related to a paucity of sturdy playwrights and a lack of recognition for their effort; but he does not believe that these problems indicate any decline or "retreat" from artistic integrity.[12]

Gassner and Quinn agree that there is literary value in the plays of the thirties; however, they do not agree as to which playwrights represent the "real hope" of the American drama. Gassner contends that Anderson and Barry represent the very "retreat" he and Flexner perceive; Quinn counters that the romantic and mystical aspect of these two writers was the very thing that places them in the forefront of the decade's dramatic advance. Joseph Wood Krutch suggests that the move from "pre-modern" to "modern" drama in this country is parallel to and synonymous with a movement from "revolutionary" drama (begun by Ibsen and Shaw some three to four decades before in Europe and carried on by O'Neill and Elmer Rice in the United States during the early and mid 1920's) to "classic" drama (represented by Chekhov and Strindberg in Europe and by Anderson and Wilder in this country) during the forties and early fifties.[13] Calling the drama an "excellent social barometer," Krutch states that its ideas and attitudes are "intended for a wide public" and reflect the concerns and expressions of the day. Although he acknowledges the contributions of such writers as Richard Sheridan and Oliver Goldsmith, Krutch points out that the eighteenth and nineteenth centuries were at once a nadir in terms of literary or artistic drama in all nations and an apex of commercial success for theatres; but in the twentieth century, after the full impact of Ibsen's drama had been felt, he claims that the theatre became the most important species as far as the dissemination of "revolutionary attitudes" is concerned.[14] And it is in the dissemination of such ideas that the division between the points of view of Gassner and Quinn most sharply exists.

Krutch's definitions of "revolutionary" and "classic" drama may be useful in reconciling this schism:

> The effect of a body of literature, especially of what we call "classical" literature, does not depend exclusively upon the argument which it presents or even upon ideas which are explicitly expounded. If it did, then the importance of literature, or at least of any except didactic literature, to society would be as slight as unimaginative people often assume that it is.[15]

Hence, he agrees with Quinn that the value of the romantic comedy and history of the thirties has an importance beyond its relevancy to social issues. However, he contends "that a first step by literature in the direction of what might finally become a salvation was taken when playwrights showed a tendency to be more interested in displaying human life against a background of moral assumptions than in presenting the argumentative defense of those assumptions."[16] Thus he defends

Gassner's point that the drama of such questioning writers as Hellman and Odets has merit because of its tendency to present life in front of a backdrop of moral and social issues, or, in Flexner's term, "reality." Krutch stops short of saying that direct demand for social redress is the major function of drama, but he submits that lively, "revolutionary" drama is not only possible in the theatre of the modern period, but that it also specifically exists in such writers as Odets and Wilder.

In Krutch's argument the differences between Quinn and Gassner are mediated. He notes:

> After all, classic drama and revolutionary drama are two different things. The plays of Sophocles, of Shakespeare and of Moliere have a certain intellectual content, but they do not, like the plays of Ibsen, make any attempt radically to alter the intellectual concepts of the audience.[17]

Both types of drama can exist in any given period, he concludes, and the question to be asked is not which type is more deserving of literary distinction but which can be said to be truly "modern."

Krutch, Quinn, and Gassner agree that the drama of the American 1930's is more than literary or historical curiosity. They agree with Eleanor Flexner to the extent that they despair of Hollywood's negative influence on playwrights, and that the successful run of a Broadway show is all too often the only determiner of its literary merit; however, they disagree with her assessment of the period as one of "retreat" and decline.

For Krutch the distinction between "revolutionary" and "classic" drama is a unique and significant one. And for Quinn, Gassner, and others, the degree of commercial success of a given play is an important part of the assessment of its value (in spite of the fact that many critics, including Gassner, rarely make a distinction between musical comedies, parlor farces, comedies of manners, and serious drama).

All these considerations, when combined with the debate over "reality" in the drama and the use of a play as a vehicle for social comment during the period, can be brought together in one central question: Does American playwriting of the 1930's have any inherent literary significance beyond its theatrical or commercial value: If so, does this significance lie in its social commentary, its theatrical technique, or in its artistic (and hence aesthetic and literary) merit?

A majority of critics suggests, more often through their silence on the subject than their outright condemnation, that the United States has produced but one playwright of even second-rate status, Eugene O'Neill. Various speculations could be offered to explain why the work of other playwrights has not been recognized. The traditional and historical view of the playwright as technician rather than professional writer, for example, did not appreciably change until the twenties, after the work of the Provincetown Players and Washington Square Players had emphasized the role of the author of plays as distinct from the role of those who produced them. Although playwrights often enjoyed recognition for those scripts in the theatre of the thirties, the idea of associating a play more closely with its production company, director, or leading actors continued from the era of Clyde Fitch and James A. Herne, who often produced, directed, and took roles in the plays they wrote. Dramatists of the thirties, with few exceptions, confined their ambitions to writing; they were still closely aligned with their production companies--the Theatre Guild, the Group Theatre, the Theatre Union--and this association often obscured their individual efforts as producing writers and artists in their own right.

The commercial nature of the theatre is also a possible reason for the critical neglect of these writers. The economic crisis of the 1930's emphasized this constant determinant of what shows would and what shows would not be produced and what shows would succeed and what shows would fail. Hence, many playwrights are dismissed because they have catered to popular taste rather than having explored new vistas in dramatic themes and experimentation.

Finally, the political didacticism of many plays of the 1930's contributed to a critical bias against favorable consideration of these dramatists. As Sam Smiley notes: "The primary purpose of the author of each of these plays was to make a drama worthy of stage production, but his concurrent goal was to awaken the social consciousness of the audience through the communication of ideas."[18] But the combination of political activism, artistic integrity, and a sensitivity to the commercial nature of the American theatre makes a strong case for regarding the playwrights of this period as serious, creative, literary artists who made a major contribution to American letters. They sought to use their pens to create commercially successful dramas which responded to the chaos and uncertainty of their times, and they attempted to do so through plays which would both survive their contemporary audiences and influence other writers and thinkers:

In 1957 Francis Fergusson summed up the attitude of many critics:

> In 1957 Francis Fergusson summed up the attitude of many critics: What seemed to be American playwriting twenty years ago says little to us now, and our great are without progeny. We have, of course, no permanent theatrical establishment; and if there is an "American Theatre" in some other sense, it has never been identified critically or historically.[19]

Prior to World War I, American theatrical offerings were almost never written by *literati.* In fact, as one surveys the history of American drama, one finds that fewer and fewer plays were written by professional writers of any ilk. Krutch, in his *American Drama Since 1918,* points out that during the nineteenth century, "plays were commonly written either to exploit the talents of popular performers or as entertainments quite frankly upon a level below that of artistic pretension."[20] This was known as the "star system," and through the first decade of the twentieth century scripts commonly came from directors, actors, managers, and even set-designers. Krutch goes on to say that even the best writers of the 1890's and early 1900's can be praised only if they are compared to their contemporary dramaturgists, not to their contemporaries in the novel or poetry.[21]

In 1910 Walter Pritchard Eaton wrote an estimation of Clyde Fitch's work for *Scribner's Magazine,* "The Dramatist as Man of Letters:"

> Now, the novel or story is written to be read, and what it does in type is all it can do. The drama is not even written; it is constructed. And it is constructed to be acted in a theatre of living men and women, with illusive scenery, artificial lights manipulated at will, the tang of actuality about it, and the mood of it created for the spectator by a thousand aids which have no connection with the printed page and do escape the reckoning of the literary critic.[22]

Here Eaton points out a fundamental truth about the modern drama: In order to write a successful play, an author must have an intimate knowledge of the technical apparatus of the physical theatre; not only must he know the potential of stage devices, he must also know their limitations and how to work effectively within them.

With only a few exceptions, such as Thornton Wilder and John Steinbeck, playwrights moved in circles populated by "theatre people" (actors, producers, directors, and technicians), not "literary people" (novelists, poets, and essayists). Although William Dean Howells, Mark Twain, Henry James, Bret Harte, William Faulkner, William Carlos Williams, Gertrude Stein, Edmund Wilson, F. Scott Fitzgerald, and John Dos Passos among other novelists and poets of the "first order" of American letters all wrote and published plays, few had any success. Probably these authors lacked a sense of what "works" on stage. Eaton writes:

> It is obvious that what is most effective in the theatre need not be most effective in type, and what is the literature of the proscenium frame need not be literature of the printed page. That a great many fine dramas are literature . . . does not prove that a great many fine dramas are not. At best it proves, perhaps, that the finest dramas transcend the theatre.[23]

The failure of great literary figures in both the nineteenth and twentieth centuries to produce successful drama can be largely attributed to their tendency to misunderstand the nature of a play as a literary work *in performance.* As S. W. Dawson writes:

> It is characteristic of drama, as of no other form of literature, that it makes an absolute and sustained demand on our attention. A poem or novel can be, indeed often must be, put down and taken up again as we are interrupted or distracted; . . . a play in performance demands our uninterrupted attention.[24]

Eric Bentley has pointed out that Broadway plays are "invariably given to the public in book form,"[25] and this should be sufficient reason for judging them as literature; but others state that a special mental attitude is required to read a play. As Alan Reynolds Thompson states:

> Alone in one's easy chair, to read a play so as to fill out
> its bare skeleton in one's imagination with vivid visualized
> action and expressive tones, is hard. Even professional
> playreaders and actors often neglect dramas of marked
> originality because they cannot fully imagine them as they
> are to be performed.[26]

Hence, drama is a peripatetic literary art; it requires sight, sound, movement, and, most important, audience reaction.

Even though the drama has often been a vehicle for sustained intellectual ideas (especially during the Golden Age of Greek theatre and again in the miracle and morality plays of the Middle Ages), this has not always been the case. In the nineteenth century, for example, the drama's main function was to entertain and only incidentially to inform. But Krutch remarks: "To attempt to define modern American drama in intellectual terms is . . . to be brought face to face with the fact that its intellectual heritage was contemporary literature as a whole, and that individual playwrights often had in common nothing more definite than some sort of participation in characteristically intellectual life."[27] Barry, Anderson, Hellman, and Odets all wrote novels and some wrote poetry with about the same success as the major novelists and poets had with the drama, but they did not go to Paris with the "lost generation"; they did not immerse themselves in some sort of literary "code," and this seems to exclude them from consideration as "American" writers. Yet they did enjoy as much success in their chosen genre as did the champions of the other two. Sometimes their tangible success was more pronounced. Because of the historical nature of the genre and the traditional view of the playwright as technician rather than artist, modern dramatists seem to have been excluded from the fruits of lasting remembrance.

In 1920 William Dean Howells wrote: "Now that Ibsen no longer writes new plays, I would rather take my chances on pleasure and profit with a new American play than with any other sort of new play."[28] Howells' remark was timely, for the "Little Theatres" were already well on their way to exploiting American talent. By 1920 Ibsen and Chekhov were dead, Shaw's best work was finished, and Sean O'Casey was only just appearing on an American stage hungry for innovation and new talent. As the decade wore on and young playwrights emerged, a change in the traditional role of the dramatist occurred. By the 1930's, for the first time in the history of the American theatre, plays were being produced by professional writers, not by actors or managers of companies who penned plays in their spare time, but by full-time artists who wrote for a living. Many, like Philip Barry, took their "training" from college courses such as Professor George Pierce Baker's "47 Workshop"; or, like Maxwell Anderson, they were practicing journalists. Clifford Odets was an undistinguished actor who yearned for the opportunity to see his first play in production, and there were many like Lillian Hellman who simply worked away at their plays until the first script sold. When this younger generation of writers joined the "carryovers" from the Little Theatres, they provided the 1930's with a cadre of experienced, professional writers.

In the 1920's the idea of authorial credit as something important to the success of a play was born in the fame and popularity of Eugene O'Neill's drama; however, during the 1930's this trend became a virtual revolution. The Hollywood practice of paying writers for scripts contributed to the phenomenon somewhat, but the Group Theatre, the Playwright's Company, and the Theatre Guild all actively supported the writer as an autonomous artist whose contribution was as important, if not more important, as that of any other member of the company. Scripts were still bought and sold on the basis of merit, but they were written without specific actors, specific directors, or specific theatres in mind. The "star system" of the pre-World War I decades was over, and the name of the playwright was frequently more important than the name of the actor, director, or production company.

The emphasis during this decade was also on *American* playwrights. The Theatre Guild took the lead from its antecedents, the Provincetown Players and the Washington Square Players, and devoted a great deal of energy to the discovery and promotion of native American playwrights. The Group Theatre, which had emphasized the separation of company from playwright,[29] joined other organizations in sponsoring contests for undiscovered writers; it was to one of these, The New Theatre League's contest, that Odets sent *Waiting For Lefty*. During the ten years of the Group's existence, it performed but one play by a foreign author, *The Case of Clyde Griffiths* by Erwin Piscator, and this was, of course, based on an American novel.[30] Although the Federal Theatre Project performed plays by a variety of foreign playwrights, most of these were historically established classics by Shakespeare and Marlowe or established successes staged as revivals. The Federal Theatre Project's major contributions to "Americanizing" the drama were the establishment of numbers of "grassroots" theatres all across the country and the discovery of several major ethnic playwrights, many of whom collaborated on "The Living Newspaper" plays.[31]

The dramatists of the thirties looked longingly at the national theatres of France and Russia, and they sought to enliven their own drama and to stimulate their own public demand for an American National Theatre by copying those established institutions, not only in terms of techniques and organization, but also by calling for and emphasizing playwriting as an autonomous, literary activity of the stage. The result was a plethora of dramatic works by native writers which can only be seen as an important development in American literature.

At no time in recent history had the relationship between the popularity and the survival of a work been more acute than during the depression years of the 1930's. Of the half-dozen or so companies organized during the decade or carried over from the previous decade, only the Theatre Guild had sufficient financial backing to hold a show open in the face of lagging audience interest or unfavorable notices. Harold Clurman's account of the Group Theatre's history is punctuated with incidents of sacrifice of salary by producer, actor, director, and even playwright in order to keep an unfavorably reviewed play open for another week or two.[32] Because drama must appeal to the widest possible audience and attract the most favorable reviews, musicals, light comedies, and revues, appealing to popular notions, flimsy idealism, and easy sentimentality could outdraw and outlast a more serious effort, regardless of whether it was "classic" or "revolutionary" in nature. Thus, writers such as John Howard Lawson, Albert Maltz, and Paul Peters often attempted to adapt the popular and acceptable forms to their social themes. Other playwrights did not, but very few enjoyed any success at all. One exception was Jack Kirkland's adaptation of Erskine Caldwell's *Tobacco Road,* which became the third longest running play on Broadway. Most critics, however, are quick to point out that audiences were more attracted by the promise of prurient sexual material and controversial language than by whatever social comment Kirkland retained from the novel. Audiences also read the damning reviews of Odets' *Waiting For Lefty* and came to see for themselves what all the fuss was about, inadvertently saving the failing Group Theatre from financial collapse by giving them a member playwright who could "pack a house" with subsequent plays.

The factors which guarantee success for a play—popular support and favorable notices--seem to reduce its value, especially in scholarly circles, for literary critics traditionally abide by an axiom that whatever is "popular" (or for that matter, easily understood) cannot have much literary merit. Krutch has pointed out that few if any literary critics pay serious attention to the literary value of the drama of their own age:

> This was true in Shakespeare's time, when few educated men would have supposed it possible that the Elizabethan drama would one day be considered the chief glory of Elizabethan literature. It is equally true today when the most earnest literary critics seldom devote their attention to any modern dramatist.[33]

James Rosenberg echoes this sentiment when he laments the fact that a Neil Simon comedy would outdraw an Ibsen play almost anywhere.[34]

While the 1930's saw a virtual hey-day for comedies by George S. Kaufman and Moss Hart, for musicals and family dramas, for the sentimental comedy of William Saroyan, it also saw the genius of Maxwell Anderson, Lillian Hellman, and Clifford Odets. Because these latter writers used techniques of showmanship and theatricality in their plays, and because their plays were popular successes as well, modern critics tend to dismiss them as popular writers rather than to consider them as literary artists. Elsewhere Gassner comments that showmanship "can never be allowed to dominate playwriting if dramatists are to achieve the penetration of the major modern novelists."[35] But without that very element the plays of the 1930's might never have run beyond opening night. Often, however, what made the plays of Anderson, Hellman, and Odets popular was less their showmanship than their incorporation of literary themes and devices such as naturalism, allegory, and social relevancy.

The thirties is, therefore, an important decade from the standpoint of the changing role of the writer from technician to artist. Gassner has declared that "the main historical reason" why an "ample body of literary drama" has not been forthcoming since the break the modern theatre made from the "pragmatic older American theatre" is that the "pragmatic theatre" did not regard the drama as literature at all:

> Another purpose of the striving to give our plays literary status was, however, achieved when playwrights acquired the status and privileges or rights nondramatic writers already possessed. During the 1930's the American stage finally became more of a playwrights' theatre than ever before in its history, affording incentive to the playwright not to truckle to popular taste, giving him some necessary measure of control over his playscript, and encouraging him to use modern content, argument and idea into [sic] his work.[36]

Historically, the 1930's demonstrated an intensification of the experimentation carried on before and during the 1920's both in the United States and abroad. Physically, the theatre was more modern. Techniques of lighting, makeup, and costume had come a long way since the nineteenth century candle-and-gas-lit theatres wherein the first drama played in historical dress was performed in 1846.[37] When William Gillette introduced the concept of "realistic action" in *Held by the Enemy* and *Secret Service* in the 1880's and 1890's, few realized that a mode of acting would so profoundly affect the writing of drama.[38] The plays of Clyde Fitch and James A. Herne offered realistic character and witty, mimetic dialogue to audiences who had never seen a drama by Chekhov or Shaw; such efforts seemed timid and naive beside the European "masters" who had been using such techniques for decades. David Belasco's "gross realism," employing live animals on stage, actual fires, running waterfalls, and absolute fidelity to verisimilar detail in set and action, smacks more of the American propensity for spectacle and pageant than serious literary innovation.[39] Gassner points out that these developments indicated a new direction for American playwriting: "The writing had a rough grain of surface realism instead of the varnish of urbane manners present in the English drama not only of Pinero and Henry Arthur Jones, but even in most of the work of their successors."[40] This shift, variously dated between 1910 and 1915 (with the establishment of the Provincetown Players), marks the beginning of a serious literary attitude in the American dramas.

Gassner also notes that during this period the stage "became a notable medium for intellectual discussion, psychological analysis, social conflict and experimentation in theatrical and dramatic art,"[41] and Travis Bogard agrees. "By 1919," he writes, "any man alert to the theatre who was not bound in by the heaviest commercial fetters should have been aware of the turn the American theatre was taking toward the province of art."[42] Therefore, it was a combination of what Gassner calls "surface realism" and others have named "Belascoism" with sustained intellectual ideas and social awareness which stimulated the American writer to further his experiments in all aspects of dramatic art.

One of the most important of these techniques was introduced by Strindberg in the early decades of the century. "Expressionism" was popularized as a dramatic mode by O'Neill and Elmer Rice in the 1920's, and a decade later it became a major part of the naturalistic plays of Odets and Anderson. According to Gerald Rabkin "the constraints of realism were rejected in favor of attempts to re-order experience and sequences of dialogue and bold innovations and scenic designs." By using the expressionist techniques introduced by O'Neill and Rice and others in the 1920's, dramatists were able to present the modern man, according to Rabkin, "in a perennial theme of alienation."[43]

Eric Bentley writes: "Experimentalism in the arts always reflects historical conditions, always indicates profound dissatisfaction with established modes, always is groping towards a new age."[44] The playwrights of the 1930's used the "experimentalism" of earlier decades to open new realms of intellectual, social, and philosophical inquiry. They used and perfected techniques developed by their predecessors; they believed *they* were a "new age"; they proceeded to do and say things no playwright had done or said before. For this reason the 1930's represents the end of one experimental age and the beginning of another.

Regardless of Flexner's complaint, a great number of American dramatists of the 1930's attempted to make their plays sounding boards for social and political reform, setting them, to borrow Krutch's analogy again, in front of a "backdrop" of social issues and moral assumptions which they considered vital to the American public. Often their characters mouthed political polemics of the day, and almost just as often, the result was more essay than art. "The protest playwrights," Michael J. Mendelsohn writes, "attempted to interpret their society. In doing so they were no different from hundreds of playwrights who preceded them. They were angrier; they were generally less subtle; they were, with few exceptions, humorless."[45] Mendelsohn's analysis is correct up to a point. The agitation and propaganda ("agit-prop") plays of the late 1920's and early 1930's were offered as straight propaganda. Performed without professional actors, stages, regular rehearsals, and often without any scripts beyond a bare outline of action, these plays did not pass for literary endeavor then and they should not now; their function was to stir workers into action. They were, to borrow Krutch's term again, "revolutionary" drama carried to an extreme.

Not all the "protest writers" wrote "agit-prop" plays, however. Some handled social issues in a more universal manner, and they attempted to offer alternative political philosophies and economic theories as panacea for the depression-torn society of their audiences and for mankind in general. When they dealt forcefully with these issues, their work was frequently condemned as propaganda; and many, Hallie Flanagan of the Federal Theatre Project, for example, found themselves under investigation by various governmental agencies both during the 1930's and in the decade following World War II.[46]

The development of modern American theatre was, according to John Gassner, "a reflection of social realities in the United States."[47] And it is true that some playwrights such as John Howard Lawson and Clifford Odets offered plays with strong leftist sentiment, and Marxist propaganda, plays which dealt with strikes, anti-fascism, and class struggle; however, it is also true that Anderson, Hellman, and others wrote plays about social evils of a different kind such as political and social corruption, housing problems, and the lack of understanding between peoples within a social framework. The approach to such problems taken in *The Children's Hour* or *Winterset* is different from that taken in *Waiting For Lefty* or *Marching Song* in that the former group depicts the problems and dramatizes their effects, and the latter group dramatizes the problem and calls for action in a demand for immediate redress. Yet the "apologists" have treated the entire decade's drama as political didacticism. When selected plays such as Hellman's *The Little Foxes* or Anderson's *High Tor* are singled out for comparison, they are regarded as unique examples of artistic accomplishment in an age committed to political activism. Just as the stigma of commercial theatre and popular writer is extended to cover all the drama of the period, so is the stigma of "leftist" propaganda often extended by many critics to cover even the most apolitical drama of the 1930's such as the historical drama of Maxwell Anderson or the romantic fantasies of William Saroyan.

Gassner has written elsewhere that "a vital theatre is communal, drawing its sustenance from the manners and interests of common folk, it explores local customs, finds a common bond in a people's legends and heroes, and celebrates both its labors and its dreams."[48] This definition is possibly a more appropriate assessment of the dramatic product of the 1930's than Mendelsohn's accusation that it was primarily "doctrinaire speeches in Marxist Morality Plays," or Flexner's complaint that it "retreated from reality."

Certainly there were an appreciable number of Marxists and Communists among the thirties' dramatists;[49] but most writers understood that a play could not succeed commercially, and hence any other way, if it fell into invective or preachment at the expense of entertainment. Certain playwrights made Herculean efforts to wed polemic and literary endeavor, not by "masking" their social or political arguments with plot and character, but by honestly examining the society they observed around them and by using such techniques as literary naturalism to demonstrate the hopelessness of individual aspirations in the face of seemingly omnipotent social forces of environment, or or the futility of dreaming in a world of nightmarish reality.

Occasionally their attempts were wildly successful, as Clifford Odets demonstrated in *Lefty* and *Golden Boy*; occasionally the arguments were not political at all, as Lillian Hellman demonstrated by attacking intolerance in *The Children's Hour*. Even the plays of Philip Barry and Maxwell Anderson made social comment, and herein lies the chief literary accomplishment of the decade. These writers sought to unite social commitment with artistic commitment. Although only a few managed to strike the proper synthesis between the two, the continuing search for a play which both entertained *and* informed marks the decade as a period of major development in the American drama. For not only did the experimentation of these writers in both form and content finally yield a mature, responsive, and relevant social drama, it also established an identity for the drama in the United States.

The traditional view of the professional writer as technician rather than literary artist, the historical view of the theatre as

commercial enterprise rather than artistic endeavor, and a reluctance to deal with writers and works of a politically unpopular nature have all combined to shove the dramatist of the 1930's
out of the mainstream of American literature. Further, any
comparison between genres must take into account the "state
of the art." Jack Poggi speaks for a number of critics:

> No body of dramatic literature comparable to the best
> American fiction and poetry has been created in this
> country. Unless one chooses to regard Eugene O'Neill
> in the same class with Walt Whitman, Mark Twain, and
> F. Scott Fitzgerald (perhaps the only reason for doing
> so is that he is the best the theatre has to offer), it is
> impossible to be very cheerful about the achievements
> of the American drama.[50]

And John Gassner laments that American drama is possibly
"the greatest *sub-literary* [his italics] drama"[51] in the history
of the Western theatre. But both these comparisons are unfair.
The novel has enjoyed a straight line of development over more
than two centuries of celebration and acclaim. Poetry has a
tradition of development and study that extends even further
in time than written literature. The drama, however, had lain
dormant for centuries as an active literary form, and the 1930's
marks a climax of its most recent emergence.

Mendelsohn has stated that the plays of the 1930's, particularly those of protest, "provided the most exciting theatre
in the period between the wars."[52] It represents a maturation
of the genre in this country. It follows a turbulent and uncertain
childhood, an angry and rebellious adolescence, and represents
a *tour de force* of professional ambitious playwrights who may
have failed as often as they succeeded (commercially speaking)
but who left a tradition of dramatic writing which pioneered
new vistas to be more thoroughly explored by the postwar generation.

No study of this decade's drama would be complete unless every one of the hundreds of productions both on and off
Broadway, both in New York and elsewhere across the country,
were considered individually. What I attempt to do is restrict
my study to plays which were actually produced in New York
between 1929 and 1939 by American playwrights and companies.
Although the playwrights in this study are by no means the only

major writers of the decade, I believe that their work is truly representative of the movements and attitudes with which I have identified them. Also, I have tried to select plays from their total bodies of work which best illustrate those movements and attitudes rather than attempting to discuss any individual writer's entire canon or career development.

When Eleanor Flexner published her arguments in 1938 she had no way of knowing that she was writing on the eve of the end of a literary era. Tennessee Williams, Arthur Miller, William Inge, and Edward Albee would all emerge from the forties and fifties to write specifically and often frighteningly "real" drama, dealing not with political or social reform, but cogently and frankly with human relationships in a manner which the 1930's writers could only approach through tactful and tasteful stylization. "To puritan eyes," Gerald Rabkin writes, "art is eternally suspect, eternally the instrument of the devil."[53] The playwrights of the 1930's actively attempted to make art an instrument of the people, a spokesman for and arbiter of their problems, and hopefully a source of their ideas for change. Maxwell Anderson spoke for many when he wrote: "Our theatre is the one really living American Art."[54]

The development of the American drama during the nineteen thirties saw the establishment of the social drama as a permanent part of the American stage. As Krutch puts it, it was drama "whose moral, intellectual or social implications involve a revolution in the attitude of audience toward moral, intellectual or social questions."[55] Playwrights of this period sought to interpret life by penetrating what O'Neill called "the unreal real . . . the surfaces of life,"[56] by revealing the truth of human relationships and the effects of social institutions on those relationships. By blending the "realism" of the stage with naturalism and expressionism these writers hoped to expose the modern human condition in order to achieve an aesthetic drama which was at once socially relevant, artistically sound, and commercially successful.

Three distinct stages of development are evident in the decade beginning with the first years of the depression: The first phase, 1929-1933, saw attempts at "hard-line" Marxist drama by such writers as Claire and Paul Sifton and Elmer Rice fail while the social comedy of writers like Philip Barry and S. N. Behrman succeeded. It moved from mild lampooning of mores and convention to biting political satire as is seen in Maxwell

Anderson's *Both Your Houses*. The second phase, 1933-1936, saw the advent of the social critics on stage as Marxist and Communist didacticians, whose plays such as Clifford Odets' *Waiting For Lefty* or Sidney Kingsley's *Dead End* synthesized the elements of agit-prop with the more acceptable forms of Broadway plays to offer a drama which declaimed, exhorted, and informed its audience but entertained it as well. As this synthesis continued to influence drama through such companies as the Federal Theatre Project, the third phase, 1937-1939, began; and a softening of the "hard-line" Marxist position gave way to attempts to synthesize political and social activism with the "well-made" play such as Odets' *Golden Boy* or Hellman's *The Little Foxes* and ultimately came full circle as Philip Barry's *The Philadelphia Story* effectively combined social comedy and social criticism into a play which illustrated the need for unity and understanding between all elements of American society on the eve on an international crisis.

Although many of the issues which are central to the drama of this decade are now long past, the contribution represented by these playwrights is significant to the development of American drama in the twentieth century. Rather than being either a "retreat" from reality or an exercise in polemic, the social drama of the thirties provided a cornerstone for subsequent writers and brought the American drama into the "modern" period.

NOTES

[1] Eleanor Flexner, *American Playwrights, 1918-1938: The Theatre Retreats from Realty,* with a Preface by John Gassner (1938; rpt. New York: Simon and Schuster, 1966), p. 26. Reprinted with permission of Simon and Schuster, a Division of Gulf and Western Corporation.

[2] *Ibid.*, p. ix.

[3] *Ibid.*, pp. 27-28.

[4] *Ibid.*, p. 17.

[5] *Ibid.*, p. 3.

[6] *Ibid.*, p. 12.

[7]Sam Smiley, *The Drama of Attack: Didactic Plays of the American Depression* (Columbia: University of Missouri Press, 1972), p. 86.

[8]See, for example, John Russell Brown and Harris Bernard, eds., *American Theatre* (New York: St. Martin's Press, 1967); this includes a collection of essays by such writers as John Gassner, Morris Freedman, and others.

[9]John Gassner, "Preface," *American Playwrights, 1918-1939*, p. vii.

[10]Arthur Hobson Quinn, "The Significance of Recent American Drama," *Scribner's Magazine*, 72 (July 1922): 7.

[11]Arthur Hobson Quinn, "The Real Hope for the American Theatre," *Scribner's Magazine* 97 (January 1935): 35.

[12]*Ibid.*, p. 33.

[13]Joseph Wood Krutch, *"Modernism" in Modern Drama: A Definition and an Estimate* (Ithaca, New York: Cornell University Press, 1953; rpt. New York: Russell & Russell, Inc., 1962), passim. Copyright 1953 Joseph Wood Krutch; copyright renewed. Reprinted with permission of Russell and Russell.

[14]*Ibid.*, pp. 2-4; here Krutch is following a pattern of critical opinion espoused by a number of dramatic scholars, viz: Sheridan and Goldsmith were largely exceptions to the rule of their own time. Phyllis Hartnoll, ed. *The Oxford Companion to the Theatre*, 3rd ed. (New York: Oxford University Press, 1967) states, for example, that Sheridan's "best play," *The School for Scandal*, is largely a derivation of the wit and manners of Restoration Comedy, although it has "none of the licentiousness" (p. 881); and it also states that both Sheridan and Goldsmith were "far in advance of the drama" of their time (p. 397). Ibsen's early poetic drama, beginning with *Cataline* (1850) and terminating with *Peer Gynt* (1867), would seem to dispute Krutch's point; however, the Norwegian's reputation was not widely known outside Europe until his first English production was staged as *Quicksands (The Pillars of Society)* in December, 1880, and he did not enjoy wide acclaim in England until the late 1890's. In the United States, the first Ibsen play to be produced which had popular impact was *A Doll's House* in 1889, (Oxford, pp. 459-461); hence, Krutch's point is that in terms of the overall theatre in England and the United States, little in the way of "revolutionary attitudes" which characterize so much of Ibsen's work (*Hedda Gabler, A Doll's House, Enemy of the People*, etc.) was being produced during the eighteenth and nineteenth centuries.

[15]Krutch, p. 110.

[16]*Ibid.*, p. 112.

[17]*Ibid.*, p. 108.

[18]Smiley, p. 113.

[19]Francis Fergusson, *The Human Image in Dramatic Literature* (New

York: Doubleday & Co., Inc., 1967), p. 3. Reprinted with permission of the author.

[20] Joseph Wood Krutch, *The American Drama Since 1918* (New York: Random House, 1939), p. 12.

[21] *Ibid.*

[22] Walter Pritchard Eaton, "The Dramatist as Man of Letters: The Case of Clyde Fitch," *Scribner's Magazine* 46 (April 1910): 490.

[23] *Ibid.*, p. 491.

[24] S. W. Dawson, *Drama and the Dramatic* (London: Methuen & Co., Ltd., 1970), p. 12. Reprinted with permission of the publisher.

[25] Eric Bentley, *The Playwright as Thinker: A Study of Drama in Modern Times* (New York: Harcourt Brace & Co., 1946), p. xiv.

[26] Alan Reynolds Thompson, *The Anatomy of Drama* 2nd ed. (Berkeley and Los Angeles: University of California Press, 1946), p. 2. Reprinted with permission of the publisher.

[27] Krutch, *The American Drama Since 1918*, pp. 10-11.

[28] Howells, William D., *The Complete Plays of W. D. Howells*, ed., with an introduction by Walter J. Meserve (New York: New York University Press, 1960), p. 123. Reprinted with permission of the publisher.

[29] Gerald Weales, "The Group Theatre and Its Plays," *American Theatre*, John Russell Brown and Harris Bernard, eds. (New York: St. Martin's Press, 1967), pp. 68-69.

[30] *Ibid.*

[31] Jane Dehart Mathews, *The Federal Theatre: 1935-1939: Plays, Relief, and Politics* (Princeton: Princeton University Press, 1967), passim.

[32] Harold Clurman, *The Fervent Years: A Story of the Group Theatre and the Thirties* (New York: Harcourt Brace Jovanovich, 1975), pp. 98-126, passim.

[33] Krutch, *"Modernism" in Modern Drama*, p. 1.

[34] James Rosenberg, "European Influences," *American Theatre*, Brown and Bernard, eds., p. 60.

[35] Gassner, *The Theatre in Our Times: A Study of the Men, Materials and Movements In the Modern Theatre*, (New York: Crown Publishers, 1954) p. 45. Used by permission of Crown Publishers.

[36] John Gassner, *Dramatic Soundings: Evaluations and Retractions Culled from 30 Years of Dramatic Criticism* (New York: Crown Publishers, 1968), pp. 248-249.

[37] Barnard W. Hewitt, *Theatre U.S.A.: 1665-1957* (New York: McGraw-Hill Book Co., 1959), p. 11.

[38] Arthur Hobson Quinn, *The History of the American Drama from the Civil War to the Present Day*, 2 vols. (New York: F. S. Crofts & Co., 1937), 2:212.

[39] Lisa-Lone Marker, *David Belasco: Naturalism in the Theatre* (Princeton: Princeton University Press, 1975), passim.

[40] John Gassner, *The Theatre in Our Times*, p. 283.

[41] *Ibid.*, p. 6.

[42] Travis Bogard, *Contour in Time: The Plays of Eugene O'Neill* (New York: Oxford University Press, 1972), p. 51. Reprinted with permission of the publisher.

[43] Gerald Rabkin, *Drama and Commitment: Politics in the American Theatre of the Thirties* (Bloomington, Indiana: Indiana University Press, 1964), p. 29.

[44] Bentley, *The Playwright as Thinker*, p. xxv.

[45] Michael J. Mendelsohn, "The Social Critics on Stage," *Modern Drama* 6 (December 1963): 284.

[46] Mathews, passim.

[47] Gassner, *The Theatre in Our Times*, p. 282.

[48] Gassner, *Dramatic Soundings*, pp. 256-257.

[49] Malcolm Goldstein, *The Political Stage: American Drama and the Theatre of the Great Depression* (New York: Oxford University Press, 1974), p. 57.

[50] Jack Poggi, *Theatre in America: The Impact of Economic Forces: 1870-1967* (Ithaca, New York: Cornell University Press, 1968), p. xix. Reprinted with permission of the publisher.

[51] Gassner, *Dramatic Soundings*, p. 249.

[52] Mendelsohn, "The Social Critics on Stage," p. 277.

[53] Rabkin, *Drama and Commitment*, p. 122.

[54] Maxwell Anderson, "A Prelude to Poetry in the Theatre," *Winterset* (Washington, D. C.: Anderson House, 1935), p. x.

[55] Krutch, *"Modernsim" in Modern Drama*, p. 42.

[56] Bogard, *Contour in Time*, p. 299.

THE SOCIAL COMEDY: DRAMA WHICH REFLECTS LIFE

A social drama, according to Gerald Rabkin, is a play which suggests "social alternatives, either reformist or radical," or a play which demands "personal or collective action."[1] The majority of the plays of social consciousness produced during the depression years fulfill Rabkin's requirements. Prior to 1933-34, however, few "radical" plays calling for"collective action" enjoyed much success at all in the commercial theatre.

During the late twenties the most successful social drama was staged in the form of high comedy which usually offered a hero with little to lose engaging in a personal rebellion against the forces of big business or industry. Although the hero was often accused, as is Johnny Case in Philip Barry's *Holiday*, of being "un-American," he generally demands his personal freedom of thought and own way of life without making a pronounced social commitment. While Barry and others, such as George S. Kaufman and his various collaborators, managed to include criticism of social programs and economic attitudes in such plays, the primary purpose of the social comedy was to entertain an audience, not inform it or arouse it to action.

In reaction to the idea that drama's sole function was to entertain, however, several playwrights, including Lawson and Elmer Rice, joined with younger and virtually unknown writers such as Paul Peters, Albert Maltz, and Claire and Paul Sifton in offering more didactic plays which were frequently communistic and always leftist in philosophy and tone. Although many of these leftist writers banded together in group-oriented companies dedicated to staging socially significant plays which put forth a collective idea, few enjoyed more than modest success even off-Broadway. Their announced intention to inform first and entertain only incidentally defeated their effort to compete with the more palatable social comedy as it had existed in the late twenties.

By 1933, however, a further development occurred. In Hegelian terms, the social comedy with its emphasis on indivi-

dual rebellion and mild reform represented a "thesis" for successful drama on the commercial stage. Against it, the louder but
less successful social critics posed an "antithesis" which demanded collective action and called for immediate social change.
A "synthesis" was created. It attempted to achieve commercial
success by entertaining its audience through romance and comedy
and managed to make significant social comment by informing
its audience of the evil and corruption the playwrights saw in the
social and economic chaos around them. The emphasis on individual action remained, but it was not a selfish or hollow demand for personal freedom. Incorporating the collective idea
and even radical action, this synthesis exhibited the hero as a
leader who stirred the masses to act.

Although such plays as Maxwell Anderson's *Both Your
Houses* (1933) and S. N. Behrman's *Rain from Heaven* (1934)
were hardly Marxist or communistic in their appeal or message,
they were seriously critical of social institutions and prevailing
national attitudes concerning everything from anti-semitism
to the self-perpetuating evil of commercial wealth. These plays
contained "calls to action," but they were couched in "well-
made dialogue" aimed at other characters on stage rather than
at the audience. The design of this drama was to create a public
arousal through knowledge and sentiment rather than through
the preachments of the turgidly political drama of the avowed
leftists; in other words, they wished to evoke what Horace called
in the *Ars Poetica* the "pleasure and profit" idea of combining
a "sermon" with a "tickle."[2]

The social drama of the thirties grew from a precocious
comedy, gently poking fun at national ills in the late twenties,
to a keen satiric comedy by 1933. It had become palatable to
audiences less because the patrons themselves were concerned
over political and economic issues than because the playwrights
learned that to use drama effectively as a weapon of social change,
they must make it both entertain and inform; it must, as John
Lily put it in his satirical prose work, *Euphues: The Anatomy
of Wit,* present social criticism in the form of "sugar coated
pills."

On November 26, 1928, at Plymouth Theatre in New York
City, a new play, *Holiday*, opened. This comedy was a major
success for Philip Barry; critics and audiences received it as
another pleasant offering by a writer who made his career in
the past decade by lightly lampooning the very rich and uphold-

ing the spirit of individuality and rebellious youth. Barry's plays of the twenties were notoriously "well-made" and professionally staged. *Holiday*, like its immediate predecessor, *Paris Bound*, follows a standard "high comedy" formula of the twenties: boy meets girl, boy loses girl, and boy finds girl, adding only the interesting twist that the girl boy finds is not the one he loses.

Johnny Case, the protagonist of the play, is a "self-made, up by his own bootstraps" attorney who has devoted most of his life to putting together a nest egg. As a result of some shrewd stock market speculation, he has made a good deal of money upon which he intends to take an extended holiday and enjoy living while he is young. On his first vacation ever he meets and falls in love with Julia Seton, daughter of a stocks and bonds magnate, Edward Seton. The discovery that Julia has family money fits in nicely with his plans since he will now be free to take Julia with him on his holiday without worrying about her welfare. But Julia, following her father's lead, dismisses such foolish notions as idle dreaming, and with her father's reluctant blessing, the wedding is planned.

Julia's spoiled and priggish nature is off-set by her sister, Linda, who is rebellious and independent in spite of the fact that she and her sister have shared the same privileges and come from the same social structure. She spends almost the entire play trying to convince Julia that Johnny's intentions to retire at thirty are sincere and urging her to go along with his plan. As the wedding is announced, Johnny is introduced to two sets of friends, the Seton Crams and the Potters, who offer him pictures of what his life will be like depending upon whether he follows his original decision to go away and enjoy his money, or whether he abides by Julia's plan for his life which includes working in his future father-in-law's company. The Seton Crams are snobbish, upwardly motivated, obnoxiously capitalistic; the Potters are more wealthy than either the Crams or the Setons, but they spend their time and money in pursuit of pleasure and unabashed fun. Predictably, Johnny finds the latter couple more to his liking. Ultimately, however, he gives in to Julia; but as she and her father plan an "itinerary" for both their honeymoon and the next five years of their lives, he rebels and leaves Julia and her father in mid-plans. He will take his holiday alone.

Realizing that Julia has completely given up on Johnny, Linda suddenly understands that she also wants to rebel against the kind of life her sister and father represent. She discovers that she believes in Johnny's dreams and his plans, and she realizes that she can escape her life in the Seton house and social circle simply by following him:

> You've got no faith in Johnny, have you Julia? His little
> dream may fall flat, you think--yes! So it may! What
> if it should? There'll be another—the point is, he does
> dream! Oh I've got all the faith in the world in Johnny.
> Whatever he does is all right with me. If he wants to sit
> on his tail, he can sit on his tail. If he wants to come back
> and sell peanuts, Lord how I'll believe in those peanuts![3]

She leaves her dumbfounded sister and father and hurries to catch Johnny's boat, escaping the world of society and capital for a world of dreams.

On the surface *Holiday* appears to be nothing more than a formula high comedy, typical in plot and character of other such plays in the high prosperity decade of the twenties. While Barry's principal characters, Johnny Case and Edward Seton, respectively represent conflicting attitudes of a working man and a wealthy capitalist, Johnny could hardly be described as a blue-collar "stormbird" of the working class; and Edward, for all his insensitivity, is not a greedy, oppressive, capitalistic demon. The points of view expressed by these and the other characters seem diluted through the material success and wealth surrounding the whole situation, and Johnny's demand for holiday—his personal rebellion—seems particularly selfish when one considers that he obtained the means of his escape through speculation and chance and that he has very little to lose by going his own way. But given the set of events which would transpire shortly after the play's run, *Holiday* can also be seen as an ironic comment on the end of a raucous party and a foreshadowing of a major change in attitude among American dramatists.

The first act of *Holiday* is set in "mid-December, this year" (p. 3), 1928. The second takes place New Year's Eve, 1928, and the final act occurs in mid-January, 1929. In the first month of the last year of the decade, Johnny Case, a "working-class stiff" who "made good," quits his job, cashes in his stocks, and leaves for an indefinite holiday on the fruits of his labor. His life to that point represents the fulfillment of every American worker's dream in the twenties. Johnny leaves behind Edward

Seton and Seton's relatives and associates, most of whom inherited their wealth, and all of whom have tied it up in an ill-fated stock market. On Black Friday, October 24, 1929, barely ten months from *Holiday's* final curtain, their affluenc and life-style would be threatened if not destroyed, almost as if in vindication of the wisdom of Johnny's decision.

It would be as unfair as it is untrue to suggest that Philip Barry had an inkling of the financial disaster pending on Wall Street. While speculation fifty years hence about the future of the Johnny Cases and Edward Setons might prove interesting and demonstrate further justification for Linda's perception and Julia's foolishness, it does not prove anything more than the fact that in 1929 Barry sensed that something in the way of misordered priorities existed in the "big business" attitude of the very wealthy in America. Joseph Roppolo notes that Barry's plays in the twenties were almost always plays of "rebellion—against family, against institutionalized morality, against society itself." But it was not blind or simply angry rebellion for the sake of rebellion alone; it was designed to "achieve fulfillment of the individual on his own terms."[4]

In his biographer's words, Barry had entered the profession "on the wave which brought the Washington Square Players and playwrights Eugene O'Neill, Sidney Howard, Elmer Rice, and George S. Kaufman to Broadway."[5] *Holiday* was his ninth production in as many years, and he was securely established by 1928 as a writer of light satire and high comedy, containing what Louis Broussard calls "a certain moralizing purpose."[6] Unlike his contemporaries, however, Barry was not a product of the collective pressures of the literary giants of the "Lost Generation." He did not join the army and march off to France with John Howard Lawson and Elmer Rice; he did not join the intelligentsia of New York's Greenwich Village as Lawson and Sidney Howard had done; and he did not come from the poverty and make-shift life that had produced O'Neill and others of that decade. Barry spent the war years in college, studying under George Pierce Baker, and he enjoyed the fruits of immediate professional success by removing himself from New York almost entirely; he came from a well-to-do family and never knew poverty and artistic frustration.[7] He was, by 1929, a professional playwright of distinction, and *Holiday* marked a high point both for his career to that date and for the social satire in the decade.

Eleanor Flexner, after dismissing some "minor hokum" in the plot, [8] finds *Holiday* to be Barry's best play largely because of his caricature of the big businessman: "Barry's savagely hilarious picture of the capitalist in *Holiday* ranks with the best of those known in the 1930's," she wrote in 1938.[9] Even though his plays were comedies, he always wrote with a purpose; Roppolo points out: "What the critics overlooked. . .was that Barry, even in his 'comedies,' was essentially serious."[10] It was not in Barry's nature to accept mass movements or leftist trends; he maintained his belief in the inherent worth of the individual and saw man as "responsible for all his actions, a creature of God, made in God's image. . .capable of illimitable self-improvement."[11] Barry also understood that this message along with whatever direct social comment he wished to make had to be presented in the form of effective and successful drama; and, as John Gassner puts it, he managed to strike a medium between "social satire and vacuous entertainment."[12]

Barry's last play of the twenties illustrates the plight of an individual who takes a stance against social convention, who throws away an opportunity for grand riches for a chance to learn more about himself and enjoy living life for its own sake. Maxwell Anderson in *Saturday's Children,* produced two years earlier, had probed much the same problem from a different point of view and with less success, and Elmer Rice and John Howard Lawson had also dealt with the problems of individual success and ambition; but none seemed to have Barry's genius for finding the balance between social comment and successful drama. Barry understood as well as most playwrights of his generation that capitalism represented a major threat to individual spirit. Flexner notes: "His antagonist is 'business' and everything it stands for: its goal, way of life, its hostility to originality and individuality. To Barry, 'big business' represents everything he abhors in life."[13] But Barry also understood that his audiences were frequently sympathetic if not aligned with big business concerns, and he viewed the social satire as both an effective and subtle method of criticizing the priorities of his age.

As a writer of comedic entertainment and as a professional in the commercial theatre of the twenties, Philip Barry stuck to his theme: the plight of the individual in a world controlled by the evils of greed and big business. Roppolo points out:

> Barry beat no drums for organized movements. Instead, and always, he found the answer to the world's problems in the individual, who, with his free will, was the source of all the evil in the world and the potential force to conquer that evil.[14]

And Flexner notes that while Barry never deals with the lower or middle class, he does concern himself with all that is evil in "a microscopic section of the population which appears to be making an injudicious use of its advantage."[15] Herein lies the strength of Barry's social comment. He deals with the people and the class he knows best, and he deals with them harshly; but the twenties were over, and a new age demanding a new social perception and a more strident social commitment was beginning.

The depression had a profound effect on Philip Barry. Turning from the satiric platform upon which *Holiday* had been constructed, he began to explore philosophical questions through a different medium which was neither comedy nor tragedy. After joining the established Theatre Guild in 1929, he produced six original plays and one adaptation by 1938; none of these enjoyed the splendid success of his twenties' plays, but all of them represent what Flexner calls his "retreat from reality." Ranging from the melancholy *Hotel Universe* in 1930 to the allegorical and melodramatic *Here Come The Clowns* in 1938, Barry floundered in metaphysical and theological questions. As his own depression increased, so did the bewilderment of his audiences, who found the confusing questions his plays attempted to answer alien and irrelevant to the social chaos going on around them. He had been classified as a writer of comedies; and, as Roppolo points out, the failure of his audiences to accept his thirties' plays was a result of their inability to accept his "serious drama" when the times seemed to call for either optimistic statements, or at least, comic relief.[16] Barry became, as Francis Fergusson states, "a pioneer of a new genre, the serious comedy";[17] but few understood his intent or his newfound sense of humor.

Had Barry stayed with the social satire he might have done well in the thirties. There were audiences aplenty for such light farce as George S. Kaufman and Moss Hart's *You Can't Take It With You*; and the British playwright, Noel Coward, found American audiences and critics most receptive to his comedies of manners; also, revivals of satirical treatments such as Charles MacArthur and Ben Hecht's *Front Page* were staged to the delight of American theatre-goers throughout the decade. Confusing and melancholy philosophical inquiry, however, was depressing to audiences who found the economic plight of their society a grave enough matter, and Barry's attempts at "serious comedy" failed. But the legacy of *Holiday's* attack on the carelessly wealthy, its assertion of the value of individual potential and courage in rebellion against conformity, and its belief in the ultimate triumph of right over wrong was felt throughout the decade.

The social drama of the 1930's would pick up these themes; however, the use of comedy as social comment would undergo dynamic changes. It would become more selective and specific in its targets than Barry had been with his sense of misordered priorities, and it would become more didactic in its social criticism. In the aftermath of Black Friday, playwrights would begin to work for the advent of a significant social drama which would address the ills of an American dream gone haywire. At first, however, they did not understand how to achieve Barry's and others' methods of staging social comment which entertained as well as informed its audience.

The idea of staging didactic social drama was not born in 1929, nor was it a direct by-product of the depression-wracked society it revealed. Social drama, protest drama, proletarian drama had existed in one form or another since the turn of the century. Admittedly, the "thesis play" or didactic drama had rarely made an appearance in the respectable houses on Broadway; however, plays which addressed social concerns often found their way into New York theatres, some by circuitous routes. In 1922, for example, O'Neill's much acclaimed *The Hairy Ape* explored class disparity, and Elmer Rice's *The Adding Machine,* produced in 1923, centered upon the plight of an individual worker who has been replaced by automation after twenty-five year's faithful service to an uncaring business. O'Neill continued to produce successful drama throughout the decade, occasionally venturing to the brink of social drama with such plays as *The Emperor Jones,* again produced in 1922, and *All God's Chillun Got Wings,* produced in 1924, which deal with problems of racism and inter-racial marriage; but his principal interest was in other directions. Although he continued to produce drama for the New York stage through 1934, little of his thirties' drama could be construed as socially significant; and after the closing of *Mourning Becomes Electra* in that year, he remained silent until after World War II. Elmer Rice, on the other hand, joined a growing minority of playwrights, including John Dos Passos and Michael Gold, in producing plays which attempted to expose the cruel realities of proverty, hopelessness, and despair beneath the din of the "Big Party" of the 1920's. Although Rice remained active in the companies and circles which produced social drama during the thirties, and although he offered a number of scripts on social themes (*Street Scene*, 1929, which won the Pulitzer Prize for that year; *Counsellor-At-Law* and *The Left Bank*, 1931; *We, The People*, 1933; and *Between Two Worlds*, 1934), Rice's career in the early years of the depression never regained the high point he achieved in 1923 with *The Adding Machine*.[18]

By far one of the most outspoken of the socially conscious playwrights of the twenties was John Howard Lawson. Although he would later become the chief dramatic spokesman for the Communist Party and a leading leftist playwright and critic, Lawson's reputation as an author of social drama was well established by 1930. *Roger Bloomer*, his first play, was produced in 1923; and, in Harold Clurman's words, it was "fairly typical of the whole post-war generation's awakening to the tragic implications of the American scene."[19] In this comment Cluman is clearly referring to the "Babbit-like" characters Lawson reveals in the play. Essentially the play is the story of the development of one young man, Roger Bloomer; however, between lines of droll comedy, his father, Bloomer, mouths platitudes intended to express the general attitude of Americans in the "Jazz Age." For example, early in the play Bloomer declares: "Poor! Who's poor? There's no poor in America." But when Roger reminds him that he always tells him what a poor childhood he had, Bloomer explains: "That's different; times have changed. I was a poor boy, I sweated and made good. People don't know the meaning of sweat these days—That's the whole cause of this social unrest. No poor in America."[20] Other American attitudes are satirized by Lawson through Bloomer. When Roger states that "Washington had an ideal, Freedom!" and asks "What was Woolworth's ideal?" his father retorts: "To sell big and sell cheap" (p. 8). The entire play takes on an expressionistic mood as dreams and actual happenings mesh in Roger's life. Leaving home, he goes to New York seeking both a job and an education; he finds neither. Ultimately led into crime by a woman he meets, he winds up in prison where he is charged in her death.   Lawson, in what he calls a "dream of pursuit," brings all the characters of the play around Bloomer in a circle as "conventions and proprieties" which threaten him.   The figures become a "mocking orgy of Sex and Obscenity" and threaten him with death.   As he defies them, they come closer to kill him, but the woman whom he had supposedly killed appears as "the dream that will not die" and protects him by driving the other spectres away.   Finally, cleared of the crime, he is left alone, "ready for manhood" (pp. 190-196).   Roger's experience makes him aware of the tragedy of accepting the twenties' vision too literally.   In the mood of the 1920's, however, Lawson's premiere play concentrated on the value of the experience of individual rebellion.

Lawson followed *Roger Bloomer* with a series of plays dealing with various aspects of social oppression: *Processional* (1925), *Nirvana* (1925), *Loudspeaker* (1926), *International* (1927), and *Success Story* (1930).   Each of these plays moved more left in perspective, but each fulfilled the requirements of the commercial establishment to be produced and tested by New York audiences and critics; that is, they contained sufficient entertainment potential in producers' opinions to draw big box office receipts, and they couched their social comment in terms that were not offensive to what the procedures believed were typical audience attitudes:

Writing in the mid-forties, Clurman recalls:

> When Lawson wrote his *Processional,* he called it a "jazz symphony," and although it dealt with the Ku Klux Klan and bloody class war, we thought of the play only from the viewpoint of its artistic style, which we approved for its novelty or disliked for its pretension.   We never dreamed of saying: "This is our world, and it bodes no good."[21]

But that was 1925; and the social drama, if it was to succeed as a commercial device, had to succeed first as a theatrical enterprise.   Making a meaningful statement about the ills of the "Jazz Age" was important; but without a commercially successful play, the message would never be delivered.   By using expressionistic technique and caricature and satire, Lawson was cunningly able to stage social comment which ideally applied the theory of "sermon and tickle."   This led Clurman to regard him as "the most promising playwright in America" at the close of the decade.

During the thirties Lawson's ability to combine theatrical technique with social comment began to break down in proportion to his growing communistic sympathies. Gerald Rabkin notes that "the necessity of social commitment" increased in his work and that from the first play, "Lawson represents the man who was always conscious of his role in society, of his debt to it, and also of its encroachments upon his individual conscience."[22] However promising his work appeared in the late twenties, Lawson's plays became increasingly didactic, and it was this growing emphasis on informing the audience at the expense of entertaining it that marked his decline (as with Rice) as a successful voice in the drama of the early depression years.

The development of social drama in the thirties was in large part an extension of the twenties' work of men like Lawson and Rice, however; and it was a response to a desire in so many young writers to deal with the problems of their time through successful Broadway plays. Lawson found himself in the mainstream of socially conscious playwrights, a mentor to some, a model to others. In addition to Rice, Lawson, Barry, and Maxwell Anderson, the years 1929-1931 saw a proliferation of younger, more zealous if less wise writers, most of whom would not see their work produced until mid-decade if at all. What they lacked in dramatic skill, however, they attempted to make up for in their unbridled enthusiasm for socially significant theatre. John Gassner notes that they tended to make "social drama synonymous with Truth, Wisdom, Knowledge, and, it would seem, Holiness itself." Gassner also states that they felt a tremendous "engagement to life in the midst of economic and political crisis."[23] They were often as confused as the critics about what the social drama should be. Douglas McDermott points out:

> They were unsure of what they were creating, and they were unsure of the proper attitude to take towards it. It is not surprising that the people involved in creating this drama should be confused about what they were doing. They were not engaged in the deliberate conscious realization of some dramatic principle; they were reacting instinctively through the medium of the drama to a serious social crisis.[24]

In spite of their zeal, however, they kept their eyes on reviews, on audiences, and on the possibility, however unlikely, of producing a successful play in the commercial theatre, a play which also made a significant social statement. In other words, they were more worried over the problem of how successfully to inform their audiences than how successfully to entertain them.

The chief problem facing these young writers, and the older ones as well, was how to "break into the business," while they increasingly dwelt on what William Kozlenko describes as "the forces at work in life . . . wars, strikes, evictions, sit-downs, unemployment, the cruelties of federal penal institutions."[25] As the most prosperous and successful company on Broadway, the Theatre Guild sponsored most of the new and experimental forms throughout the twenties, and its penchant for the *avant-garde* made it the most likely choice to stage the new social drama. But while the Guild was "the most enduring 'art theatre' in American theatrical history,"[26] it had become more mature, more conservative since its founding by the Washington Square Players in 1918. Throughout the thirties it would remain a durable theatrical company, producing six plays a year; but it managed to maintain its "high-mindedness and self-conscious pursuit of art,"[27] it's reputation for "tastefulness" by shying away from drama that seemed too radical in its social comment. While the Guild had produced such plays as *The Adding Machine* in the past and would go on to stage Lawson's *The Pure in Heart* and Paul Peters and George Sklar's Marxist revue, *Parade*, in the thirties, it remained staunchly committed to its own fiscal solvency and sense of what was good box office in its play selection. *Parade,* in fact, was the last social drama the Guild produced. Coming in 1935, that revue topped the list of Guild-produced failures in the medium of leftist social drama. But aside from these and a few other plays, the Guild became reluctant to produce revolutionary or proletarian drama largely because its audiences were simply not sufficiently interested in such "dull material" and would not support such productions.[28]

The Guild was also inclined to produce more plays by foreign dramatists than by American writers. In the twenties, only nineteen Americans are represented out of eighty-one Guild productions. Although that figure changed to a ratio of thirty-two American plays to twenty-one foreign scripts in the thirties, there still was too little room for new American talent in the Guild's season.[29] The Theatre Guild was, however, willing to throw its support and some monetary backing behind newly emerging theatre companies which sponsored as yet unknown American playwrights.

Sam Smiley delineates three types of commitments among the social dramatists of the thirties: to multiform social concerns, to rigidly specific political systems and parties, and to leftist theatrical companies.[30] While the young writers of the early years of the depression had not yet clearly aligned themselves with political parties, and while the social concerns were largely those of the newspaper headlines, the late twenties and early thirties saw the formation of several leftist theatrical companies committed to plays of social significance. The New Theatre League, The Theatre Union, and the Group Theatre were all created out of a desire to successfully promote socially relevant drama. Some of them, such as the Theatre Union, were less concerned with aesthetic quality than social or political programs; however, the largest and longest lived of these new companies, the Group Theatre, placed its major emphasis on the combination of social comment and art. Rabkin writes: "Whatever the final verdict as to the durability of American drama in the thirties, there is no doubt that much of this accomplishment was due to the efforts of the Group Theatre."[31]

In his personal memoirs of the history of the Group Theatre, *The Fervent Years,* Harold Clurman points out that the Group wanted to go beyond the Guild in its relationship to its plays:

> They [the Guild] set the plays out in the show window for as many customers as possible to buy. They didn't want to say anything through plays, and plays said nothing to them except that they were amusing in a graceful way, or, if they were tragic plays, that they were "art."[32]

The goals of the Group were simple: it wished to advance the theatre by exposing American writers, improving on the quality of acting and directing, and maintaining a socially relevant theatre which would respond to the needs of its age. In short, it wished to create a national theatre.

During its decade-long history the Group, under the direction of Clurman, Cheryl Crawford, and Lee Strasburg, produced twenty-five plays, only one of which was not by an American author; and it counted among its contributors Paul

Green, Maxwell Anderson, Sidney Howard, John Howard Lawson, William Saroyan, and an early one-act effort by Tennessee
Williams.   Additionally it introduced, almost single-handedly,
the Stanislavski method of acting, ensemble playing, and the
idea of staging plays in theatres where ticket prices would make
drama accessible to audiences who had never seen plays before.
Taking for its motto "Theatre is an art which reflects life,"[33]
the Group was a leftist theatre in the sense that it staged social
drama.   Only six of its twenty-five plays were blatantly Marxist,
however; the majority of the rest were considerably left of center,
but the Group never espoused a particular political philosophy
or aligned itself with any social or political programs.   It was,
as Malcolm Goldstein points out, "liberal but not radical . . .
They were more interested in revolutionizing the stage than
the national political structure."[34]   From the first, however,
critics and audiences regarded the Group as one of the major
leftist theatre companies not only because its organization and
structure suggested the collective idea—actors, directors, writers,
and technicians all lived in a communal manner and all collaborated on decisions regarding play selection and production—
but also because its early productions all seemed to contain
Soviet propaganda, communist philosophy, and calls for revolution.   *Red Rust,* its premiere performance under the auspices
of the Theatre Guild, was a pro-Soviet play, and it joined with
1931—and *Waiting for Lefty* in characterizing the Group as a
leftist company.

It would be inaccurate to characterize the Group as a company dedicated to staging proletarian or politically didactic
drama on an exclusive basis, however.   Throughout *The Fervent
Years* Clurman denies *any* leftist bent in the Group; but John
Russell Brown notes: "They saw themselves as a social unit
working within (and sometimes against) society as a whole,
and the product they offered had to be something more than a
unified and artistic whole. It had to say something significant
and useful to and about society."[35]   In other words, the Group
was dedicated, as Rabkin points out, to "producing a play which
spoke in the authentic voice of its time."[36]   But this did not
mean that they were dedicated to establishing angry, proletarian
theatre for purposes of informing instead of entertaining.   In
fact, Clurman turned down Molly Day Thatcher (Elia Kazan's
wife) when she approached him about founding just such a theatre
within the Group, because, as Clurman states, he feared it would

become an organ for the Communist Party.[37] But the liberal attitudes among the actors and writers within the Group created an atmosphere of leftist social comment in many of the organization's plays. Writing of the "preoccupation with social, economic and political matters" among the members, Clurman asks:

> Where had it come from—from the inside or the outside? None of the people around us were connected directly with business, industry, labor, or politics. It did't matter what sides were taken. In truth, there were as yet no sides.[38]

As a major theatrical force in the thirties, the Group Theatre felt a responsibility to make social comment, however; and it seems natural that they were the first to attempt a drama which would address the specific issues of their time. The question was, could they do so and succeed as a commercial theatre company?

On December 10, 1931, the Group opened its first production without direct aid from the Theatre Guild. Claire and Paul Sifton's *1931*—a play in fourteen scenes, attempted earnestly to criticize civic and social attempts to deal with the problems of the depression. Adam, the protagonist, is a truck driver who loses his job and, as a result, breaks off his engagement to marry The Girl because he can no longer afford to support himself, let alone her and a family. As his savings ran out, he starts panhandling on the street, and eventually he turns his hand to robbery but loses courage at the last minute. He goes back to The Girl with his problems, and they console each other until they finally succumb to their love and sleep together. Shamefully, he leaves her again, and soon he loses his health and enters a hospital. The Girl, her honor gone, is fired from her job and soon is out on the street also, since she cannot afford to pay rent. She turns to prostitution. Adam, now recovered, tries again to find work and finally lands a twelve-dollar-a-week job. Elated, he seeks out The Girl and asks her to marry him, but she tells him she is infected with social disease and cannot. Together they elect to join the Communists, who are planning a rally in a square nearby, and hand-in-hand they go off to the meeting. *1931*—closed in nine days.

In both its theatrical organization and in its early productions, the Group Theatre represented the collective idea. Though plays such as *1931*—revolved around the actions of a hero and heroine, the characters' names, Adam and The Girl, indicate that they were allegorical in nature, representative of Everyman and Everywoman victimized by the economic turbulence of the age. The solution to their dilemma, to join the Communists' rally, is obviously metaphorical, since it will not allow them to regain their former economic security or good health; however, it does suggest that by participating in a social action, they can possibly rectify the evils in society which brought about their problems in the first place, thus making the world a better place for others. Their choice to participate in a collective action rather than an individual rebellion speaks to the playwrights' sense of selflessness and sacrifice which was popularly believed to be part and parcel of the working-class character in the early thirties.

Reviewers found the play an exaggeration of depression horrors in spite of its emotional impact and quality of production. Percy Hammond wrote of the scenes containing long unemployment lines:

> It was a depressing sight, and I was melancholy last night as I left the theatre to walk through Broadway to this desk. But on my way I was confused by other long lines of men at the Paramount, the Rialto and Loew's. None of them was cold and hungry. They were warmly clothed, and they had the price of admission. No symptoms of destitution were present.[39]

Hammond's skepticism over the urgency of the play's message was apparently shared by the typical New York theatre-goer, for Clurman recalls that most of the business was "balcony business"; however, he sensed a curious phenomenon about the balcony audience; he sensed "a kind of fervor in the nightly reception of *1931*—that was intense with a smoldering conviction uncharacteristic of the usual Broadway audience." On the last night of the run, however, the balcony was packed, and Clurman recalls an incident which he found confusing at first and later significant:

> . . . that night there was something of a demonstration in the theatre, like the response of a mass meeting to a

particularly eloquent speaker. As the actors—surprised
and moved—were taking curtain calls, a man in the balcony shouted, "Long live the Soviet Union!" Franchot
Tone, on the stage, shouted back, "Hurrah for America!"
Both outcries might be described as irrelevant, but evi-
dently there was something in the air beyond theatrical
appreciation.[40]

That "something in the air" Clurman would later recognize as
a "new audience," one which he believed would support the emerging new theatre in its attempts to explore social problems through
art.

Years later, when the Group would be accused by the leftist
critics of not being political enough in its dramatic selection,
Clurman responded that it had never been the aim of the Group
to become a political theatre, "but to be a creative and truly
representative American theatre," and this meant staging the
best drama they could find as well as finding and pleasing the
"new audience" which Clurman and others had sensed that closing
night in 1931. The Group had staged, as Clurman points out,
the "first depression play in *1931*—not from any political bias
but from a sense of what was going on in our day, so in the future
we could do more socially conscious plays than any other theatre
then functioning."[41] The commitment of the Group, as Rabkin states, was moral rather than political: "The Group's dedication to plays which reflected contemporary social issues sprang
from its conception of theatre as a social as well as an artistic
institution." While the members regarded their role as social
commentators as an important one, they also recognized the
importance of their plays as art, and they were as equally committed to commercial success as they were to social consciousness. Rabkin continues: "Theatre was commune, but it was
not necessarily revolutionary commune . . . Although it rejected
Broadway values, it is significant that it worked within the Broadway framework."[42] *Red Rust* and *1931*—taught the Group a
valuable lesson about the social drama; however, as Philip Barry
and other socially conscious writers of the twenties knew very
well, the social commitment of a play had to be in proportion
to its commercial value as a theatrical enterprise, else not only
would the aesthetic value of the piece suffer, but the play would
probably close quickly and no one would be able either to appre-
ciate it as art or to understand it as social comment.

The Group's third production was not a social statement of the strength of *Red Rust* or *1931-; House of Connally* by Paul Green achieved the first major success for the company, but only after Green agreed to rewrite the ending, changing the play from a melodramatic tragedy to a comedy. Throughout the decade the Group would continue to function; and with some exceptions, such as Sidney Kingsley's *Men in White*, Clifford Odets' *Golden Boy,* and William Saroyan's *My Heart's in the Highlands,* most of their productions met with only modest success and frequently closed quickly, bringing the threat of financial disaster ever closer. With the special exception of *Waiting For Lefty,* already a success when the Group took over production, the organization shied away from "strictly working-class plays" after *1931*—and their attempts at more politically—oriented plays such as Lawson's *Gentlewoman* met with such disastrous failure that they began to move more toward plays which tempered social comment with quality writing rather than political diatribe.[43]   It would be fair to say that in spite of its ultimate collapse in 1941, the Group accomplished in the thirties what the Provincetown Players and Washington Square Players had accomplished in the teens and early twenties.   It promoted American playwrights and introduced several, such as Odets and Saroyan, in the same way the earlier companies had introduced O'Neill and others. The members brought about a change in acting techniques and production methods that rivaled the innovations of the earlier groups; they brought a number of new actors and directors to the stage such as Will Ghere (later Geer), Lee J. Cobb, and Elia Kazan; they produced controversial scripts by unknown American writers and worked constantly for the artistic integrity of the playwright; and they, like their spiritual predecessors, brought the American drama to a higher state of artistic maturity. Risking commercial failure for their philosophy but striving always to explore social concerns and issues of their day, the Group failed only in its major, announced goal: the founding of a permanent national theatre. However, they never ceased seeking Clurman's "new audience" through the social drama.

The Group Theatre was not alone in its attempts to stage drama which called for mass response. Other plays such as *Stevedore* by Paul Peters and George Sklar and *Black Pit* and *The Crime* by Albert Maltz would continue to promote the idea of collective action, and these would rarely focus on a hero except in the most allegorical sense. But audiences still demanded to see the nobility of a single individual standing alone against corruption, injustice, and economic inequity. As the depression continued and prospects for a return to normalcy dimmed, however, the national mood became more receptive to drama which criticized specific social ills; but pro-soviet or pro-communist drama still had difficulty in finding its audiences. The social satire and militant didactic drama were not capable of answering the demand: one was too indirect and lacked specificity; the other was too direct and demanded too much in the name of alien-sounding philosophies. In March, 1933, however, a new play by an established writer earned audience and critical approval. Not only did it manage a biting critique of the American political system; it managed to do so with the grace and dignity of the older mode of the social comedy.

Both Your Houses by Maxwell Anderson represented a return for that playwright to a type of drama he had temporarily abandoned, the political and social satire. Anderson's career had been launched in 1924 by a collaboration with Laurence Stallings, *What Price Glory?*, a biting anti-war satire which has been called "the first realistic picture of war the American stage had seen."[44] Ostensibly it was the story of a love-triangle between two veteran marines, First Sergeant Quirt and Captain Flagg, who are stationed on the Western Front of World War I, and the licentious and voluptuous Charmaine de la Cognac, daughter of an inn-keeper in a rear outpost. *What Price Glory?* examines the values and beliefs of men who have made war their business and who expect to die at any given moment. In fast-paced dialogue and rapid action often bordering on a slapstick, Quirt and Flagg fight, argue, and do their best to rival each other in every way, especially in Charmaine's favors. Beneath their bickerings, however, lies a profound respect between the two soldiers that no woman and no argument can alter. As the play closes, Quirt, wounded and able at last to "best" Flagg by remaining behind the lines with honor and pursue Charmaine without his rival's interference, turns his back on her and joins his company as it is ordered back to the trenches without the much needed rest it has been promised. Alfred Shivers sums up the playwrights' message: "Because the object of the heroes' quarrel is a mere trifle of a slut, we are ready to believe that the object of the whole bloody war itself is no less inglorious and foolish."[45]

What Price Glory? was a smashing success with audiences and critics. On opening night the New York City Police, United States District Attorney, and representatives of the Marine Corps were present, ready to close the show and bring lawsuit if there was any obscene language or slander against the American armed forces. In a program note, Anderson explains the rough language to the audience: "The soldiers talk and act much as soldiers the world over . . . . Oaths mean nothing to a soldier save as a means to obtain emphasis." He went on /to say that the play represented a new "truth" about war: "In a theatre where war has been lied about, romantically, effectively—and in a city where the war play has usually meant sugary dissimulation—*What Price Glory?* may seem bold." But he asks the audience to "bear with" the language of the play in order to discover the truth of the play's message.[46] No legal action was taken against the show, and the play continued to enjoy a successful run. In his first major effort, therefore, Anderson "prepared the way for a more intense realism in the theatre."[47] And during the twenties he would continue to explore that realism as well as other dramatic modes.

Between 1924 and 1931 Anderson enjoyed only two more successess: *Outside Looking In* (1925) and *Saturday's Children* (1927). Both these plays dealt humorously with social problems. The less successful ventures, *First Flight, The Buccaneer,* and *Gypsy* experimented with other dramatic modes and mediums such as poetic tragedy, romantic fantasy, and historical drama. *Elizabeth the Queen,* produced with much acclaim in 1930, represented his major success in the latter category, and he would continue to produce plays in that vein throughout his career. One other collaboration, *Gods of the Lightning,* was written with Harold Hickerson; based on the Sacco-Vanzetti trials, the play had only modest success, but it has been called by modern critics "the decade's most forceful play on a specific incident."[48] Anderson's interest in social issues is often present, even in his most fantasized drama. In his historical plays, he searched for circumstances in the past to fit contemporary themes and problems. He believed the best way for theatre to treat social problems was through metaphoric, historical allegory rather than direct political rhetoric.

Like Barry, Anderson understood that a play must have commercial success first; then its statement, it message, could be transmitted. "No audience is satisfied with a play which doesn't take an attitude toward the world," he writes.[49]   His dramatic theory, writes Mabel Driscoll Bailey, "is simply a re-assertion of one of the oldest aesthetic principles on record—that art is a vehicle of communication."[50]   It was a lesson the young playwrights such as the Siftons had not yet learned even by 1933, and it was a lesson such organizations as the Group Theatre were only beginning to learn, but Anderson demon-strated that commercial success and social comment were as possible in the thirties as they had been a decade earlier. He also demonstrated that it was not necessary to cast such com-ment in the guise of historical metaphor. He returned to his earlier successful mode, the social satire, and attacked corrup-tion in the American Congress.

Both Your Houses is, in Lawson's terms, "a burning in-dictment of American political methods."[51]   And Malcolm Goldstein states that its "comic dialogue and fabricated romance" almost completely "blunts the play's leftist edge," but it is never-the-less a poignant social comment which could win audiences and communicate its message at the same time. Set in the office and meeting room of the United States House of Representa-tives' Appropriations Committee, the action centers on the com-mittee's deliberations over a bill ostensibly designed to provide a dam and irrigation to Nevada farmers. H. R. 2007, however, has been overloaded with "pork barrel" sections and graft-laden riders, some designed to please individual committee members and some offered to attract support from other House members when the bill is brought to a vote.

Most of the items on the bill are ludicrous, ranging from appropriations for money to dredge dry river beds in Iowa to a stipend to finance out-of-work farmers who will set up patrols on the Canadian border to watch for the encroachment of Japa-nese Beetles, even though, as one member points out, Japanese Beetles cannot survive that far north. Other riders are nothing more than graft, such as a measure for building an unneeded veteran's hospital in Baton Rouge to aid one member's financial holdings in the area, or sending the Atlantic Fleet to its summer docking near another member's real estate development and "chain of speakeasies" on Long Island. Only a few items seem to be genuinely attached to the bill for the public good, such as an item calling for the enlargement of the nursing force under the Department of the Interior, including "fifteen thousand for the dissemination of birth control information and contra-

ceptives."[52]   But even this seemingly altruistic action is tainted, for the particular member who proposes it will have the
opportunity to make all the additional appointments and garner favors in return.[53]

The main characters of *Both Your Houses* are all Congressmen: Simeon Gray, the committee chairman, attempts to reason
with the members and hold the total cost of the bill down; at
the outset he is the single member who apparently has nothing
to gain from the bill. Solomon Fitzmaurice is the eldest of the
committee members; he is outraged by the degree of graft and
corruption he witnesses in his fellow legislators, but he is not
inclined to disavow his own demands even when Simeon tells
him that sending the Atlantic Fleet to Sol's real estate development on Long Island might make the bill sound "fishy." Sol
declares: "Fishy! My God, a little honest smell of fish on that
bill would hang over it like an odor of santity!" (p. 19). Sol
represents a crusty and seasoned politician. He is not "slick"
in his dealings with people, as are other members of the committee; on the contrary, he readily admits that he is corrupt and
blames the system of the Congress for corrupting him; he states
at one point: "the sole business of government is graft, special
privilege and corruption—with a by-product of order. They
have to keep order or they can't make collections" (p. 103).
But he is not completely irresponsible; a nagging sense of integrity always prevents him from going too far in the direction
of total corruption: "No, I'm all wrong," he admits. "But what
I'm mostly wrong about is I don't steal in a big enough way.
Steal apples and they put you in jail—steal a nation and the hosts
of heaven come down and line up under your banners" (p. 104).
But greed usually gets the better of Sol as it does of all the committee members, and he aligns himself with them in their grab-
bing pork barrel practices.

Alan McClean is the protagonist of *Both Your Houses.*
Newly elected on a promise of reform, Alan is as naive as he
is honest, and he is shocked over the load of graft the bill has
taken and at the nonchalance with which the committee continues to spend millions of unneeded dollars. By accident, he
learns that the one member of the committee who appears to
be honest, Gray, also has special interests in the building of an
asylum-prison near his home town. Thoroughly disgusted, Alan
resolves to fight the bill and kill the entire program if necessary,
even though it means his constituents will not obtain their much

needed dam. Alan is reluctant to expose Gray's personal graft because it will destroy the chairman's reputation and because Alan is courting Gray's daughter.

Making an alliance with Bus, his new secretary, Alan tries at first to reason with the committee. Failing this, he decides to go ahead and expose Gray as well as the other members of the committee for what they are, corrupt perpetrators of graft and special interests: "They can be had—and they're going to be—" he resolves, "right on this bill they are! Why damn their god-damn eyes—" Alan's attempts to amass opposition to the bill come to grief, and his appeals to Sol to support his action in the name of the voters' interest also fail: "I have found no word in the English language and no simile or figure of speech that would express the complete and illimitable ignorance and in-competence of the voting population," Sol tells him (p. 102). Undaunted, Alan tries to load the bill so heavily that it runs too much over cost for anyone in his right mind to support it: but this also backfires, for when everybody has an interest in the bill, nobody will vote against it: "You give everybody what he wants, including the opposition, and lo! there ain't no opposition," Sol jubilantly declares (p. 170). Alan's plans to defeat the bill have failed. Even a presidential veto is out of the question due to the overwhelming majority of both houses who now have their own personal graft riding on the bill.

Brooks Atkinson notes that *Both Your Houses* "lacks the reckless gusto of *What Price Glory?* and the literary distinction of *Elizabeth the Queen*" but offers the most successful political satire before 1935, possibly the best of the entire decade.[54] Its political punch was softened by its timing, however. By March, 1933, Roosevelt's "New Deal" administration had taken office, and the play's exposure of the corruption of the Hoover administration, particularly of the much contested Hoover Dam bill, was "old business." Anderson wrote that since those he intended to lampoon were already out of office, the play "seemed quite pointless."[55] But audiences and critics disagreed; *Both Your Houses* was awarded the Pulitzer Prize for 1933.

As a social drama, *Both Your Houses* represents a synthesis of the themes and structures present in both the social satire of the twenties and the newer and less successful didactic drama. There is still the individual hero, alone in his rebellion against the forces of evil, in this case political corruption; but unlike the Johnny Cases who selfishly demand a personal escape from

the tendrils of business and society, Alan McClean emerges as
a leader of what he hopes will be a collective action of the people
to overthrow these "empire wreckers," to replace them with
something better. Unlike Adam and The Girl, he does not turn
to political "patent medicine" for the solution, but issues a
"call to action" to Americans to rectify the ills of a democracy
gone awry:

> I'm not the person to give you a warning. I'm not a poli-
> tician. I'm a Nevada school-teacher. I don't know your
> tricks—you showed me that tonight, and I won't forget
> it. But I didn't lose because I was wrong. I lost because
> I tried to beat you at your own game—and you can al-
> ways win at that. You think you're good and secure
> in this charlatan's sanctuary you've built for yourselves.
> You think the sacred and senseless legend poured into
> the people of this country from childhood will protect
> you. It won't. It takes about a hundred years to tire
> this country of trickery—and we're fifty years overdue
> right now. That's my warning. And I'd feel pretty damn
> pitiful and lonely saying it to you, if I didn't believe there
> are a hundred million people who are with me, a hundred
> million people who are disgusted enough to turn from you
> to something else. Anything else but this (pp. 178-179).

In this speech Alan reveals himself to be what Bailey sees as
Anderson's ideal dramatic protagonist. For Anderson, she writes,
a hero "must discover something in himself or in his environment
about which he had been unaware or had imperfectly understood."[56] McClean comes to Washington and realizes that his
school book ideas about government have little to do with political realities. He also discovers a capacity in himself for political chicanery which digusts him, even if he does try to use it
for the ultimate public good. But his realizations and discoveries
of political corruption do not lead him down the road Adam
takes to a "red" rally; on the contrary, when he is defeated,
he threatens to take his case to the people through the press.
The committee members tell him that such an action would
treasonous, but Alan declares: "How can one speak of treason
against this government? It's one vast, continuous, nation-wide
disaster" (p. 174). And when another member accuses him of
following the advice of one of the janitors and becoming a Com-

munist, Alan explodes: "I'm not a red! I don't like communism or fascism or any other political patent medicine! If I did, I'd say what Ebner says—go right ahead the way you're going. You're doing all you can to bring it on" (p. 175). Both in his "call to action" and in his denial of communistic beliefs, Alan emerges as more of a Jeffersonian Democrat than a Marxist flag waver.

Vincent Wall points out two reasons why Anderson does not embrace a revolutionary attitude in *Both Your Houses:* "First, Anderson is too much of an individualist; and second he is too convinced that government is and always has been exploitive."[57] And Anderson's solution, as Rabkin points out, is not to worry about tearing down "transformable institutions," but to eliminate the "evil in the black heart of man."[58] Anderson himself characterized what he called "the prevailing fallacy of the age": "Villains were made villains by circumstances, and we must fight the circumstances, not the poor wretches whose anti-social actions caused trouble."[59] The sagacious Solomon Fitzmaurice articulates this point in the closing lines of the play. Though he has opposed Alan from the first, he senses that he and the other members of the committee are up against a new generation of young people who refuse to play by the old rules: "This generation that's growing up now, it's a generation of vipers. You can't compete with 'em without becoming a viper. Why, they're born with teeth and claws nowadays" (p. 109). Also, Sol begins to realize that Alan's efforts of the past few days have had no effect on the committee; they will continue to pass porkbarrel and graft-laden bills, especially now that they have learned a new way around the opposition. "It'll blow over," he tells them. "As a matter of fact, the natural resources of this country in political apathy and indifference have hardly been touched. They're just learning how to pay taxes. In a few years you'll really give them taxes to pay" (p. 179). But even this cynicism cannot dispel his admiration for Alan's efforts, and in the closing lines of the play he cautions the committee that their day of personal corruption might be drawing to a close:

> SOL
> . . . On the other hand, he's right about you. I always told you boys you were a bunch of crooks! And some day they're going to catch up with you.
> WINGPLATT
> Well, how about yourself, you two-faced swindler?

SOL

I'm too old, Wingie. They won't get me. No—I don't
hardly expect it in my time. (he pours himself a drink.)

BUS

Maybe. (pp. 179-180)

Bus' last word speaks the greatest optimism Anderson has to
offer in *Both Your Houses.*

Anderson's *Both Your Houses* also represents a synthesis
of the two other modes of social drama in the early years of the
depression because it neither ignores the possibility of radical
change nor advocates a particular political doctrine. Wall points
out that Anderson "believed in the class struggle and even feels
that the capitalist system is worse than the Marxists claim that
it is."[60] But Anderson also knew that a play which openly
attacked the Congress would not succeed on Broadway unless
it did so in the mode of tasteful entertainment. Leftist critics,
predictably, were not overly enthusiastic about the play. Referring to Alan's "call to action," John Howard Lawson sniffed:
"platitudinous and weak—any honest (or dishonest) man might
and has said the same thing."[61] But *Both Your Houses* effectively
manages to combine elements of the other modes in other ways.
The names of the characters are symbolic: Solomon, the "wise"
if misguided character; Gray, the "shaded" character, neither all
good nor all bad; and, of course, McClean, the "good" character,
as yet untainted by the corruption of public office. This recalls
both the dramatic tradition of representational, flat characters
found in medieval morality plays where characters such as "Faith," "Hope," "Friendship," and "Riches" played against characters named for the seven deadly sins, as well as the more recent use
of such names as "Adam" or "The Girl" to simply depict random
individuals in a modern world. The "call to action," however,
tepid though it may have been in leftist eyes, was something
new to successful social comedy. Taking the focus away from
the individual and accenting the collective idea, Anderson's
hero seeks to inspire "a hundred million" to support his protagonist's fight against evil.

Anderson was never one who subscribed to what McClean
calls "political patent medicine," politics calling for radical action.
He recognized that such calls for extreme measures in drama
only alienated audiences and distorted the value of the theatre
as a place where an attitude toward the world could be expressed.

Further, he had little respect for organized political dissent as it existed in the early years of the depression because, as Wall points out, Anderson believed the "radicals are always too busy fighting among themselves even to present comprehensive strategy that could outwit entrenched greed."[62] Instead, Anderson borrowed from both the didactic political drama and the older, proven social comedy to provide a social drama that both entertained its audience and directly addressed social problems.

After *Both Your Houses* Anderson returned to his experiments in poetic and tragic modes. *Winterset, The Wingless Victory,* and *Key Largo* are all essays into social drama, but these latter plays lack the specificity of *Both Your Houses* both in the problems they analyze and in the solutions they offer. Anderson maintained his belief in the courage and potential of the individual, and he continued to resist politically inspired drama even after it became possible to achieve commercial success with it, but *Both Your Houses* is one of the best examples of acceptable social drama of the early thirties. Not only does it gather the tools and devices of earlier social drama, it foreshadows elements which would become cliched in the socially conscious plays of subsequent years.

Sam Smiley states that the social drama of the thirties was written with three express purposes in mind: "(1) enlightening spectators about conditions, motivating forces, or responsibilities; (2) persuading them to accept social doctrines; and (3) provoking them to social actions."[63] By 1933 the social drama was still in its formative stages as far as Broadway was concerned. The most successful plays still did not directly address the ills they might have exposed. But, as Douglas McDermott points out, "the social drama of the thirties was not an accident but an intention,"[64] and the writers who had the most success were those who understood best what audiences would want and in what form they would want it. By 1933 the depression was not the only social issue on the minds of both playwrights and audiences. The rise of Nazism in Germany and growing antisemitism abroad and at home also caused several writers to attempt plays which exposed and condemned such atrocities and attitudes. But the time was not yet ripe for the social dramatist to emerge as both militant propagandist and artistic creator.

Still, in the major successes of the years early in the depression, the movement toward serious social criticism was well begun. A year after *Both Your Houses* another playwright,

S. N. Behrman, produced *Rain From Heaven*, a biting criticism of American and English anti-semitism and growing fascism which flourished in the name of capitalism. Behrman's reputation as a writer of light, social comedy launched the play; however, its successful run was sustained by an audience increasingly attracted to drama which addressed contemporary issues. William Kozlenko, speaking of *Both Your Houses, Rain from Heaven*, as well as other social drama, notes that many felt that the translating of vital social problems into dramatic writing meant that the art must become propaganda; however, he writes: "the theatre need not be a platform from which abstruse political doctrines are disseminated at the sacrifice of the character's emotions."[65] Anderson and a few others had proven by 1933 that a synthesis of didactic, even angry, analyses of social problems and light, satric treatments of those same problems could be accomplished through a well-made, carefully constructed dramatic medium which both entertained and informed.

Notes

[1]Gerald Rabkin, *Drama and Commitment: Politics in the American Theatre of the Thirties* (Bloomington: Indiana University Press, 1964), p. 78.

[2]The idea of combining entertainment with information in art, specifically poetic art, actually goes further back than Horace's work. Several critics see it as a part of what is now characterized as the "Aristotlilian and Platonic Debate" in matters of philosophy and rhetoric. The Stoics had much to say about it prior to Horace's writing, and such philosophers as Boethius discussed it. In drama, the idea finds expression through the Renaissance works of John Lily, principally *Euphues: The Anatomy of Wit* (1579) and his court romances, *Alexander and Campaspe* (1584) and *Sapho and Phalo* (1584) through which he demonstrated the idea of the "sugar coated pill" by revealing court scandals in his plays; in both *The Defense of Poesie* and *An Apology for Poesie* (both 1595) Sir Philip Sidney discusses the same principle. The "classic-modern debate" picks up much the same idea, but modern applications of the "sermon" and "tickle" combination can be found in the works of George Bernard Shaw, among others. An

exceedingly contemporary and particular application of the idea can be found in the current television program, *Sesame Street*, produced by Public Broadcasting Systems, wherein grammar, math, and other information are dispensed to children through an entertaining program. For a history of the ancient discussion of the idea, see William K. Wimsatt, Jr. and Cleanth Brooks, *Literary Criticism* (New York: Random House, 1957), pp. 91-92.

[3]Philip Barry, *Holiday: A Comedy in Three Acts* (New York: Samuel French, 1928), p. 204; subsequent citations from this play will be noted parenthetically in the text.

[4]Joseph Patrick Roppolo, *Philip Barry* (New York: Twayne Publishers, Inc., 1965), p. 63. Reprinted with permission of Twayne Publishers, a division of G. K. Hall and Co., Boston.

[5]*Ibid.*, p. 45.

[6]Louis Broussard, *American Drama: Contemporary Allegory from Eugene O'Neill to Tennessee Williams* (Norman, OK: University of Oklahoma Press, 1962), p. 57.

[7]Roppolo, p. 46.

[8]Eleanor Flexner, *American Playwrights: 1918-1938: The Theatre Retreats from Reality*, with a Preface by John Gassner (New York: Simon & Schuster, 1938), p. 34.

[9]Roppolo, p. 24.

[10]*Ibid.*, p. 8.

[11]*Ibid.*, p. 10.

[12]John Gassner, *The Theatre in Our Times: A Survey of the Men, Materials and Movements in the Modern Theatre* (New York: Crown Publishers, 1954), p. 326.

[13]Flexner, p. 249.

[14]Roppolo, p. 124.

[15]Flexner, p. 250.

[16]Roppolo, p. 8.

[17]Francis Fergusson, *The Human Image in Dramatic Literature* (New York: Doubleday & Co., 1957), p. 68.

[18]Phyllis Hartnoll, ed., *The Oxford Companion to the Theatre*, 3rd ed. (London: Oxford University Press, 1975), p. 799.

[19]Harold Clurman, *The Fervent Years: A Story of the Group Theatre and the Thirties* (New York: Alfred A. Knopf, 1945; rpt.; New York: Harcourt Brace Jovanovich, 1975), p. 19.

[20]John Howard Lawson, *Roger Bloomer: A Play in Three Acts* (New York: Thomas Seltzer, 1923), p. 5; subsequent citations from this play will be noted parenthetically in the text.

[21]Clurman, p. 18.

[22]Rabkin, pp. 128-129.

[23]John Gassner, *Dramatic Soundings: Evaluations and Retractions Culled from 30 Years of Dramatic Criticism* (New York: Crown Publishers, 1968), p. 388.

[24]Douglas McDermott, "Propaganda and Art: Dramatic Theory and the American Depression," *Modern Drama* 11 (May 1968): 73.

[25]William Kozlenko, ed., *The Best Short Plays of the Social Theater*, with an introduction by William Kozlenko (New York: Random House, 1939), p. vii.

[26]Malcolm Goldstein, *The Political Stage: American Drama and the Theatre of the Great Depression* (New York: Oxford University Press, 1974), p. 101.

[27]*Ibid.,* p. 116.

[28]*Ibid.,* p. 107.

[29]*Ibid.,* p. 105.

[30]Sam Smiley, *The Drama of Attack: Didactic Plays of the American Depression* (Columbia, MO: University of Missouri Press, 1972), p. 42.

[31]Rabkin, p. 86.

[32]Clurman, p. 26.

[33]Rabkin, p. 72.

[34]Goldstein, p. 16.

[35]John Russell Brown and Bernard Harris, *American Theatre* (London: Edward Arnold; rpt.; New York: St. Martin's Press, 1967), p. 72. Reprinted with permission of Edward Arnold, Ltd.

[36]Rabkin, p. 72.

[37]Clurman, p. 30.

[38]*Ibid.,* p. 91.

[39]Percy Hammond, quoted in Clurman, p. 70. It should be noted that the theatres Hammond mentions are motion picture theatres, not playhouses. The average price of a ticket to a screening in New York in 1933 was 23 cents, and this was up from previous years when the cost of a ticket ranged from 5 cents to 20 cents, depending on the quality of the picture (A or B) as well as the number of features, short-subjects, etc., which were shown; see Cobbett Steinberg, *Reel Facts: The Movie Book of Records* (New York: Vintage Books, 1978), p. 368; Steinberg also reports that in 1931 over seventy-five million people attended a motion picture screening weekly. Similar statistics for theatrical attendance have been compiled by Jack Poggi, *Theatre in America: The Impact of Economic Forces, 1870-1967* (Ithaca, NY: Cornell University Press, 1968).

[40]Clurman, pp. 71-72.

[41]*Ibid.,* p. 73.

[42]Rabkin, p. 136.

[43]Goldstein, p. 85.

[44]Tom F. Driver, *Romantic Quest and Modern Query: A History of the Modern Theatre* (New York: Delacorte Press, 1970), p. 296.

[45]Alfred S. Shivers, *Maxwell Anderson* (Boston: Twayne Publishers, 1976), p. 51. Reprinted with permission of Twayne Publishers, a division of G. K. Hall and Company, Boston.

[46]Maxwell Anderson and Laurence Stallings, *Three American Plays by Maxwell Anderson and Laurence Stallings* (New York: Harcourt, Brace & Co., 1926), p. 3.

[47]Mabel Driscoll Bailey, *Maxwell Anderson: The Playwright as Prophet* (New York: Abelard-Schuman, 1957), p. 52.

[48]Goldstein, p. 8.

[49]Maxwell Anderson, "The Basis of Artistic Creation in Literature," *The Basis of Artistic Creation* (New Brunswick: Rutgers University Press, 1942), p. 4.

[50]Bailey, p. 11.

[51]John Howard Lawson, *Theory and Technique of Playwrighting* (New York: Hill and Wang, 1960), p. 146.

[52]Maxwell Anderson, *Both Your Houses: A Play in Three Acts* (New York: Samuel French, 1933), p. 38; subsequent citations from this play will be noted parenthetically in the text.

[53]Many of the ideas treated satirically in *Both Your Houses* were stock in trade of political comedy in American drama. In 1887 Mark Twain's earlier collaboration with G. S. Densmore, *The Gilded Age* (a melodramatic adaptation of his novel by the same title which was written in collaboration with Charles Dudley Warner and published in 1875) was rewritten and staged as a sequel, *The American Claimant, or Mulberry Sellers Ten Years Later* with William Dean Howells helping Twain out this time. Twain later wrote a prose fiction adaptation of the play, *The American Claimant*. Both versions deal with political incompetence and corruption. Twain's interest in the drama was quite strong; he originally conceived of *The Prince and the Pauper* as a play although it was never produced as such; he collaborated with Bret Harte on *Ah Sin* in the 1880's; *Pudd'nhead Wilson* was adapted by Frank Mayo in 1895 to Twain's delight; and Twain wrote several scenarios and full plays which were never published nor staged. *The Adventures of Tom Sawyer*, *The Adventures of Huckleberry Finn* and *A Connecticut Yankee in King Arthur's Court* are among the successful stage and screen adaptations of his works; an one opera, *Frog of Calaveras County*, by Lukas Foss has been staged from one of his prose stories. For more information on Twain's desire and ability in the theatre, see Arthur Hobson Quinn, *The History of the American Drama from the Civil War to the Present Day*, 2 vols. (New York: F. S. Crofts & Co., 1937), 2: 114-115.

[54]Brooks Atkinson and Albert Hirschfeld, *The Lively Years: 1920-1973* (New York: Association Press, 1973), p. 87.

[55]Maxwell Anderson, *Dramatist in America: Letters of Maxwell Anderson: 1912-1958,* ed. Laurence Avery (Chapel Hill: University of North Carolina Press, 1977), p. 239.

[56]Bailey, p. 170.

[57]Vincent Wall, "Maxwell Anderson: The Last Anarchist," *American Drama and Its Critics: A Collection of Critical Essays*, ed. Alan S. Downer (Chicago: University of Chicago Press, 1965), p. 165.

[58]Rabkin, p. 265.

[59]Anderson, "The Basis of Artistic Creation in Literature," p. 6.

[60]Wall, p. 165.

[61]Lawson, p. 151.

[62]Wall, p. 165.

[63]Smiley, p. 205.

[64]McDermott, p. 81.

[65]Kozlenko, p. vii.

DRAMA AS WEAPON

Marxist and communist theatre in the United States began at almost the same time as the establishment of "modern" drama in America by the Provincetown Players and the Washington Square Players. By the early years of the decade of the Great Depression, playwrights and critics of a leftist political bent openly called themselves Communists and Socialists, and they advocated revolutionary social change both in direct calls for action and in their open admiration of the Soviet Union. Gerald Rabkin states that in the years 1930-1934 the young radicals "felt compelled to act, and Marxist philosophy and the Communist Party as an organization, seemed the most effective means of realizing this desire; in short, they accommodated themselves to what they felt were revolutionary necessities."[1] Such leftist publications as *The Daily Worker* and *The New Masses* devoted considerable space to dramatic criticism, especially from the pens of John Howard Lawson, Eleanor Flexner, and Michael Gold. From their reviews and columns these critics joined other leftist voices in demanding what Rabkin calls "collective alternatives both social and theatrical."[2] They sought a more direct address of social problems and a more definitive answer to questions concerning social ills than were provided by the comedies of Maxwell Anderson and S. N. Behrman.[3]

Lawson's plays of the twenties stand out as the most successful examples of leftist playwriting on Broadway during that decade. After 1930, however, his politics began to encroach upon his aesthetics to the extent that his plays became Marxist and communist diatribe thinly disguised as drama. After the Group Theatre's unsuccessful production of *Success Story* in 1932, he went into a decline as a playwright from which he never recovered, although his voice as a critic was louder than ever. Other communist playwrights also attempted to stage leftist drama on Broadway in the first few years of the decade. Michael Blankfort, George Sklar and Paul Peters produced plays which dealt with strikes, class consciousness, pacifism, anti-

fascism, and the decay of the middle class; but they failed to
find success on the Great White Way just as Claire and Paul Sifton
had failed with their premiere "Depression play," *1931*—and for
the same reasons: most people did not believe things were yet
bad enough to be sympathetic with radical doctrines and calls
for revolutionary change; and those who did, Clurman's "new
audience," were either still in the balcony or were not coming
to the theatre at all.

Off-Broadway, however, leftist revues and brief allegory
plays were frequently staged. They had been enjoying modest
success since World War I, often in no more auspicious surroundings than either the Provincetown Players or Washington Square
Players had originally used, such as barns, old warehouse buildings, and empty houses. Between 1925 and 1928 the popularity
of leftist plays among off-Broadway audiences increased dramatically, and "worker's theatres" began to spring up nation-
wide. The Prolet-Buehne and Worker's Laboratory Theatre of
New York were among the largest of the companies whose special-
ty was the agit-prop (agitation and propaganda) play, and a
survey of titles such as *Work or Wages, Unemployment, The
Miners Are Striking,* and *Vote Communist* suggests the nature
and content and purpose of such plays.

Agit-prop finds its antecedents in the street theatre of East--
ern Europe. In the United States during the mid-twenties, however, it was tailored especially to fit the needs of socialist groups
which were trying to organize and unionize industrial workers.
The plays were usually staged at union rallies or, if no organization yet existed, during shift-changes, lunch breaks, or even
company picnics. Scripts were sketchy if they existed at all;
sets were minimal; and there were no professional actors. The
workers themselves played roles, often improvising from a rough
character sketch. The plays generally took the form of allegory,
with the "capitalist" appearing as a fat, overdressed, greedy
fraud and the "worker" as an attractive, shabby but clean, paragon
of honesty and innocence who suffered because he was exploited
by his employer. The purpose of the agit-prop sponsors was
clear: they wanted to bring about a raising of social consciousness
among the worker-audiences. The plots of the plays were simple
and based almost completely on action rather than idea: they
usually consisted of a series of short scenes depicting a steady
worsening of the worker's plight at the hands of the corrupt
capitalist. Each scene was usually designed to evoke an emotional

response from the audience by means of such devices as the death of the worker's child, the moral or physical ruination of his wife or sister due to their oppressed state, or his own death due to unsafe working conditions, inescapable poverty, or exhaustion. But most often the melodramatic structure would dissolve at the end of the play when one or more characters would offer a "call to action" which could range, depending on the occasion, from a call for a union to a call for a strike to even a call for revolution. In this sense these plays fulfilled their purpose of agitation and propaganda perfectly.

Some agit-prop plays had full scripts, and these along with formal dramas by socialist writers such as Michael Gold's *Hoboken Blues* and Basshe's *Earth* were toured with the same actors playing the principal roles for every performance. This led to charges of fraud by right-wing organizations, but Malcolm Goldstein insists:

> There was nothing fraudulent about these bands of worker-actors. They were exactly what they proclaimed to be: part-time performers willing to give up their leisure time for the purpose of jarring other workers into class consciousness through their plays.[4]

As the years 1929-1930 brought economic chaos and unemployment home to the working class, the popularity of agit-prop grew; and frequently bankrupt movie houses and old city auditoriums would be used to stage plays for out-of-work and disgruntled blue-collars. By 1932 there were so many of these worker's troupes around the country that a "spartakiade," a national conference, was held in New York where sixty-seven plays were produced by individual agit-prop companies. The result of the conference was a journal, *Worker's Theatre,* to permit the publication of the more popular scripts and the exchange of ideas and news between troupes.

Essentially, the agit-prop play dealt with labor problems or unemployment. There were some exceptions such as *Scottsborough Limited,* which was based on a sensational example of injustice and racism,[5] and some few agit-prop productions were concerned with corruption in political organizations; but the "strike play" was the most popular, since it almost always demanded the climactic "call to action." Sam Smiley finds that three themes were most frequently employed by the writers:

the change in the world from capitalism to socialism and the establishment of "socialized productive relations and the rise of a nonpropertied proletariat"; the inevitable conflict between the "reigning bourgeoisie" and rising proletariat; and a "unity of action" resulting from the "harmonious cooperation with the predictable historical course of events and from a recognition of the material forces at work."[6] From the platforms of meeting halls and union gatherings the Communists preached their philosophy and agitated for social change.

No other dramatic form of any age exhibited a stronger social concern than agit-prop theatre. More so than almost any other art form, the worker's theatres criticized social institutions, demanded social change, and created social concern. Whether the agit-prop can be called "drama" or not is open to debate. William Kozlenko states:

> Its major interest was in action; its unique quality was to excite and convince its audience *emotionally*. Little thought was given, as a rule, to the development of character, to the living man with his complex individual contradictions.[7]

Attempts by such writers as Claire and Paul Sifton, Lawson, and others to adapt the form for the more sophisticated theatre of the commercial stage met with dismal failure, and only by synthesizing the agit-prop with acceptable dramatic forms could the ideas of leftist writers emerge onto Broadway.

By mid-1933 the worker's theatres were still growing in popularity among the blue-collar classes, but they had not managed to emerge successfully onto the established Broadway scene. By late that year, largely because of Moscow directives, the "hard-line" of the communist writers softened; *Worker's Theatre* became *New Theatre,* and the Theatre Union took over the production activities of the Worker's Laboratory Theatre. Agit-prop and other forms of propagandistic theatre began to dissipate. As 1934 began, the movement toward the Popular Front had started, partially to attract better talent to a leftist position that would be less revolutionary in its themes and partially to capitalize on the popularity of the success of the satiric but less dogmatic social drama which was finding its audience on Broadway.[8] "Little by little," Goldstein notes, "and possibly at the urging of their superiors in the Party, the magazines' writers were adopting the view that appeals to the masses could be effective even if low-voiced, and that didactic drama could work for social betterment without clamoring for a revolution."[9] The primary significance of this change was that the worker-directors, actors and especially writers would be replaced by professionals, some of whom were not politically aligned at all.

Several reasons have been proposed for the movement toward a Popular Front by American Communists, especially insofar as that move affected drama. Rabkin suggests that Moscow, recognizing the growing threat of Hitler's fascistic state, saw the need for the United States' popular support and realized that many Americans would be more likely to support an anti-war platform if the revolutionary propaganda was toned down: "With the advent of the Popular Front, many liberals found in anti-fascism a cause in which they could affiliate with the communists, since the communists were, in any case, themselves talking very much like New Dealers."[10] Drama was still, as the motto of the Theatre Union proclaimed, "A Weapon," but taking its lesson from writers such as Anderson and Behrman, the leftist playwrights began to understand that they needed to cover their iron fist with a velvet glove. "One necessary step," writes Goldstein, "was to guard against the use of the very term 'communism' in all but the most central party-sponsored or party-controlled enterprises."[11] Whereas Lawson never seemed to understand this tenet, the younger playwrights, Sklar, Blankfort, and others, gradually came to realize that their plays had to do more than exhort and declaim in order to succeed, no matter how much their authors believed in their messages. "For a meaningful protest movement, action is essential," writes Michael Mendelsohn, "and there is precious little evidence that all the doctrinaire speeches in the Marxist morality plays ever made a convert."[12] To propagate their ideas effectively in the direction of the Popular Front, the "hard-line" Marxists realized that they had to convert the agit-prop play into acceptable drama; in order to reach the audiences of Broadway, they would have to entertain as well as inform. The most significant manifestation of their efforts was the establishment of the Theatre Union.

Michael Goldstein calls the Theatre Union the "most professional of the new groups of the 1930's."[13] Existing from November 1933 until it folded under financial pressure in 1937, the Theatre Union offered Popular Front ideology ranging from the mild liberalism of Lynn Riggs and Sidney Howard to the "hard-line" communism of H. W. L. Dana and Joseph Freeman. Blankfort, Maltz, Peters, Sklar, and Lawson were all members of the Union, as were journalists, actors, Socialist organizers, and nondramatic writers.[14] During their four years of production they staged such American plays as *Black Pit, Stevedore, Peace on Earth* and *Marching Song,* and the European scripts, *Sailors of Cattaro, Fontamara,* and Bertold Brecht's *The Mother.* They took over several failing plays from other leftist companies, and they attempted to support leftist writers and production companies who asked for their help. It was their intention to combine the amateur communist theatre with the professional experience of writers who were not necessarily Marxists but who supported the Popular Front movement.[15] This is clearly stated in their published manifesto which promised that they would produce plays that "deal boldly with social conflict . . . that confront the majority of the people." They wished to speak to those "whose lives are caricatured or ignored on the stage." Warning that this would be a "new kind of professional theatre," they promised lower ticket prices to bring "thousands of people into the theatre who have never seen a professional play, or who have not gone into the theatre for years."[16] In short, they sought a synthesis of the militant agit-prop and acceptable social theatre. But turning propagandistic, didactic drama into palatable and successful theatre was an ambitious project, and the Union was troubled from the start.

The Communist Party itself became a part of the Union's difficulty. Party interference and unsolicited advice continually caused the members to publish replies and reminders that they were a functioning theatrical organization which produced professional drama, not a political party which sponsored agit-prop plays. While they looked upon themselves as a "revolutionary theatre," they were not doctrinaire. They wanted to reach "thousands who had never been to the theatre before," but they also wanted Broadway audiences—in other words, they sought the "new audience" Clurman had sensed the closing night in *1931*—.

The major problem, however, was where to find suitable plays. "The most difficult single problem that the Theatre Union had to face because of its ideological commitment was the discovery of plays that were both politically aware and dramatically sound," writes Rabkin.[17] But even when scripts were located, the Union was plagued by a host of other problems. Often actors would refuse to deliver certain lines if their personal political philosophy was contradicted, and what Lawson and others called "reactionary verdicts" of the critics crippled the Union's box office. They never attempted to hide their "Marxist assumptions," as Goldstein points out; they took class exploitation and the use of the Soviet Union as a positive model for granted.[18] The Union was, in Rabkin's words, victimized by its own assumptions:

> From the outset the Theatre Union was involved in necessary contradictions. It attempted to create a theatre of protest which would express the "worker's point of view," i.e. a class-conscious Marxism, while, in actuality, this point of view was never that of any significant segment of the American working class.[19]

In fact, the American worker, in spite of his desire for better wages, safe working conditions, and job security looked askance at alien political doctrines which called for an overthrow of the goverment; staunchly conservative, the average American worker primarily was interested in his own piece of the American dream.[20]

The chief significance of the Theatre Union was its attempt to synthesize agit-prop and "hard-line" leftist or communist formal drama and bring that synthesis together with acceptable Broadway drama to produce a socially conscious but entertaining play based on Marxist assumptions. It would not be the last company to do so. Leftist theatres such as the Actor's Repertory Company, the Mercury Theatre, the Theatre Arts Committee, and, longest-lived of all, the New Theatre League, would continue to stage socialist and communist plays until the Nazi-Soviet non-aggression pact of 1939 would end all possibility of audience sympathy with leftist positions in the United States. But in the years 1930-1934, the desire of the Union to find a successful synthesis, to stage well-written proletarian drama which could succeed in the commercial theatre provided a foundation for the high point of "drama as weapon" reached in the years 1935-1936.

Sam Smiley notes that of the 1,540 plays professionally produced in New York during the entire ten years, only 100 or about eleven percent were directly engage;[21] but Doris Falk points out that thirty-one of the Broadway productions for 1935-1936, about twenty-one percent, were on social or political themes; given the number of productions which were either revivals, ethnic drama, musicals and revues, or comedies of manners, the percentage of social drama for that one season is significant.[22] The sudden interest of audiences and critics in social drama was due, in part at least, to a deepening of the national despair and a lack of change in the national condition. In spite of the optimistic forecasts of Roosevelt's New Dealers, the depression had worsened; and hopes for "just around the corner" prosperity had all but vanished. Unemployment and labor problems had spread from being working class concerns to affecting every citizen. Gone were the well-dressed lines outside the theatres in Times Square that critics had noticed when they left *1931—*, and gone was a sense of security and confidence in existing social institutions. Harold Clurman recalls the change in the city:

> The town was visibly down at the heel; it seemed to shuffle
> feebly as if on chillblained feet. The comfortable middle
> class began to show faces pitted with worry, and the in-
> tellectuals I knew no longer seemed so concerned about
> the validity of Joyce's experiments in prose or the spiritual
> hollowness in Eliot's wasteland, where everyone was sick
> from having read too many books. They were beginning
> to worry over rent and the bills at the A & P.[23]

The depression had become a reality for Broadway audiences by 1935; and while many managers still felt that people would not want to pay to see the same troubles they faced at home dramatized on stage, calls for the theatre to take action as a socially responsible institution began to be heard from all dramatic companies. Hallie Flanagan, who was the director of the controversial Federal Theatre Project, wrote in November, 1935:

> The theatre aside from the rapidly developing left-wing
> groups has remained curiously oblivious to the changing
> social order. It is time that the theatre is brought face
> to face with the great economic problems of the day,
> of which unemployment is one.[24]

But the play which would move the social drama "uptown" to come "face to face" with social problems such as unemployment and labor issues would not come from the left-wing Theatre Union or other groups or from Flanagan's organization or

from the overtly Marxist writers and their antithetical mode;
nor would it come from the established writers of the commercial theatre.   It would come from an almost unknown actor
who, in response to a New Theatre League contest for new scripts
from undiscovered American playwrights, would lock himself
in a hotel room for three days and emerge with what Smiley
calls "the most incendiary emotive appeal of all the exhortative
plays," *Waiting For Lefty.*[25]

"Clifford Odets," writes Gerald Rabkin, "scrawled his
name across the page marked 1935 in American dramatic history."[26]   Few plays and fewer playwrights of any nation or
era have evoked so much critical debate and argumentative analysis as have Odets and his first play.   Gerald Weales notes: "Odets
is so identified with the 1930's that a mention of his name elicits
stock responses, the recollection of a time when literature was a
weapon and leftist optimism almost mandatory."[27]   Emerging
from the ranks of the Group Theatre where he had spent most
of his time playing bit parts, Odets is called both "the voice of
his day, reflecting, even more than he proclaimed or knew, the
urgent need of the people in his time and place"[28] and "a radical, a revolutionary, a red" who, in the guise of iconoclastic
theatre merely pandered the same bill of Marxist goods to a
higher-brow audience.[29]   *Waiting For Lefty* is alternately praised
as the "definitive specimen of the whole proletarian drama in
America" and damned for its "artistic crudity."[30]   Its immediate impact and subsequent popularity, however, establish
it, Goldstein states as "not only the high point in agit-prop drama,
but, to glance ahead, the only play supporting communism to
become a part of classic American literature."[31]   Rarely (O'Neill's
The Emperor Jones is the only other example I can think of)
has a one-act play been the focus of so much literary and critical
attention.

Waiting For Lefty opened January 5, 1935, at the Civic
Repertory Theatre in New York.   Although Odets was a Group
Theatre actor and although he had a play, *Awake and Sing!*,
already in production under the Group's direction, *Lefty* was
staged by the New Theatre League as a benefit for the leftist
theatre's organ, *New Theatre Magazine.*   Harold Clurman and
other Group members attended the opening, but they were not
prepared for the audience's reaction to their friend's play.   "The
first scene of *Lefty* had not played two minutes when a shock
of delighted recognition struck the audience."   Clurman recalls:

"The actors no longer performed, they were carried along as if by an exultancy of communication such as I had never witnessed in the theatre before." Although he points out that the taxi strike of February 1934 had been a "minor incident in the labor crisis of the period" and that few if any of the audience had ever been connected to a union strike meeting at all, he states that, as the action of the play built, the audience became more and more caught up in the spirit of the cabbies' complaint.[32]

The play opens at a meeting of the strike committee of the taxi-driver's union. The meeting has been called to decide whether the drivers' present union leadership is truly representative of the workers' needs. Harry Fatt, the union head, who is obviously working for the interests of management, is attempting to persuade the strike committee and members in attendance that to go out on strike would be foolhardy. The committee members are seated in a semi-circle around a lighted center area on stage, but Fatt addresses the audience who are presumably seated where the attending membership would be. Actors are placed throughout the house, from where they deliver cat-calls and arguments to Fatt's rhetoric, irritating the union boss' gunman who leans against a corner of the stage and rouses himself whenever a member seems to become hostile. From the opening scene, therefore, the audience has a sense of involvement either from Fatt's direct remarks to them or from the answers he receives from actors seated among them.

The action begins immediately as Fatt is discovered, "hot and heavy under the collar, near the end of a long talk, but not too hot."[33] He warns the audience-membership against listening to the "reds" who call for strike. Voices from the audience heckle him, calling for Lefty, the newly elected chairman of the strike committee, who is late for the meeting and to whom the cabbies look to lead them against Fatt. Finally the members of the committee rise to speak, and one by one they give their reasons for wanting to strike, each reason developing into an autonomous scene played out in the spotlight within the semi-circle of their chairs, with only a minimum of props and set pieces. The committeemen are visible throughout, but Fatt is most prominent, "smoking his cigar and often blowing the smoke in the lighted circle" (p. 7). With the exception of the "Labor Spy Episode," the entire play takes place within this area until, finally, one of the members, Agate, rises to call the membership to action.

After each committee member has played out his story, Fatt stands again and threatens the assembled membership. He calls them "reds" and tries to use his gunman to silence one member, Agate, who continues to speak. But Agate turns to the audience and offers a defiant argument to Fatt's warning:

> These slick slobs stand here telling us about bogeymen. That's a new one for the kids—the reds is bogeymen! But the man who got me food in 1932, he called me Comrade! The one who picked me up where I bled— called me Comrade too! What are we waiting for...Don't wait for Lefty! He might never come. Every minute—

Suddenly a man runs in and announces that Lefty's body has been discovered; he has been murdered, presumably by Fatt's henchmen, and Agate turns again to the audience-membership:

> AGATE (*Crying*):   Hear it, boys, hear it?   Hell, listen to me!   Coast to coast!   HELLO AMERICA!   HELLO. WE'RE STORMBIRDS THE WORKING-CLASS.   WORK- ERS OF THE WORLD....OUR BONES AND BLOOD! And when we die they'll know what we did to make a new world!   Christ, cut us up in little pieces.   We'll die for what is right!   Put fruit trees where our ashes are!

The scenes of the play are all recalled as the characters from each committee member's story assemble behind Agate and call to the audience:

> (*to audience*): Well, what's the answer?
> ALL: STRIKE!
> AGATE: LOUDER!
> ALL: STRIKE!
> AGATE and OTHERS ON STAGE: AGAIN!
> ALL: STRIKE, STRIKE, STRIKE!!! (p. 31)

It was Odets' hope that with the planted audience-actors join- ing in the chant that the climax would totally involve the audience in the play and that, instead of applause, the final curtain would bring about a massive chanting of "STRIKE, STRIKE!"   He was not disappointed.   Clurman notes that the audience was not only moved to a loud, vocal response; they were "delirious": "[The audience] stormed the stage which I persuaded the stunned author to mount. People went from the theatre dazed and happy: a new awareness and confidence had entered their lives."[34] By March, 1936, the Group Theatre had taken over the production and moved it "uptown" to Broadway. *Waiting For Lefty* had become a major theatrical event. Odets had done what Lawson and the Theatre Union had failed to do: he had brought successful proletarian protest drama to Broadway.

However, not all the critics were pleased. Edith Isaacs wrote that *Waiting For Lefty* was "sensitive but muddy," and went on: "*Lefty* is of no real worth as drama. Yet there are thousands who seem not to have known or to have understood or to have felt what taxi drivers might be thinking or feeling or suffering until they saw this play."[35] And in his critical biography of Odets, Edward Murray states: "The ecstasy that attended performances of *Waiting For Lefty* had nothing to do with dramatic art."[36] Even Gerald Weales, who frequently defends *Lefty* by calling it "almost an institution,"[37] insists that "its form is clearly agit-prop."[38] Malcolm Goldstein, Gerald Rabkin, and others also tend to agree that Odets' first play is little more than didactic drama which happened to cause a momentary sensation. But more perceptive critics realize what Clurman noted the night of the play's sensational opening, that Odets was addressing broader issues than a single taxi strike and that *Lefty,* for all its resemblance to agit-prop, was, in Morgan Himmelstein's words, "realistic human drama."[39]

Whereas the 1934 taxi strike gives *Waiting For Lefty* its unity and the occasion of the union meeting brings together all the drivers to share their common plight, the stories acted out in the individual scenes are based on conflicts which grow out of other issues besides a corrupt union and the desire for better wages. In "Joe and Edna," for example, the issue at hand is less whether Joe should act as a worker, a cabbie, and strike for better wages than whether he must strike in order to live up to his role as a husband and provider. Bitter and disillusioned with her husband's inability to feed and clothe his family as well as his loss of self-respect, Edna badgers him into making a decision to strike or to lose her to another man. Joe's plight goes beyond questions of labor and capital; they are personal, and they are tied to his hesitancy to make a decision and save his marriage and his family from the general hardships of the times.

In Edna's final speech, she transfers the oppression by the taxi company boss from mere exploitation of workers to the ruination of a whole family:

> . . .I never saw him in my life, but he's putting ideas in my head a mile a minute. He's giving your kids that fancy disease called the rickets. He's making a jelly-fish outa you and putting wrinkles in my face. This is the subject every inch of the way! He's throwing me into Bud Haas' lap. When in hell will you get wise—. (p. 12)

Joe's motivations to strike for better wages, therefore, are more related to his personal dilemma than to his role as a cabbie who is oppressed.

In Scene III, "The Young Hack and His Girl," Odets returns to the theme of social pressures and the relationship between a man and a woman, only this time the conflict is that the cabbie, Sid, is unable to marry his girl, Flossie, because his wages as a cabbie are so low. But the central issue of Scene III is larger than Sid's need for more money; he believes that if he had a chance to go to college as his brother has, he could make something significant out of his life. However, his brother went to school largely because of his athletic ability, and he gave up whatever opportunities his education afforded him to join the Navy. Therefore, Sid must drive a cab to help support the family and can never hope for a chance to advance himself intellectually. Odets emphasizes the personal misfortunes of Sid and Flossie by scarcely mentioning the fact that Sid is a cabbie; what is important in the scene is that a young man with a great potential is being wasted by a society which cares little for individual worth.

Aside from these two scenes, the "Labor Spy Episode," and the climax scene, Odets does not deal with the taxi strike or with further stories about the hardship of being an underpaid cabbie at all. Instead he introduces other problems into the play that are not only unconnected to labor but concern middle class professionals rather than working-stiffs who drive taxis. Anti-semitism and the closing of badly needed charity wards are treated in one scene; pacificism and the development of inhumane and possibly illegal weaponry are examined in another. The scenes are unified because the victims of such evil have now turned to cab driving rather than sacrifice their

integrity, their honesty, or even their nationality in order to
follow their chosen professions; and now, faced with further
oppression and exploitation at the hands of Fatt and his henchmen, they urge the membership not to stand for such subjuga-
tion by a corrupt handful of evil men.

Harold Clurman, basing his conclusion on his theory that
drama is "an art of direct communication grounded on shared
moral values,"[40] points out that Odets' play was "the birth
cry of the thirties. It was a call to join the good fight for a greater
measure of life in a world free of economic fear, falsehood, and
craven servitude to stupidity and greed."[41]   Odets emphasizes
this point in "Intern Episode," where Dr. Benjamin is fired from
his position in spite of his seniority. The reason he is let go,
he deduces, is because he is Jewish. But Odets goes even further
in his indictment of racial bigotry and greed, for when Benjamin
declares that the members of the board who fired him are also
Jewish, Barnes tells him: "I've remarked before—doesn't seem
to be much difference between wealthy Jews and rich Gentiles.
Cut from the same piece!" (p. 27).   Clurman also states that
the call for "STRIKE!" is not simply a demand for shorter hours,
higher wages, or better working conditions; it is a "strike for
greater dignity, strike for a bolder humanity, strike for the full
stature of man."[42]   And Odets affirms his belief in man's inherent worth when in the "Lab Assistant Episode" his protagonist,
Miller, quits his job and punches his boss in the mouth rather
than take a job spying on a scientist who is working on classified
government weapons projects.

By including non-working-class characters in his examination of social problems, Odets was able to depict the problems
of both hungry workers as well as abused and frustrated middle
class professionals, all of whom suffer from the same corruption
in social institutions, business, and government. Odets combines
them physically in the play, for not only have they suffered
from the same social problems in the past, but now, as cabbies,
they are also united as oppressed workers, and they stand together against a common foe represented by Fatt and his gunman.

In the six scenes of the play, Odets dramatizes the importance of fundamental human values: integrity in "Lab Assistant
Episode"; familial responsibility in "Joe and Edna"; tolerance
in "Interne Episode"; honesty and fair play in "Labor Spy Episode"; and love in "The Young Hack and His Girl" and "Joe

and Edna." This combination Goldstein and others call "robust naturalism,"[43] or the pitting of a character or group of characters against indefatigable odds. *Waiting For Lefty* uses the metaphor of a taxi strike to show elements of both the working and middle classes joined in a rebellion against common exploitation and oppression in all aspects of society.

In spite of its aesthetic value, there is much evidence to support the assertion that *Waiting For Lefty* was simply an agitation and propaganda piece which found its moment and was dragged onto Broadway. In terms of structure, the play's ties with any of the strident Marxist agit-prop plays of the late twenties and early thirties are strong. In the first place very little set is required; the plot is simplistic and relies on episodic, melodramatic scenes which are only loosely related to the "incident" which occasions the cabbies' meeting. Also, the names of characters are symbolic. Fatt, a union stooge who has grown comfortably obese from his two-faced dealings; Joe, the typical working-stiff, whose name is synonymous with the American "Everyman"; Agate, the hard, unyielding member who calls for action even when Lefty, the missing leader who espouses the philosophy of the left, does not appear. Additionally, Odets makes an overt move toward involving the audience not only by direct address and planting members of the cast in the house, but also by insisting that they join in the call for "STRIKE!" at the end of the play.

Gerald Weales has traced elements of *Lefty* directly to certain agit-prop plays such as *Newsboy* ("Come into the light, Comrade.") by Gregory Navikov; and the "Joe and Edna" scene closely resembles a scene from *America America!* by Alfred Kreymborg. Such liftings, Weales points out, do not constitute "literary cannibalism" but are correspondent with the "art as weapon" slogan of the times. Odets used situations and slogans from agit-prop plays the same way a craftsman would make use of existing tools.[44] Other parallels and similarities can be found in character and situation to such plays as *Minute Red* by John E. Bonn or *Hands Off!* by Nathaniel Buchwald; but once again, such similarities exist in dozens of leftist and proletarian plays of the period including John Howard Lawson's *Gentlewoman* and *Pure in Heart* (1933) and Michael Blankfort's *The Crime* (1936).

More than any other device in the play, however, the "call to action" which closes the play characterizes *Lefty* as agit-prop.

Douglas McDermott points out that the social dramatists, especially Lawson and Blankfort, realized that the stimulation of the audience's emotions was important; therefore, a "call to action" is almost always used at the end of proletarian, protest plays in order to release the pent-up emotions of the audience and allow the writer and actors to control the situation.[45]   In this sense, such a device is, in Weales' words, "a cousin to Aristotelian catharsis," in that it calls for an identification of the audience with the plight of the cabbies in their oppressed and subjected state.[46]   Such a response as Odets witnessed on *Lefty's* opening night was more than simply a ratification of the social statement he was making about the plight of taxi drivers; it was a recognition on the part of the audience that the oppression which is evident on the stage is extended into their own lives.   At the call to "STRIKE!" they released their emotions out of fear of the same social evils which assail the characters and out of pity for the Joes and Sids and Dr. Benjamins who have been oppressed for so long.

Odets knew that such a device could work.   He had experienced just such an emotional arousal himself.   Clurman recalls an evening in 1933 when he and Odets attended a film:

> When we had seen the film *[Weavers* based on Hauptmann's] and we were ready to leave, a man in a navy-blue flannel shirt with a suit and face that matched it, came out and addressed the audience with a simple conviction that must have been hard to maintain under the circumstances.   He was a radical of some kind—the real article, not its phony counterpart—and he urged strong political action against the terror of the crisis, the unemployment, hunger, destitution of the day.   Odets applauded with sudden spontaneity,—as if unprepared to do so and himself surprised that he had.   I was no less surprised, but did not question him.   I understood that his applause was not so much a matter of intellectual approval as almost a physical movement of union with the speaker who had uttered words that needed to be spoken one way or another.

This 1933 experience, so similar to the agit-prop plays and even to the social satires such as *Both Your Houses* in its attempt to raise the consciousness of an audience to the point of spontaneous demonstration through a "call to action," is closely imitated in the "STRIKE!" scene of *Waiting For Lefty.* Whether such a scene is a "cousin to catharsis" or not, the incident had an effect on Odets. Clurman realized the degree of that impact on the playwright when he attended the same theatre's staging of *Waiting For Lefty* two years later at a benefit for striking workers.[47]

It would be a mistake to dismiss *Waiting For Lefty* as merely an agit-prop play which found its moment. In spite of the structural similarities, there are fundamental differences. In the first place, agit-prop plays had their chief value in their ability to address immediate social problems and offer specific solutions. The taxi strike of 1934 was "old business" by the time *Lefty* was even written. Even though it would be performed at benefits for subsequent strikes by hack drivers all over the country, it would also be staged for striking workers in other industries, and it would be staged by theatrical groups who had nothing to do with labor in areas which had no labor unrest whatsoever. *Lefty's* impact goes beyond the plight of a single group of men struggling for decent wages; Odets adopted an assumption of the left: that the honest worker was a victim not only of oppressive employers but also of a corrupt government and dishonest labor leaders. Additionally, by handling problems in the play not connected to labor, he broadened the focus to the extent that the specific problem addressed by the play's format, the taxi strike, became almost an afterthought in the desire of the characters to protest their situation in general.

A second significant difference between *Lefty* and agit-prop is in Odets' depiction of character and situation. In agit-prop, characters are pure stereotypes and situations are almost cliched. In *Waiting For Lefty* characters such as Joe and Edna, Sid and Flossie, Dr. Benjamin and Miller begin to take on dimensions of personality which are well-rounded and not altogether predictable. When Joe finally makes up his mind to strike, for example, he looks to Edna for assurance that she will still be there when he returns; and although she never wavers in her determination to force him into a decision, she gives that assurance to him. Also, when Sid and Flossie come to the realization that their lives can never be joined in happiness, instead of making a Marxist stand, Sid buries his head in Flossie's lap and weeps. Throughout the play, the characters give insights into personalities which are more complex than the flat types of agit-prop.

The scenes of *Lefty* also differ from those of agit-prop. First of all, even though every scene's protagonist is a cabbie, the series of events they play out does not always lead to the inevitable conclusion to strike; secondly, each scene is a separate story, and the relationship each has to the others is only that each shows a different aspect of social problems. In an agit-prop play the scenes would proceed from one case of social injustice or capitalist oppression to the next, each becoming more serious and more emotional until the "call to action" is the only possible alternative. Furthermore, only one social situation would usually be treated at a time.

A third major area where *Lefty* differs from agit-prop is in the number and kind of communist or Marxist sentiments it expresses. Aside from the end of "Interne Episode" where Dr. Benjamin stands with "clenched fist raised high" and an occasional use of the epithet "Comrade," there is very little indication that any of the characters in the play have any inclination to accept communist doctrines. In fact, in his last lines, Benjamin refuses Barnes' advice that he go to the Soviet Union to continue to practice his medicine because hospitals are socialized there, declaring: "No! Our work's here—America!" (pp. 28-29). And Fatt's constant accusation that anyone who wants a strike is a "red" usually arouses anger in the committee members. Joe's indecision about whether he should strike or not is primarily based on a fear that he will be branded a "red" and be unable to work in the future, and even Miller in the "Lab Assistant Episode" asserts that it is better to be a cabbie in America than a communist somewhere else. Odets' strongest leftist statement, however, occurs in a scene eliminated from the collected editions of *Six Plays by Clifford Odets* published in 1939. Whereas the other characters had refused to be called "reds" or to embrace Marxist teachings at all, in this scene, Phil, a young actor who has been rebuffed by a producer, is offered a dollar by the office stenographer. She tells him he can take it and buy either ten loaves of bread or "nine loaves of bread and one copy of the *Communist Manifesto*. "Learn while you eat. Read while you run . . . ." He exhibits confusion, and she offers to give him a copy, quoting: "And I saw a new earth and a new heaven; for the first earth and the first heaven were passed away; and there was no more sea." He still does not understand:

PHIL: I don't understand that....
STEN: I'm saying that the meek shall not inherit the earth!
PHIL: No?
STEN: THE MILITANT! Come into the light, Comrade.[48]

But this statement and this scene, considered "too sectarian" by Odets when he published the play, is mild compared to the propagandistic bombast of agit-prop plays such as *Vote Communist*.

Ultimately the committee accepts the appellation "red," but Agate turns it into an ironic identification which has almost no political connotations:

(*To Audience*): What's the answer boys? The answer is, if we're reds because we wanna strike, then we take over the salute too! Know how they do it? (*Makes Communist salute.*) What is it? An uppercut! The good old uppercut to the chin (p. 30).

Such a statement is hardly in keeping with the militant tone of the agit-prop calls for revolution and acceptance of Marxist ideals.

Agit-prop plays were almost always written to create an arousal in an audience over a specific set of circumstances or events. For that reason they were usually staged by workers or people directly concerned with the event in question, usually written by someone intimately familiar with the particulars of the circumstances and usually performed for an audience whose interests were directly connected with the outcome of the play. They were, as Weales points out, "as ephemeral as the daily newspaper"; but *Waiting For Lefty* fits none of these categories. It was supposedly written for a contest and performed as a benefit for the New Theatre League, not in support of any kind of union strike; it was staged by actors, not worker-actors, and it was performed for an audience of no particular class or occupation. Testifying before the House UnAmerican Affairs Committee in 1952, Odets claimed not only that the supposed contest for which *Lefty* was submitted was a "hoax," but also that he had been approached by the New Theatre League because the selection of plays they had was so poor that they had nothing to stage for the planned benefit. He also stated that he personally knew nothing about taxi driving or unions and had never been near a strike meeting, especially the 1934 New York taxi strike.[50] Elia Kazan, testifying for the same committee at the same time, submitted that Odets wanted to write an "entertainment" for United Front meetings and rallies, and that Odets told him that his sole purpose in writing *Lefty* was to provide the Group Theatre's repertoire with some one-act plays designed for benefit performances just as Kazan and Art Smith had done in writing their own agit-prop play, *Dimitroff*.[51] But, significantly, when the Group Theatre took over production of *Lefty* and moved it "uptown," Odets refused to pair his play with the Kazan-Smith piece, even though *Dimitroff* was a proven success off-Broadway, and chose instead his own untried one-act, *Till the Day I Die*, an anti-fascist melodrama of more traditional form. This selection, more than anything else suggests Odets' intent to divorce *Lefty* from its agit-prop antecedents.

Michael Mendelsohn notes that *Lefty* is not simply a "leftist drama" even though it is frequently "militant, propagandistic, and strident."[52] What sets it apart from even the more formal Marxist drama such as was being staged by the Theatre Union was its attempt to address a broader spectrum of the population than merely the working class. Weales writes: "[*Lefty*] burst its bounds, escaped its audience, fed into the mainstream of American drama, dragging its author along."[53] It is unlikely that any play, particularly an agit-prop vehicle for communist dogma, would have won so much acclaim so easily unless it had something more than its similarity to the polemical bombast being staged by "hard-line" leftists in their Marxist "morality plays" at union meetings and in off-Broadway theatres. Odets had clearly struck a nerve, and the "new audience" Clurman had sensed in the balcony of *1931*—'s closing night had found its way into the orchestra. It supported the young playwrights work because he addressed social ills through a series of legitimately dramatic and emotional scenes; in short, *Waiting For Lefty* informed its audience, but it also entertained it, and this combination was sufficient to sustain its commercial success.

Although Leftist critics see Odets' play as a significant step toward bringing "hard-line" Marxist drama to Broadway once and for all, Lawson despairs of Odets' "romantic" ideas about social change, but admires the play as an aesthetic work. He writes that Odets' naively envisions the forces of social advancement as dependent upon personal recognition such as Dr.

Benjamin's decision to stay in America and "Get some job to keep alive . . . and study at work and learn my place—" (p. 29); or a "realization scene," such as Miller's sudden understanding that his promotion and raise include spying on his co-workers; or a "conversion scene," when all the cabbies turn to revolutionary action as a last alternative.[54] "In *Lefty*," Lawson writes, the chief conversion occurs when the announcement is made that Lefty is dead: "Lefty's death is unprepared and undramatized, yet it seems to be the culmination of a series of relationships which are the core of the action, the essence of the social conflicts around which the play is organized."[55] Speaking as a playwright and theorist, Lawson sees great potential for Odets' future work in *Lefty*, but speaking as a Communist, he is disappointed in the inability of the younger writer to master a "more profound and sustained conflict."[56] In short, Lawson and other leftists wanted the drama to agitate and propagandize more and entertain less. Yet it is in the aspect of its entertainment value that the key to *Lefty*'s great success lay.

Waiting For Lefty "fails as agit-prop," Gerald Weales writes, "because it succeeds too obviously as a play."[57] This success grows out of Odets' ability to combine a series of abstract human values and emotions with concrete social concerns in a compendium of six scenes that climax in a burst of emotional response. Although the ending speech of Agate and its assumed audience participation are bombastic and didactic in the Marxian sense, McDermott points out: "Such an ending was a necessary commitment of the social playwrights' dynamic conception of reality, and in no way detracted from his art."[58] On the contrary, by combining elements of the militant agit-prop with a keen sense of emotionally evocative drama, Odets achieved an effective combination of propaganda and art: "propaganda in that the author has a thesis which he espouses," that the oppressed must band together and fight against those who oppress them, "and a work of art in which he probes the inner and outer life of his characters."[59] Through the lives of Joe, Edna, Dr. Benjamin, Miller, Agate, and the rest of the cast, Odets demonstrates that specific social ills can be exposed by using characters who have dimension, situations which are unique to those characters, and a set of values and emotions which are shared by all people everywhere; then he penetrates the surface realism to expose their human nature. While it is not exactly what Joseph Wood Krutch called "revolutionary" drama, it does begin to

move away from his formula for "classic" drama wherein the
emphasis is almost totally on situation. *Waiting For Lefty* is
about a strike, but it is also about people; and in its explorations
of those people and their struggle and their values, it takes a
major step toward moving American drama in the thirties toward
its "revolutionary" form.

The appeal of Odets' first play spread rapidly. Over sixty
towns immediately began staging it, and performances were
played nationwide as late as 1940.[60]   The sensation it caused
was almost unprecedented in American drama in the thirties, and
although some critics continued to sniff that it was nothing more
than agitation and propaganda, a growing number began to recognize that it was something new, not only to Broadway, but also
to dramatic structure in general. *Waiting For Lefty* goes beyond
political diatribe and the stirring of an audience through rhetorical and emotional appeal.   Odets' realization, in Kozlenko's
words, "that the implicit motivations of a human being are themselves dynamic and that when shown in relationship with his
background, the dramatization of his conflict becomes at once
individual and social,"[61] created in *Lefty* something more than
a political harangue, an agit-prop play that moved to Broadway.
Although it speaks to a time now far removed in specific concerns and sentiments, it attempts to comment on its age with an
eye toward making changes; and although its message and language
seem antiquated and trite, its portrayal of human values and
human conflicts transcends its time. *Waiting For Lefty* manages
to fulfill its literary obligations as well as its political thesis. It
comes, as Malcolm Cowley puts it, "as close to being a classic
as anything that emerged from the proletarian school."[62]

Odets' successful combination of agit-prop devices with
acceptable Broadway drama in *Waiting For Lefty* gave new hope
for those playwrights who had been attempting to achieve such
a synthesis for years. Suddenly the social drama as protest play,
as didactic or thesis play, was welcome in the Great White Way,
and the success of Odets' blend of the agit-prop structure and
quality playwriting indicated that audiences were at long last
ready to accept social commitment in their drama. But New York
audiences were not going to stand for being harangued from
the stage night after night.   "Hard-line" leftists still were not
able to move their radical messages onto Broadway stages. Odets'
synthesis of the two forms—acceptable human drama with strong
social commitment and agit-prop diatribe, with "call to action"—

was more of a milestone than a plateau; and American writers continued to search for a perfect synthesis of protest drama and acceptable playwriting.

Till the Day I Die, ground out hurriedly to accompany *Lefty* when the latter moved to Broadway, became the model for the anti-fascist plays which would follow. Odets' second one-act, a melodrama in seven scenes, contains characters, situations, and slogans which would become clichés by the time World War II began. The underground fighters in the play include the hero, Ernst Tausig; his sweetheart, Tilly; and his brother, Carl. Like most anti-fascists of the pre-war years, they are essentially pacifistic and resort to violence only when they are forced to. Even when the greater organization suspects Ernst of treachery and informing on them, they punish him with censure and ostracism rather than a death sentence.[63] The Nazis who arrest Ernst in the first scene are also prototypes for standard characters in subsequent anti-fascist plays and films. They fall into three categories: Detective Popper, who represents both the Gestapo and its sadistic, barbaric cruelty; Captain Schlegel, who stands for the ambitious young officer corps, loyal to Hitler and in control of the fate of the German people; and Major Duhring, who performs his duty to the military but kills himself because his conscience will not permit him to follow blindly the ideology and orders of a madman and his henchmen (pp. 135-136). The rest of the soldiers of Germany fall generally into one of these categories, although there is little likelihood that those who share Duhring's sentiments will follow his example rather than give in to Nazi pressure.

Harold Clurman is kind when he notes that *Till the Day I Die* is "a little artificial yet not without some qualities of youthful sweetness and idealism."[64] As several critics point out, the play depends unnecessarily on stage violence for much of its impact. In Scene III, for example, two troopers have a grisly contest of strength to see which can fell a standing prisoner with one blow (pp. 125-126); and this follows the brutal smashing of Ernst's fingers with a rifle butt in the previous scene. Edith Isaacs agrees with those critics who find the play too violent and states that this lack of subtlety is a major flaw of Odets' script.[65]

The mental violence perpetrated by the Nazis is far more frightening than the physical abuse carried out by back-alley hoods. After Ernst's arrest for "questioning," for example, he is well-treated; Popper smashes his hand against orders. He is then made to stand in the room where other prisoners are interrogated, and those who are released carry the tale that he is cooperating with the Nazis. He is also taken along on raids of underground strongholds, and those who escape see him seated prominently in the front of the Gestapo car, as if he is guiding them. What the escapees do not see, however, is that Ernst is bound by chains to the seat and forced to sit upright in plain view. From time to time he is released; the Nazis follow him, hoping that he will lead them to his comrades in an attempt to cleanse his own name. Thus the Gestapo is able to round up suspects and create mistrust and suspicion among the underground all with one effort.

   This game of mental violence does not stop with the enemies of the Nazi state, however. Even within the Party itself, ambitious men spread suspicions about their peers and superiors: "I think that Popper must have Jewish blood. He hasn't the brains of a trained flea," Schlegel hints to Adolph at one point (p. 119). Such lines give Odets the opportunity to illustrate both the moral depravity of ranking Nazis as well as their blind anti-semitism.

   Another complaint frequently lodged against *Till the Day I Die* is that Odets offers no alternative to fascism but communism: "If you do not like the philosophy of communism," Isaacs writes in her review, "you will not like the theme of *Till the Day I Die*."[66] But Odets' advocation of a communist alternative (he became a member of the Party in the winter of 1935) is less a result of his personal politics than of his astute realization that in Nazi Germany in 1935 the Communist Party was probably the only group capable of effectively organizing opposition to Hitler's Reich. The burning of the German Parliament in 1933 had been blamed on Communists; and, aside from the unorganized and helpless Jews, the most strongly persecuted group in Germany during the mid-thirties was the Communist Party and its affiliates. Odets indicates that for the average German in 1935 there were only three alternatives: to join the Nazis and go along with their programs, however cruel; to accept death, along with the Jews and Major Duhrings, whether at the hands of the Gestapo or by suicide; or to join the only possible opposition, the Communists. These are not optimistic alternatives, perhaps, but in 1935 there was little to be optimistic about in Germany.

This point is emphasized when Ernst makes what can only be described as a "call to action" speech at the close of the play. Because Gestapo tactics have made him a danger to his comrades and useless to the underground, he follows Duhring's example; but before his suicide, he exhorts his comrades to continue the fight:

> These guns are complicated pieces of machinery. (*Has picked it up.*) Our Germans make them like works of art. (*Weighs the gun in his hand.*) Tilly, Carl, our agony is real. But we live in the joy of a great coming people! The animal kingdom is past. Day must follow the night. Now we are ready: we have been steeled in a terrible fire, but soon all the desolate places of the world must flourish with human genius. Brothers will live in the soviets of the world! Yes, a world of security and freedom is waiting for all mankind! (*Looks at them both deeply. Walks to door to room L.*) Do your work, comrades. (*Exits.*) (p. 154)

The tone of this speech is considerably milder than Agate's demand for "STRIKE!" at *Lefty*'s curtain; in fact, it recalls Alan McClean's exhortation at the end of *Both Your Houses* more than it does the militant "call to action" of the agit-prop plays. Like McClean's speech it is delivered to other characters on stage rather than to the audience in true agit-prop fashion. Like both Agate and McClean, however, Ernst is positive and optimistic in his closing lines; and except for the single reference to the "soviets of the world," there is almost nothing in the speech that an American capitalist might not agree with in the depressed years of 1935-36.

The choice of *Till the Day I Die* as a companion piece for *Waiting For Lefty* indicates that Odets had a conscious desire to exploit the synthesis he had stumbled onto with his first one-act. Although Ernst and the underground members are Communists, Odets carefully avoids writing leftist platitudes for them to mouth except insofar as they react to the extreme rightism of the Nazis. Just as the leftist philosophy in *Waiting For Lefty* is toned down to represent the only positive alternative rather than a radical and impulsive demand for social change, the characters in *Till the Day I Die* are more memorable as anti-fascists than as communist revolutionaries. The chief activity of the underground, for example, seems to be distributing leaflets with anti-Nazi propaganda in them. They are not militant in either their announced programs or their plans for revolution; in fact, Ernst's concepts of life after revolution are based on values which are more humanistic than economic. In one speech he describes his experience in Russia:

> My present dream of the world—I ask for happy laughing people everywhere. I ask for hope in eyes: for wonderful baby boys and girls I ask, growing up strong and prepared for a new world. I won't ever forget the first time we visited the nursery in Moscow. Such faces on those children! Future engineers, doctors; when I saw them I understood most deeply what the revolution meant. (p. 112)

Such a vision is a far cry from militant Marxist bombast; it is even a long way from the "reluctant dragon" position of Joe, Dr. Benjamin, and Agate in *Lefty*; for the characters in Odets' first play are ultimately willing to become stridently "red" if that is the only way they can realize their dreams. Ernst's role as an anti-fascist dreamer rather than militant revolutionary is emphasized immediately after this speech, however; the Gestapo knocks at the door and he is led away without a struggle.

In spite of its flaws, *Till the Day I Die* made a significant move from the kind of anti-fascist statement offered by S. N. Behrman in a play such as *Rain From Heaven*. Behrman's characters, both those who opposed the fascist ideals and those who supported them in the name of capitalism, were upper and middle class individuals; Odets' characters cut across class structure. Ernst, Tilly, and Carl, as well as their comrades in the underground, could be working class people or from other strata; Popper, Duhring, and Schlegel also represent all levels of German society. Again the attempt to universalize a social problem by touching all levels of social strata and intellectual ability indicates a synthesis between agit-prop and the older social drama.

Critical reaction to *Till the Day I Die* was generally negative, but the strength of *Waiting For Lefty* carried the piece along and kept it from closing. American Nazis did not find the play as ineffective as the critics, however. In California Will Geer's production of the two scripts resulted in his being kidnapped and severely beaten by "Friends of the New Germany" hoodlums, and Odets was forced to add an "extra heavy lock" on his and Clurman's New York apartment.[67] Still, even a cursory reading of *Till the Day I Die* reveals that it is not as well written as *Lefty*. When Odets abandoned the mode of incorporating the audience and using the more strident motif of *Waiting For Lefty*, his scenes appeared to be too episodic and his characters tend to flatten out into stereotypes. There is no opportunity in *Till the Day I Die* for the characters to indicate that they have any depth or complexity of personality at all. None of the scenes approach the poignancy of the love story briefly played out in "The Young Hack and His Girl," for example; instead the love story between Ernst and Tilly is played down to the extent that they rarely show any affection for each other, and when they do it is more in the nature of friendship than passion. They are totally devoted to their cause. Also, the wife of Major Duhring, Hedvig, has none of the complexity of Odets' earlier example of the "woman behind the man," Edna. She resembles Edna in that she is ambitious for her husband, but she lacks Edna's insight into her husband's problems, for Hedvig cannot perceive that her husband is unhappy with his role as a Nazi henchman and is close to suicide.

Although *Till the Day I Die* has elements which suggest the quality of writing Odets demonstrated in *Lefty* and would show again in subsequent plays—his sensitivity to dialogue, ability to build dramatic intensity in short scenes, and use of devices such as suspense, discovery, and recognition—his one-act is finally little more than a thesis melodrama with "good guys" and "bad guys" and would probably have been forgotten except for its companion piece. The play is significant, however, for its theme and for its introduction of a subject which had been dealt with only in metaphoric ways or through incidental dialogue or through the social satire of the past: the threat of Nazism and the confrontation of fascist-communist ideology.[68]

During the same session *Waiting For Lefty* and *Till the Day I Die* made their debuts on Broadway, other writers also achieved some success with dramas effectively synthesizing the militant ideals of the left with the palatable drama of the commercial theatre. The communist line had become almost completely devoted to the Popular Front movement by mid-decade, and in spite of attempts to stage militant proletarian drama such as Lawson's Theatre Union production of *Marching Song* in 1937, there were relatively few attempts to stage a play which could "out-Lefty *Lefty.*" Plays based on themes of pacifism such as Irwin Shaw's *Bury the Dead,* a macabre comedy about World War I corpses which refuse to be buried, created a sensation in audiences concerned about and divided over Hitler's rapidly growing territorial ambitions and bellicose actions, the Spanish Civil War, and Japan's conquests in Asia. Many plays of the period contained lines referring to such international problems, but the social dramatists had discovered that Clurman's "new audience" was more concerned with domestic problems than with foreign armies and alien wars.

Sidney Kingsley's *Dead End* was produced nine months after *Waiting For Lefty* opened, and in it Kingsley employs many of the same techniques which stirred and excited Odets' audiences. The characters of Kingsley's play also possess allegorical names: Gimpty is an unemployed artist who is crippled from childhood rickets; he spends each day sitting by New York's East River where he watches a group of young boys swimming in the garbage-filled water and idling away their youth collecting smokable cigarette butts and engaging in petty thievery and minor crime. The play takes its name from its setting, the end of a street which runs into the river between two buildings: one a tenement where some of the boys live and the other an exclusive apartment house from which wealthy people enter and exit. Gimpty expresses his bitterness over his own infirmity throughout the play. He tells Drina, older sister of one of the boys:

> Drina, the place you live in is awfully important. It can
> give you a chance to grow, or it can twist you—*he twists*
> *an imaginary object with grim venom*—like that. When I
> was in school they used to teach us that evolution made
> men out of animals. They forgot to tell us it can also
> make animals out of men.[69]

In this speech Gimpty expresses a basic tenet of literary naturalism which has its antecedents in Hippolyte Taine's and Emile Zola's works in Europe and Stephen Crane's and Theodore Dreiser's fiction in the United States: that the environment he has grown to manhood in has left him twisted and unable to rise to his potential in life, either physically or spiritually. As he watches the boys play in the garbage and filth around him, he understands that they are turning into animals, and his anger increases: "When I see what it's doing to these kids I want to

tear down these lice nets with my fingers" (p. 81). Again, he
recognizes that without a decent environment, none of the boys
he watches has a chance to make anything of himself.

Gimpty is also bitter because he is in love with Kay, a girl
from modest surroundings, but not as poor as his. Kay has learned that by using her good looks, she can raise herself in society;
she has become the mistress of a man named Hilton, who owns
and lives in the fancy apartment building and sails his yacht
up and down the river. Kay and Gimpty meet occasionally in
secret, but she is not bright enough to perceive either that he
truly loves her or that she is happier when they are together
than when she is with Hilton. But Kay fears Gimpty's bitterness as much as she is attracted to his love for her. She pities
him and tells him that she never really knew how poor people
could be until she saw his apartment with its wet walls and filth.
Her comments make him feel ashamed, and he tells her that
even though it is not right "that anybody should live like that,
. . . a couple of million of us do." And the fault, he tells her,
lies with a system that condones grand buildings for grand cities
but places no priorities on decent housing for a city's people:

> Yeah, right here in New York...New York with its famous
> skyline...its Empire State, the biggest God-damned build-
> ing in the world! The biggest tombstone in the world!
> They wanted to build a monument to the times. Well,
> there it is, bigger than the pyramids and just as many
> tenants. *He forces her to smile with him. Then he sighs
> and adds hopelessly.* I wonder when they'll let us build
> houses for men to live in? (p. 80)

Kay refuses to leave Hilton and marry Gimpty, for she fears
he will pull her down with him; she sympathizes with his bleak
vision of the world, but she recognizes the futility of his anger.

The Gimpty-Kay love story is actually a subplot of the
play, emerging between the scenes of the boys' pranks and near-
criminal mischief, which revolve around the teasing and tor-
menting of Phillip, a rich boy whose apartment is in the fancy
building opposite the tenement. But the two plotlines come
together when a known and wanted criminal, Baby-face Martin,
returns to his old neighborhood to find his mother. Seeing an
opportunity to obtain enough money for his and Kay's happiness, Gimpty puts aside the memories of fear he used to have

for the now famous criminal and turns him in to the police. In what must be the most brutal scene in American drama, the detectives track Martin to the dead-end alley and onto center stage where they gun him down, one of them standing over the lifeless corpse and emptying his revolver into it.

Although he has the reward for turning Martin in, Gimpty still cannot convince Kay to marry him. She tells him that money alone cannot change the bitterness in him; and, further, she says that she has come to accept what she is, a wealthy man's mistress. She recognizes that she would probably return to that way of life even if she did marry Gimpty. Kay's realization that her decision to escape Gimpty's poverty and her own background by an immoral life-style is irrevocable recalls The Girl in *1939—*, whose streetwalking has rendered her unfit and unworthy of Adam's love. But the severity of The Girl's plight has been softened in *Dead End* to a conscious choice on Kay's part rather than the physical necessity brought about by an incurable social disease.

Gimpty's depression after Kay's refusal and departure on Hilton's yacht is short-lived, however. Drina's brother, Tommy, has led the gang of boys in beating Phillip; and when the wealthy boy's father, Griswald, comes to his son's rescue, Tommy stabs him in the hand. Griswald's wounds are superficial, but he insists on pressing charges against Tommy, and Gimpty perceives that if the youth is jailed he will soon turn tough and wind up like Baby-face Martin, dead in an alley:

> Yeah...Martin was a killer, he was bad, he deserved to die true! But I knew him when we were kids. He had a lot of fine stuff. He was strong. He had courage. He was a born leader. He even had a sense of fair play. But living in the streets kept making him bad. . .then he was sent to reform school. Well, they reformed him all right! They taught him the ropes. He came out tough and hard and mean, with all the tricks of the trade. (p. 112)

Recognizing that Tommy has all the qualities he has just described and all the potential to go bad as well, Gimpty decides to use the reward money to bail the boy out and give him a second chance; presumably, Gimpty will help Drina keep her brother off the streets so that he will not turn out like the dead gangster.

Dead End has strong naturalistic tones throughout, both in its theme and its resolution which emphasize the influence of environment and uncontrollable forces over the fates of individuals. The money which will save Tommy comes from Martin's destruction, for example, as if to say that the product of the environment can ironically be the means to conquer it as well. When Fat Lady, tormented by the boys, lashes out at them that they are "little savages" who inherited wickedness, Kingsley emphasizes the naturalistic theme as Gimpty shouts out: "Inheritance? Yeah. You inherit a castle thirty stories over the river, or a stinkin' hole in the ground! Wooden heads are inherited, but not wooden legs...nor legs twisted by rickets" (p. 62). And at another point he characterizes his own childhood development and fears:

> *Stares down at the blackwater swirling under him. He begins to talk faster and faster, trying to push back into his unconscious the terror that haunts him, to forget that afternoon if only for a few seconds.* It reminds me of something...What is it?...Oh yeah...when I was a kid. In the spring the sudden sun showers used to flood the gutters. The other kids used to race boats down the street. Little boats: straws, matches, lollipop sticks, I couldn't run after them, so I guarded the sewer and caught the boats to keep them from tumbling in. Near the sewer... sometimes, I remember...a whirlpool would form...dirt and oil from the street would break into rainbow colors... iridescent...*For a moment he does escape.* Beautiful, I think...a marvel of color out of dirty water. I can't take my eyes off it. And suddenly a boat in danger. *The terror in him rises again.* I try to stop it...too late! It shoots into the black hole of the sewer. I used to dream about falling into it myself. The river reminds me of that...Death must be like this...like the river at night. (pp. 134-135)

But *Dead End* is not purely naturalistic because the hero is not destroyed by the forces. True to the formula of social drama, he is only made more solidly resolute by the ordeal, more strident by the defeats he suffers; and although he is crippled for life he is determined to fight against the crushing social forces by saving Tommy from a similar or worse fate.

Kingsley's play was enthusiastically accepted by audiences, although many critics quarrelled over its dramatic quality. The biggest objection was to the language of the boys in the gang, but Kingsley and others maintained that he was striving for more than "surface realism" and that such brutal language as well as brutal action gave the play its power.[70] Malcolm Cowley agrees: "It is Kingsley's antisentimental treatment of slum dwellers that gives the play its strength, whether he is dealing with criminals or those who abide by the law."[71] But the chief critical complaint of the time was that the play lacked focus; in other words, was the Gimpty-Kay affair the major plot of the play or was it the fracas between the boys and Griswald? What the critics did not seem to understand was that *Dead End*'s main character was the city itself. As Brooks Atkinson states: "Callous, imperious, hostile, contemptuous, complex, it overwhelmed all the human actors and also Mr. Kingsley's play."[72] Just as *Lefty* uses brief vignettes to create an emotional response, a basis for Odets' larger social criticism, Kingsley uses both the love story and the action of the mischiefious boys graphically to illustrate a contest which goes on between a gigantic and villainous city and the people who fight for their very existence within and against it. Like the strike in *Lefty*, the struggle for a decent life in lice-infested slums amid polluted rivers on dead end streets is a metaphor for a greater social issue: the struggle for a chance to be honest and happy in a society which places higher priorities on how wealthy a person is or where a person comes from rather than on what he can do or who he might become. *Dead End* is about a city and urban housing problems, but it uses the human drama played out among the characters to emphasize its social point. Just as Joe, Edna, Miller, Sid, and the other characters of *Lefty*'s scenes demonstrate the impact of social problems in their inner lives, Gimpty, Kay, Tommy, Drina, and the other characters of *Dead End* provide the audience with dramatically sound romance, conflict, and graphic dialogue to illustrate Kingsley's social message. Although *Dead End* lacks the strident agit-prop structure of *Lefty* or other radical plays, it treats the social issues of housing and unemployment in a similar fashion by combining social commitment and thesis with an entertaining and palatable dramatic form. Just as Odets had done in *Waiting For Lefty*, Kingsley took a specific social concern and made it a universal matter. Common to both plays is the belief that a refusal to surrender in the face of overwhelming odds is the only possible alternative to present troubles. Although *Dead End* contains no "call to action," it does create an emotional and moral response as the crippled, unemployed artist hobbles off to the jail to give away his money for the salvation of a small boy.

If the critics were confused over the nature of Kingsley's play, the audiences were not. *Dead End* was vigorously acclaimed by its patrons and enjoyed a long run.[73] The new-found synthesis had a name by the end of the 1935-1936 season; it was called the "new theatre," and it apparently had permanently located Clurman's "new audience." Writing in 1939 of the 1935-1936 season, Krutch states: "Very soon any sharp distinction between the writer for the New Theatre and the writer for the general public ceased to exist."[74]

In spite of their Popular Front motivations, radical leftists were not at all satisfied with the synthesis discovered by Odets, Kingsley, and others. John Howard Lawson, whose association with the leftist theatre had been a long and active one by 1936, published *Theory and Practice of Playwriting* in that year, a book devoted at least in part to the mechanics and philosophy of constructing socially relevant drama. "The essential character of drama," he writes, "is social conflict in which the conscious will is exerted: persons are pitted against other persons, or individuals against groups, or groups against other groups, or groups against social or natural forces."[75] Lawson sought a return to "poetic drama," not the blank verse of Maxwell Anderson's *Night Over Taos* or *Elizabeth the Queen*, but "imagistic dialogue" such as John Dos Passos wrote in the twenties.[76] Lawson believed that playwriting required a sense of both the history of the genre as well as a fundamental recognition on the part of the writer and the audience that a thesis was being stated. In a 1935 paper, "Technique and the Drama," delivered to the American Writers' Congress, he summarized this idea:

> There are three basic principles of play construction: conflict, action, unity. The application of these principles is complex, and requires careful definition and analysis . . . (a) conflict and action involve the exercise of the conscious will toward a goal; (b) this involves social judgments and social purpose; (c) it may be then assumed that the dramatist's conception of social meaning and purpose will determine the exact form of conflict; (d)

> then construction is not merely a pitcher into which
> the social content is poured, but it is the core of the social
> content itself.[77]

But Lawson, however influential his theories may have been
on his contemporaries, had not produced a successful play since
the start of the decade. *Success Story, Gentlewoman,* and *Pure
in Heart* had all failed; and, while he blamed the critics rather
than his technique,[78] he still failed to recognize that entertainment was as fundamental to dramatic success as social significance.   The very devices he complained about in both Odets'
and Kingsley's plays—the development of character, the exploitation of action devices such as realization, discovery, and physical
violence, the concentration on human emotions such as love,
and values such as integrity—were the very items which brought
audiences in to see the plays and caused the critics to recommend
them.   Odets and Kingsley had learned a valuable lesson from
the social satire, that while the "sermon" might be their major
interest, the play would not succeed at all without the "tickle."
    In the wake of *Lefty* and *Dead End,* the synthesis of "hard-
line," leftist, agit-prop protest plays designed to raise social
consciousness through acceptable dramatic form began to weaken.
Lawson and other leftists and their companies became aware
that Odets and Kingsley among others had found the "new audience," and they had found them in the orchestra seats "uptown."   In response to this realization, the Theatre Union moved
onto Broadway among the successful and established companies
and writers.   For its premiere it chose a new script by Lawson,
Marching Song.
    Opening in February 1937, two years after *Waiting For
Lefty, Marching Song* represented both an example of the techniques Lawson expounded in *Theory and Practice of Playwriting*
and a return to the subject matter—the American working class—
which had brought him success a decade before in such plays
as *International* and *Processional.*   In spite of all his work with
the Communist Party and leftist organizations, however,
Lawson revealed, as Goldstein puts it, "that he did not know
that class well enough, for all the genuineness of his concern,
to write a convincing play about it."[79]   Lawson was out of
touch with the very people toward whom his thesis was directed;
his concern for communist ideology over the years had altered
his awareness of the very problems such a philosophy was sup-

posed to relieve. Further, because he hoped to avoid what he perceived as a weakness in Odets' and Kingsley's approach to social issues, he failed to treat the problems he examines in the play on a level where a mixed audience could respond. The middle class audiences found the play vaguely insulting, highly inflammatory, and pointedly communistic.

Marching Song adopts a naturalistic formula in accordance with Lawson's theory: a proletarian hero, Pete, is pitted against the forces of economic exploitation, in this case a factory and its owners. A violent situation erupts as the workers go out on strike; but Pete hesitates, afraid of losing what little he has and fearful of the "reds" who clamor for revolution. Finally, after his baby dies, he relents and casts his lot in with the revolutionaries, recognizing that while triumph of the "cause" is at best a risky gamble, defeat while fighting is better than continued exploitation and slow death without dignity.

Early in the play Lawson establishes Pete as an American working class "Everyman," a basically honest man who has fallen away from his own ideals due to his oppressed state:

> PETE (*Slowly, as if he had just realized it.*) My life is gone; a man without a life is dead. A man wants a radio an' a car, go to the movies, bounce his kid on his knee. (I been a good egg, played baseball, had a high batting average, shot pool with the boys.)...(*He sits on concrete base C.*) Jenny an' me married in twenty-eight. I met her in August. (*HANK sits beside him.*) (Nobody could keep his eyes off her, when she went down the street you'd think she had a brass band with her the way men followed.) We went courting in the fall of the year. We walked in the deep woods, we rolled in the red leaves like horses in a pasture. (I'd tear her flesh till she'd bleed, kiss the blood away. I had no more shame than a stallion trumpeting my strength.) She had me walking on air...Listen, I'm talking about Jenny; did you look at Jenny just now? (*HANK nods.*) When this dump closed in thirty-two, I had a thousand dollars saved. Jenny an' me argued ourselves sick. I wanted a partnership in a garage; an' she wanted her own house. I was all set for the garage, ready to sign; when I come home that night our kid was dead. Remember little Pete, three years old, drowned in the swamp? I bought the house for Jenny

to hide her grief in....

HANK You can't leave Jenny, Pete.

PETE There's no love among the dead...Saturday I borrowed money from you for a doctor and medicine for
the baby. (HANK *nods.*) I didn't go for the doctor.
I stopped for a drink. I got stinko on white mule at Hen-
nessey's....Then I went to spend the last two bits on a
woman, in one of them cribs on Central Street. The
thing sitting on the bed waiting for me was the Malacci
kid, Giuseppa, thirteen years old, lives on our street.
There she was, naked, with her teeth smiling, painted
like an Indian, even the buttons on the front of her painted. (*He indicates the breasts.*)

HANK She's the oldest of eight, and her father dead.

PETE I come home blind, tried to kill my kid—lift her
in one hand, smash her brains out. Jenny tore the kid
away from me and ran out of the house. I fell down
in the garden, went to sleep with my face in the mud.[80]

Lawson's hero has, at this point in the play, "hit bottom"; a
"good man," Pete has "gone bad" because of forces he cannot
understand or control.

Pete and Jenny share the same plight as Joe and Edna in
Lefty, and, to a certain extent, Gimpty and Kay in *Dead End.*
But Lawson's worker's wife is different in her attitude from
the militant and agitating Edna. Jenny bursts out at Pete when
he confesses his inability to face up to the forces which threaten
him:

> You think I want a house to die in? You think I want
> to sit there dying till you come in with liquor and per-
> fume on you? I got a heart in me and the house was
> my heart 'cause it's you, the house was you and no other
> thing. You talked to me about love one time. When was
> that? Is there memory in you? (p. 111)

The result of Jenny's tirade is the same as Edna's threat to leave
Joe and Kay's rejection of Gimpty: Pete resolves to fight with
the forces, even though defeat seems inevitable.

The representatives of capital, of the factory, are thinly
disguished fascists. The benevolent but dutiful Duhring-type
has disappeared, but the malevolent intellectual and back-street

hoodlum remain. Doc, the intellectual of the right, attempts to use twisted logic to convince Pete and the other workers that he is really afraid of their power: "I envy you," he tells them. "You're a realist. I'm just a dreamer...you're a man of cruelty and force. You have no illusions—" (p. 129). But in his attempt to talk them around to his way of thinking, he reveals that he has a more pernicious nature than the henchmen and gunmen the owners have hired to break the strike, for he begins to use patriotic platitudes in order to bring them over to his side. He asks Pete and the others if they really know "what it means to be an American citizen?"; and he asks them if they love their country's flag or if they are "against God." Finally, telling them that the American worker is "the salt of the earth," Doc launches into a speech of racial theory which clearly aligns him with a Nazi ideal of Aryan superiority:

> (*His enthusiasm increasing, moving about the stage, addressing one man after another*) Our civilization is doomed to death and decay unless we wake up....Did you ever hear of the white man's burden? (*He continues to move about the stage seeking the attention of one man after another.*) There's not many white men in the world, so few it makes you nervous. Now the radicals come along, and stir up all the dark people to take the world away from us, make it like darkest Africa. (*Turning back to* PETE) You're an American worker. You could be rich. We could *all* be rich if it wasn't for the aliens that take our bread away from us. (p. 132)

Doc proceeds to argue that Jews, Negroes, Egyptians, Russians, Moors, and Mongolians are all inferior to the American white man: "They're all out of the same barrel, popped out of the same womb, up in the jungle where the Nile begins—" he rants at Pete. But Pete continues to vacillate, unable to decide whether throwing his lot in with the "reds" would end his life and his dreams. Finally, he refuses to go along with Doc's bigoted philosophy, and the rightists try another tack; they begin to appeal to Pete's nostalgic recollections of his time in the army during World War I. At first Pete slips into confused recollections, but suddenly he begins to awaken to the true nature of his memories: "I done nothing since, learned nothing," he tells them, "just bragged about being a hero, puffed myself up over a lousy medal...I got this for killing sixteen men in a dugout....Six of them so weak they couldn't stand up." The memory jolts him into an awareness of what Doc and the henchmen are trying to get him to do: "That's what you want now, kill again, kill for the white race, kill the hungry men..." And finally he makes up his mind about which side he is on: "I don't know where I stand, walking in a fog; but I ain't with you—not me. Take the Goddamned medal..." Pete's final refusal of Doc's attempts at perverted reason angers the fascistic intellectual. He orders the thugs to "Teach him a lesson," and Pete is mercilessly beaten (pp. 132-133).

After things go from bad to worse, Lawson's protagonist finally joins the "reds" and begins actively to fight against the social forces which oppress him. Like Odets' characters, Pete shows a reluctance to embrace communism and Marxist teachings; however, Lawson's hero differs from Joe, Dr. Benjamin, and Agate in that his decision to join the fight and the revolution is not simply a last alternative; it is a full political and philosophical commitment. Lawson posits a major tenet of leftist dogma: there are two major forces, fascism and communism; one is bad, and the other is good. For those who oppose fascism, there is no middle ground; there is only a full commitment to the only ideology strong enough and militant enough to defeat the Nazi terror.

Pete's decision is an individual one. He is moved to action because he has lost everything: his job, his baby who was killed in the fighting, and his wife, for Jenny no longer loves or respects him. After his decision, however, Lawson subordinates the importance of his individuality. Shifting to another worker, Bill Anderson, who has argued for continuing the strike and joining the "reds" all along, Lawson puts the "call to action" into his lines. Binks, a company thug, challenges him: "You think you're big," he taunts. But Anderson's reply establishes the collective philosophy of the leftist writers of the thirties: "Me?...Big...*As if the idea has just occurred to him.* Yeah, I'm big. There's a hundred million of me!" (p. 157). Lawson's "call to action" evokes the same numbers and same tone of Maxwell Anderson's call at the end of *Both Your Houses.* But whereas McClean's "hundred million" would rise to throw out corrupt politicians, Bill Anderson's people would presumably rise to overthrow capitalism, industrial exploitation, and the bigotry and special malevolence of fascism.

Marching Song was one of the last major attempts by a self-proclaimed Communist to stage a successful leftist drama on Broadway. As a synthesis of the militant agit-prop and the more moderate social drama of the early thirties it indicates the degree to which the proletarian drama had weakened by 1937. One might speculate that if it had been produced two years earlier in lieu of *Lefty*, it might have displaced Odets' play as the most important protest drama of the decade; however, even in 1935 audiences were less willing to respond to a melodramatic plot and highly stylized rhetorical argument than they were to the forceful experimentation they found in *Lefty*. Also the blatant endorsement of communistic and revolutionary tactics offered by *Marching Song* was unpalatable. It was one thing for frustrated cabbies to say that they would be striking regardless of whether they were called "reds" or not; it was quite another for striking workers to "man the barricades" in a class revolution. Further, by 1937 the depression had deepened to the extent that the optimism which could move audiences at the end of *Both Your Houses* or even *Till the Day I Die* to applaud and hope for a better future seemed hackneyed and a bit naive. And finally, the official governmental line toward Communist Party activities had begun to harden, in spite of the efforts of the Popular Front; and as union organizations and continued strikes brought violence and hardship into the households of middle class Americans in the form of higher prices and shortages, there was less sympathy for the working class American in 1937 than there had been two years earlier. The failure of *Marching Song* to capture the imagination of Clurman's "new audience" can be attributed to a general weariness among those who attended the theatre of being harangued about social issues and international revolution and abstract political theories; they had enough to concern them at home.

Possibly no play nor group of plays came closer to achieving a synthesis of protest drama and palatable social drama than did the "Living Newspaper" productions of the Works Progress Administration's Federal Theatre Project. As "one of the largest coordinated theatrical experiments in the history of the world," the Federal Theatre Project was established August 29, 1935, under the authority of Harry Hopkins and the direction of Hallie Flanagan.[81] It would exist for four years, stage twelve hundred productions, and cost the government a mere $46,207,779, a modest figure when the number of brand new companies, troupes,

and theatrical personnel involved in the Project is considered.[82]
The project's director, Flanagan, came to the Federal Theatre
from Vassar, where she had been a professor of drama, and the
course of the company's history was largely shaped by her philosophy and ideas. She maintained "that if the theatre were to be
a vital social force, it could not afford to ignore the implications
of social change. The theatre . . . had to grow up."[83] And while
this philosophy guided virtually every aspect and every program
of the Project's activities, it was through the "Living Newspaper"
that audiences experienced the main thrust of the Project's social
commitment, presented in innovative and often iconoclastic
forms.

The Federal Theatre Project was a unique concept in theatrical companies. Unlike the Group Theatre, founded on an aesthetic principle of staging successful and socially significant drama,
or the Theatre Union, founded on an ideological principle of
staging protest and proletarian drama which was also commercially successful, the Federal Theatre Project was founded upon
economic necessity alone. Its goals and accomplishments were
formidable. It sought to, and actually did, stimulate community
theatre and dramatic training all over the country; it established
the National Service Bureau, which read, wrote, and translated
plays, sent synopses and scripts to community theatres for try-
outs, and conducted theatrical research; it published the *Federal
Theatre Magazine,* which coordinated and established communi-
cations between theatres nation-wide; it created the Federal
Theatre of the Air, producing about two thousand radio scripts;
it offered benefit performances to aid flood victims, out-of-work
farmers, the generally destitute, and the infirm; and it established
playwriting contests in Civilian Conservation Corps camps and on
college and university campuses. In spite of handicaps such as a
prohibition against advertising in competition with the commercial
theatre and an "overt" WPA board censorship, the Federal Theatre
Project used its various divisions to stimulate foreign language
companies, to establish ethnic theatres such as the Anglo-Jewish
and Negro Theatres, to produce experimental theatre such as
the poetic drama theatres and the children's theatres; and, by
converting bankrupt movie and opera houses, they literally
brought plays to communities where a staged drama had never
been seen before.[84]

The chief goal of the Project was to put actors, directors,
technicians, and writers back to work. Proof that this goal re-

mained foremost in the Project director's mnd may be found by surveying the wide variety of plays the Federal Theatre staged. The Project revived Shakespeare, Moliere, and Sophocles; it produced new plays by new writers, including *Murder in the Cathedral* by T. S. Eliot; it revived more recent drama by George Bernard Shaw, Eugene O'Neill, and even John Howard Lawson. But its most sensational contribution to the development of American drama was the "Living Newspaper," although this was but a single program of the Federal Theatre Project's New York unit and represents less than twenty percent of that unit's total activity. Ironically, the "Living Newspaper," more than anything else, brought an end of the Federal Theatre Project.

Hallie Flanagan was aided in her directorship of the theatre by established playwrights and directors, among whom was Elmer Rice; and it was their intention to do more than simply revive plays and keep theatrical people working. Rabkin writes: "They wanted to create out of the fact of unemployment a theatre which would not only serve the entire nation in many ways, but which would be expressive of the attitudes and needs of the age."[85] The "Living Newspaper" plays evolved as the best vehicle for attaining this goal. Flanagan and Rice sought to develop a dramatic medium which would respond to the needs of all the people, which would make those people the very subject of drama. She writes:

> The "Living Newspaper" can make it part of its theatre business to show what is happening to people, all sorts of people in America today. Not that our plays should be restricted to a study of one-third of our nation which is ill-housed, ill-clad, and ill-nourished, though these millions are so inescapably a part of America today that they are subjects for drama, drama with the militant ring of the Second Inaugural.[86]

Not only did the "Living Newspaper" require elaborate sets, large casts, and the professional activity of multiple writers and directors, it also reflected what Flanagan saw as a fundamental attitude necessary for a positive solution to the problems of the depression. She states:

> The history of the "Living Newspaper" illustrates the fact that in a larger sense, also, the Federal Theatre is

a pioneer theatre, because it is part of a tremendous re-
thinking, and rebuilding of America. Being a part of
a great nationwide work project, our actors are one, not
only with the musicians playing symphonies in Federal
orchestras; with writers recreating the American scene;
with artists compiling from the rich and almost forgotten
past the INDEX OF AMERICAN DESIGN; but they
are also one with thousands of men building roads and
bridges and sewers; one with doctors and nurses giving
clinical aid to a million destitute men, women and children;
one with scientists studying mosquito control and re-
forestation and swamp drainage and soil erosion.[87]

But aside from putting people to work in the spirit of the American labor community, Flanagan made no mistake about the
fact that the "Living Newspaper" was also intended to be a
social drama:

These activities represent a new frontier in America, a
frontier against disease, dirt, poverty, illiteracy, unemployment, despair and at the same time against selfishness,
special privilege and social apathy. The struggles along
this frontier are not political in any narrow sense. They
would exist under any administration. Taken collectively
they illustrate what William James meant when he talked
about a moral equivalent for war.[88]

But unlike the leftist writers of protest drama or playwrights
of social drama, the "Living Newspaper" would reply on no
ideology, no political stance; instead, it would use the facts
and figures of the American scene as they were reported in the
press, in almanacs, encyclopedias, and bureaus of vital statistics.
    Although some of the "Living Newspaper" scripts were
singly authored such as *Ethiopia,* others, *One-Third of a Nation*
and *Triple-A Ploughed Under,* were "edited" from the combined
efforts of several writers. As Sam Smiley notes, it was a new
technique of playwriting, based on journalistic methods rather
than on solo artistic performances:

Each "Living Newspaper" had a staff similar to that of
a large metropolitan daily, with a chief editor, managing
and city editors, copyreaders, and reporters. . . They in-

vestigated the circumstances behind conditions rather than surface news. Each of the "Living Newspapers" was different in history and technique. All, however, depended on a large staff who dug into mountains of details, carted away tons of facts, and then refined the information into an exciting but economical dramatic presentation.[89]

The "Living Newspaper," therefore, utilized the maximum number of theatrical personnel to dramatize current events and make a rational social statement.

The titles of "Living Newspaper" plays suggest a close relationship to agit-prop plays: *Ethiopia, Triple-A Ploughed Under, Power, Spirochette, Highlights of 1935,* and *Injunction Granted* all suggest the nature of the content and focus of the plays. Other aspects of the structure of the plays suggest antecedents in the worker's theatre: the frequent use of allegorical names or even mere titles such as "Landlord," "Commissioner," or "Tenant" for characters; the placement of actors in the house among the audience to stimulate audience involvement; direct address of the audience by speakers who are pleading a rhetorical issue; and the frequent choice of inflammatory subject matter such as labor problems, agricultural issues, and corruption in government and business also align the plays with the militant agitation and propagation intent of the travelling worker's drama. However, conspicuously missing from "Living Newspaper" plays are political doctrine, calls for radical action, or ideological diatribe. The plays did nothing more than present the facts, and the facts were carefully documented in the printed scripts so there could be no question as to their authenticity. At no time was any "Living Newspaper' play deliberately used as a platform for socialist or Marxist or Communist Party propaganda, although the authors, editors, actors, and others connected with the Project might have had leftist sympathies which emerged in the productions. John Gassner states that the charges were false that the Federal Theatre plays were ever propagandistic and that when "propaganda was evident," it "was propaganda emanating from the desires of the American people, propaganda that is legitimate in any genuine democracy, propaganda, indeed, for a working democracy."[90] The events dramatized in "Living Newspaper" plays were real events; there was no need for analogous invention of situation to stimulate audiences into awareness.

Antecedents for the techniques of the "Living Newspaper" can be traced to the "epic theatre," the cabaret political theatres of Berlin and Paris, cinematic formats and approaches to subject matter, the radio-loudspeaker motif, and a general montage effect of expressionist drama. Generally the plays were built on an episodic structure, a real event giving rise to a fictional vignette, written to illustrate the impact of actual occurrences on average individuals, a structure not unlike the experiments of John Dos Passos in his impressionistic novels, *Manhattan Transfer* and *U. S. A.* John Gassner points out:

> The "Living Newspaper" combined the comic strip of
> Casper Milquetoast, gusty American Journalism, the
> brash loudspeaker technique of radio advertising, and
> other native elements into earnest sociological drama
> in which amusement, excitement and information were
> simultaneous.[91]

It was Odets' and Kingsley's synthesis carried to its penultimate degree. But instead of using a year-old taxi strike or the shooting of a fictional gangster as the crucible, or to use Lawson's term, the "pitcher" into which the "social content is poured," the "Living Newspaper" used current events, those which were on the minds of any audience member who had chanced to read a recent newspaper, view a newsreel, or listen to the radio news, events which affected almost everyone present.

Hallie Flanagan told the American Federation of Arts that the purpose of the "Living Newspaper" was to dramatize a new struggle—the search of the average American today for knowledge about his country and his world; to dramatize his struggle to turn the great natural and economic and social forces of our time toward a better life for more people.[92] Almost without exception, and, incidentally, without advertising or attracting major reviewers, every "Living Newspaper" play was a success.

The United States government was not as receptive to such notions as were the audiences who applauded the "Living Newspaper" plays, however; and the project ran into trouble right away. *Ethiopia,* a biting anti-war editorial by Elmer Rice based on the Italian invasion of that African country, was censored so harshly that Rice resigned from the Project altogether. *Triple-A Ploughed Under,* written by seventy writers, directed by fifteen directors and staged by one hundred actors, dealt with the plight of American farmers who had to plough their crops under to maintain market prices even though people were starving. It brought about cries from some Congressmen of unfair and misrepresentational depictions of farm life in the United States. E. P. Conkle's *Prologue To Glory* managed to circumvent censorship by placing its social comments on justice and humanism in the mouth of young Abe Lincoln, and it was of sufficient quality to make the Burns Mantle "Ten Best" list for 1937-1938. But the play which comes closest to demonstrating the ideals of the project as Flanagan stated them is *One-Third of a Nation;* ironically, it was also the play which finally provoked the government to cancel the entire Federal Theatre Project.

Edited by Arthur Arent, *One-Third of a Nation* requires a cast of almost two hundred actors and an extremely elaborate set, including a cut-away section of a tenement slum which burns down in the first scene of the first act and again in the last scene of the second act. After the slum burns, an investigation is held to determine who is responsible for the fire and the deaths of those who could not get out in time. The Loudspeaker calls forth questions and encourages the Commissioner as he questions various city, state, and federal bureaucrats about the responsibility of each, finally determining that the fire must have been the fault of no one person; for although the building was a firetrap, substandard in every way, the confusing tangle of law, regulation, and bureaucracy prevented anyone from doing anything about it until it was too late and the building was destroyed and people died.

Most culpable in the eyes of the former tenants is the landlord, Schultz, who admits to the Commissioner that the building is falling apart but confesses that he bought it on speculation; he cares little for the structure, for that is worthless. What he values is the land it sits on. The Commissioner, anxious to blame someone, asks him why he failed to bring the house up to standard fire codes. The landlord replies that there are three reasons: ". . . first, I don't have any money. Second it's not any worse than any other tenement on the block; and third, if I do have the money and do fix it up I have to raise the rent to get my money back."[93] At this point the Loudspeaker gets into the act and offers to buy the house if it is such a bad investment that the landlord will not maintain it; but there is a catch: Loudspeaker will only offer him what he paid for the house in 1924. Schultz refuses the offer, and he is accused of speculating and causing the standard of living of "six million people" to suffer. This, he readily admits is true: "I tell you, it's land, land, *land*! That's where the money is! And I don't sell mine without a nice big profit" (p. 23).

Finally Rosen, a tenant whose wife and children died in the fire, speaks up; Schultz follows the example of the inspectors, commissioners, and city officials who passed the blame from one to another; he blames history. While he offers Rosen sympathy, he refuses to allow the burned-out tenant to blame him: "You'll have to go back into history and blame whatever it was that made New York City real estate the soundest and most profitable on the face of the earth!" he tells Rosen (p. 23). The fire which destroyed Schultz's building actually occurred on February 19, 1924, a fact which is meticulously documented in the script. But the event of a fire in 1924 is not the issue of *One-Third of a Nation*. From that year, the play goes back to the founding of New York and follows Schultz's demand to find out who is at fault for slum conditions in the twentieth century.

Scene III of Act I begins with the Loudspeaker announcing the movement back through time to November 20, 1705, when the Governor of New York deeded King's Farm to Trinity Church "to own, and to improve for the great glory of the Church and for other pious uses" (p. 25). From that auspicious beginning, the scene traces the development of the land, with the Loudspeaker announcing dates, famous historical events and people as they influence the disposition of the land, and various political shenanigans which raise the land's worth. As the scene progresses, the first private investors come into the picture, and people begin to pay rent to remain on the land owned by other people.

The remainder of the play moves forward in history, dealing with both actual historical events which affect housing changes on Manhattan Island as well as with the effects of those changes on individuals who live there. Slowly the buildings that were rented to tenants become more and more run down, and the area begins to decay; disease and catastrophe haunt the slum dwellers, and the landlords become more and more wealthy, not from the small rents they charge for their substandard housing but from the increased worth of the land on which that housing stands. Throughout the march of time the Loudspeaker quotes statistics, laws which were passed both to change conditions and to protect conditions from change, and historical events which bring about change that laws and statistics cannot alter. The specific questions about the law or interpretations of the events, and the Loudspeaker always obliges.

Finally the play progresses past the 1924 fire to the depression. The characters who have been studied in previous scenes are revisited through subsequent generations, and a rent strike is organized in the Bronx in 1933. In the fifth scene of the second act the year is 1938, and the tenants continue to agitate for better housing. As the Loudspeaker announces that three billion, one hundred and twenty-five million dollars have been appropriated for the Army and Navy during the past four years, one of the tenants, Little Man, confers with another, Mrs. Buttonkooper, about their plight. As they talk over the injustice of a government spending so many millions on war they become increasingly agitated. Mrs. Buttonkooper finally decides that if everyone hollers together, loudly enough, the government might awaken to the needs of its people and "admit in Washington it's just as important to keep a man alive as it is to kill him!" Joined by the other actors, she leads a shout which at first might appear to be a "call to action":

> MRS. BUTTONKOOPER: NOW! (*Shouting.*) We want a decent place to live in! I want a place that's clean and fit for a man and woman and kids! *Can you hear me--you in Washington or Albany or wherever you are! Give me a decent place to live in! A home!* (p. 120)

But unlike Odets' "STRIKE!" scene, this call is not directed at an oppressive company or corrupt officials, nor is it directed, as is Alan McClean's closing threat in *Both Your Houses,* toward the population at large. It is a demand that the existing system work, not, as in the "hard-line" Marxist plays, that it be changed or, as in the more extreme agit-prop plays, that it be torn down entirely. Further, the call for better housing becomes ironic, for no sooner are the words out of Mrs. Buttonkooper's mouth when a voice from the slum yells, "Fire!" and this tenement, just as the one in Act I, Scene I did, goes up in flames, just as such a building did in March, 1938. The Loudspeaker makes the final comment on the play and the situation: "Ladies and gentlemen, this might be Boston, New York, St. Louis, Chicago, Philadelphia—but let's call it, 'one-third of a nation' " (p. 121).

Goldstein calls *One-Third of a Nation* the "most skillful"

of all the "Living Newspaper" plays; it was also the last.[94]   The
Hearst Press led an attack on the whole Federal Theatre Project,
calling it, and specifically the "Living Newspaper," "an adjunct
to the New York leftist literary junta."[95]   In a sense the Project
became the scapegoat for all leftist and social drama of the decade,
not because it was more radical than the others, but because
its social statements were more than a little critical of existing
governmental and capitalistic institutions, and especially because
those statements were being financed with tax dollars.

Finally the criticism became loud enough for the Dies Committee of the House of Representatives to investigate the entire
Project and recommend that it be suspended.   In its investigation
of the eight hundred thirty separate titles of the twenty-four
hundred productions of the Project, eighty were named by witnesses as being leftist and subversive, including fifty-two plays
which were either stock revivals by Shaw, Barrie, O'Neill and
others, classics by Sophocles, Shakespeare and Moliere, transla-
tions by Brecht, Ibsen and Checkhov, and five plays not produced by the Federal Theatre at all.[96]   Flanagan, who had spent
almost the entire four years writing and speaking against charges
that the Federal Theatre Project was a communist organ, had to
petition for permission to testify in defense of the Project. Once
before the committee, who had steadfastly refused to attend any
performances but preferred to rely on testimony of witnesses
concerning the nature and content of productions, she found
herself not only having to identify Christopher Marlowe for
Congressman Starnes, but also having to state, "for the record,"
that the "greatest dramatist in the period of Shakespeare, immediately preceding Shakespeare" was not a communist.[97]

But the "Living Newspaper" was the chief target of the
critics.   And while the right attacked it as being too subversive,
the influential voices on the left found it to be too conservative
to defend.[98]   Pressure from the right continued, and the committee, concerned only with "the record" and with finding sedi-
tious intent on the part of the project's directors, steadfastly
refused to hear any evidence in support of the Project.

Gerald Rabkin points out: "Although social plays constitute only a small percentage of its prolific record, the phenomenon of the federal Theatre was itself indicative of a social atmosphere in which art and political commitment were intimately
interrelated."[99]   But that "interrelationship" was responsible
for ending what was possibly the largest and most successful at-

tempt at establishing a national theatre in the history of American drama. Criticism of the New Deal, "propagation of radical ideas and blasphemy," writes Rabkin, "was not to be endured."[100] On June 30, 1939, the Federal Theatre Project was officially dissolved by Act of Congress due to a "lack of funds."[101]

The ending of the Federal Theatre Project brought to a close the movement of the radical theatre in the thirties. The plays of the "Living Newspaper" had carried the synthesis of form and content discovered by Odets and Kingsley beyond merely entertaining and informing the audience; it had become a major force in theatrical development. Although theatre-goers quickly tired of leftist diatribe, no matter how well-staged it may have been, a breach had been opened in the wall around the established theatre. Social drama which did not moderate its stance through comedy or manners could now boldly take the stage without fear of automatic failure. When *Waiting For Lefty* burst onto the 1935 season it represented something fresh and new, a synthesis of the militant agit-prop and the capricious and often satiric social comedy. *Dead End, Idiot's Delight, Bury the Dead, Tobacco Road,* and other plays marked further successful combinations of these forms, departing from an old direction wherein entertainment had to be a first priority and information came second if at all. Occasionally the playwrights went too far, as Lawson did in *Marching Song,* and demonstrated that an imbalance of any kind in the two priorities was unacceptable. However, the "Living Newspaper" plays carried the synthesis as far as it could be taken. If success can be judged in reaction, either from audiences or from the social institutions a play criticizes, then the killing of the Federal Theatre Project ironically represents its greatest triumph.

Following the dictates of the Hegelian dialectic, however, this synthesis soon gave rise to a new antithesis, and from the combination of these final two modes of playwriting in the thirties, yet another synthesis of social drama was formed. McDermott defines naturalism in the theatre as a play which calls for an "historically specific depiction which furthers the aim of ideologically remoulding and educating working people in the spirit of socialism."[102] Such plays as *Waiting For Lefty* had already accomplished that end with commercial success, and audiences seemed to want something more, something McDermott dubs "sociological realism," or a play with "characters which represent various ideas, issues and classes," set in the midst of "real situations."[103]   Recognizing the dependence of *Lefty* and *Dead End* and even plays such as *One-Third of a Nation* on situations such as strikes and crises in housing and on the roles the characters fulfilled rather than the dimension of their personalities, the last synthesis of the decade would place "real" people into "real" situations and strive to penetrate surface realism and interpret the meaning behind the life it imitated. This movement would take the American drama into the realm of what Krutch called the "revolutionary drama" of the modern theatre.

Notes

[1] Gerald Rabkin, *Drama and Commitment: Politics in the American Theatre of the Thirties* (Bloomington, IN: Indiana University Press, 1964), p. 25. Reprinted with permission of the publisher.

[2] *Ibid.*, p. 28.

[3] For a discussion of the views of leftist literary critics in the early years of the depression, see Daniel Aaron, *Writers on the Left* (Oxford: Oxford University Press, 1977), pp. 231-268.

[4] Malcolm Goldstein, *The Political Stage: American Drama and Theatre of the Great Depression* (New York: Oxford University Press, 1974), p. 29. Reprinted with permission of Oxford University Press.

[5] *Scottsborough Limited* should not be confused with John Wexley's *They Shall not Die* which opened in New York at the Royale Theatre in February of 1934. Both plays deal with the much publicized Scottsborough, Alabama, rape case wherein nine Negroes were charged with raping a white woman in spite of overwhelming evidence of their innocence, but Wexley's play is a more formal drama and enjoyed a moderately successful run for a protest or propaganda play, in the early years of the depression. See Brook Atkinson and Albert Hirschfeld, *The Lively Years: 1920-1973* (New York: Association Press, 1973), pp. 88-91.

[6] Sam Smiley, *The Drama of Attack: Didactic Plays of the American Depression* (Columbia, MO: University of Missouri Press, 1972), p. 136.

[7] William Kozlenko, ed., *The Best Short Plays of the Social Theatre*, with an introduction by William Kozlenko (New York: Random House, 1939), p. viii.

[8] Rabkin, pp. 49-50.

[9] Goldstein, p. 39.

[10] Rabkin, p. 27.

[11] Goldstein, p. 151.

[12] Michael J. Mendelsohn, "The Social Critics on Stage," *Modern Drama* 6 (December 1963): 284-285.

[13] Goldstein, p. 59.

[14] *Ibid.*

[15] Rabkin, p. 46.

[16] Goldstein, p. 59.

[17] Rabkin, p. 52.

[18] Goldstein, p. 61.

[19] Rabkin, p. 50.

[20] The Politics of the American worker and working class are examined through documents and literary responses in Daniel Aaron and Robert Bendiner's *The Strenuous Decade: A Social and Intellectual Record of the Nineteen-Thirties*, Documents in American Civilization Series (New York: Anchor Books, 1970), pp. 137-411.

[21] Smiley, p. 26.

[22] Doris V. Falk, *Lillian Hellman* (New York: Frederick Ungar Publishing Co., 1978), p. 29.

[23] Harold Clurman, *The Fervent Years: A Story of the Group Theatre and the Thirties* (New York: Alfred A. Knopf; rpt; New York: Harcourt Brace Jovanovich, 1975), p. 113. Reprinted with permission of Alfred A. Knopf.

[24] Hallie Flanagan quoted in Goldstein, p. 251.

[25] Smiley, p. 132.

[26] Rabkin, p. 170.

[27] Gerald Weales, *Clifford Odets: Playwright* (New York: Pegasus, 1971), p. 15. Reprinted with permission of the author.

[28] Clurman, p. 181.

[29] *Ibid.*, p. 154.

[30] Edward Murray, *Clifford Odets: The Thirties and After* (New York: Frederick Ungar Publishing Co., 1968), p. 23.

[31] Goldstein, p. 54-55.

[32] Clurman, p. 148.

[33] Clifford Odets, *Six Plays of Clifford Odets: Waiting for Lefty*, with a preface by the author and three Introductions by Harold Clurman (New York: The Modern Library, 1939), p. 5; subsequent citations from this play will be made parenthetically in the text. Reprinted with permission of Grove Press.

[34] Clurman, p. 148.

[35]Edith J. R. Isaacs, "Merry Feast of Playgoing: Broadway in Review," *Theatre Arts Monthly* 18 (April 1935): 328.

[36]Murray, p. 23.

[37]Weales, p. 40.

[38]*Ibid.*, p. 47.

[39]Himmelstein quoted in Murray, p. 23.

[40]Clurman, p. 320.

[41]*Ibid.*, p. 148.

[42]*Ibid.*

[43]Goldstein, p. 52.

[44]Weales, p. 30.

[45]Douglas McDermott, "Propaganda and Art: Dramatic Theory and the American Depression," *Modern Drama* 11 (May 1968): 73.

[46]Weales, p. 49.

[47]Clurman, p. 115.

[48]This scene is excerpted in Goldstein, p. 53.

[49]Weales, p. 46.

[50]Goldstein, p. 51.

[51]Weales, p. 36.

[52]Michael J. Mendelsohn, *Clifford Odets: Humane Dramatist* (Deland, FL: Everett Edwards, 1969), p. 21.

[53]Weales, p. 37.

[54]John Howard Lawson, *Theory and Technique of Playwriting* (New York: Hill & Wang, 1960), p. 254. Reprinted with permission of Susan Amanda Lawson.

[55]*Ibid.*, p. 253.

[56]*Ibid.*, p. 254.

[57]Weales, p. 49.

[58]McDermott, p. 76.

[59]Kozlenko, p. x.

[60]Clurman, p. 156.

[61]Kozlenko, p. viii.

[62]Malcolm Cowley, "While They Waited For Lefty," *Saturday Review,* (June 1964): 61.

[63]Clifford Odets, *Six Plays of Clifford Odets: Till the Day I Die,* with a Preface by the author and three Introductions by Harold Clurman (New York: The Modern Library, 1939), pp. 143-147; subsequent citations from this play will be made parenthetically in the text.

[64]Clurman, p. 153.

[65]Edith J. R. Isaacs, "Going Left with Fortune," *Theatre Arts Monthly* (April 1935): 328.

[66]*Ibid.*, p. 331.

⁶⁷Clurman, p. 156.

⁶⁸Elmer Rice had authored and produced *Judgement Day* in 1934, a play dealing with the Richstag Trials. The failure of that play after only a few nights' run indicates the degree to which American audiences were slow to awaken to the Nazi threat in Germany.

⁶⁹Sidney Kingsley, *Dead End: A Play in Three Acts* (New York: Random House, 1936), p. 50; subsequent citations from this play will be made parenthetically in the text. Reprinted with permission of Random House, Inc.

⁷⁰Atkinson, p. 109.

⁷¹Goldstein, p. 377.

⁷²Atkinson, p. 107.

⁷³Burns Mantle, ed., *The Best Plays of 1936-1937: And the Yearbook of the Drama in America* (New York: Dodd Mead & Co., 1937), p. 239.

⁷⁴Joseph Wood Krutch, *The American Drama Since 1918* (New York: Random House, 1939), pp. 8-9.

⁷⁵Lawson, p. 163.

⁷⁶John Howard Lawson quoted in Goldstein, p. 230.

⁷⁷John Howard Lawson quoted in Rabkin, p. 156.

⁷⁸John Howard Lawson, *With a Reckless Preface: The Pure in Heart and Gentlewoman* (New York: Farrar & Rinehart, Inc., 1934), pp. vii-xviii.

⁷⁹Goldstein, p. 232.

⁸⁰John Howard Lawson, *Marching Song* (New York: Dramatists Play Service, 1937), pp. 35-36; subsequent citations from this play will be noted parenthetically in the text. Reprinted with permission of Susan Amanda Lawson.

⁸¹Rabkin, p. 96.

⁸²John Gassner, *Dramatic Soundings: Evaluations and Retractions Culled from 30 Years of Dramatic Criticism* (New York: Crown Publishers, 1968), p. 355.

⁸³Hallie Flanagan quoted in Rabkin, p. 100.

⁸⁴Several works treat the history and evolution of the Federal Theatre Project in detail. Possibly one of the most complete studies is Jane Dehart Mathews, *The Federal Theatre: 1935-1939: Plays, Relief, and Politics* (Princeton: Princeton University Press, 1967).

⁸⁵Rabkin, p. 128.

⁸⁶Flanagan quoted in Goldstein, p. 25.

⁸⁷Hallie Flanagan, "Introduction," *Federal Theatre Plays,* ed. Pierre de Rohan (New York: Random HOuse, 1939), p. xii. Reprinted with permission of Random House.

⁸⁸*Ibid.,* p. xiii.

⁸⁹Smiley, p. 55.

[90]Gassner, p. 358.

[91]*Ibid.*, p. 356.

[92]Flanagan quoted in Goldstein, p. 278.

[93]Arthur Arent, ed., *One-Third of a Nation, Federal Theatre Plays,* ed. Pierre de Rohan, with an Introduction by Hallie Flanagan (New York: Random House, 1938), p. 21; subsequent citations from this play will be made parenthetically in the text. Reprinted with permission of Random House.

[94]Goldstein, p. 282.

[95]Rabkin, p. 101.

[96]*Ibid.*, p. 105.

[97]*Ibid.*, p. 122.

[98]*Ibid.*, p. 123.

[99]*Ibid.*, p. 105.

[100]*Ibid.*, p. 123.

[101]*Ibid.*, p. 121.

[102]McDermott, pp. 77-78.

[103]*Ibid.*

CLIFFORD ODETS: MIDDLE CLASS NATURALISM

From 1935 until the end of the decade the social drama underwent a dialectical change. The synthesis achieved by Odets in *Waiting For Lefty* and expanded by others in subsequent seasons began to lose its impact. Among other problems facing playwrights, old and new, was declining audience interest in any play, especially in those which emphasized exhortation over entertainment. Malcolm Goldstein, among others, has suggested that the motion picture and radio had begun to capture audiences which were likely to have attended the theatre in previous years; and since most of the Broadway hits were being rapidly filmed by Hollywood studios, there was even less incentive for patrons to support an expensive and less accessible enterprise such as the theatre. Moreover, Hollywood was offering top salaries to technicians, actors, directors, and especially writers if they would abandon, temporarily at least, the legitimate stage for the silver screen.[1] While the spirit of Clurman's "new audience" still existed, the social attitudes which concerned it were changing. The result was a steady decline in the number of new plays opening on Broadway. Eighty-nine new scripts were introduced in the season 1935-1936, but by 1939-1940 the annual figure had dropped to sixty. But Goldstein notes that while there were fewer and fewer productions, the quality of the plays seemed to improve.[2] The crisis in the theatre's fiscal situation began to take its toll among the various companies as well. The Theatre Union folded completely; the Group Theatre and once prestigious Theatre Guild were frequently on the brink of bankruptcy; and new companies, such as the Playwright's Producing Company, founded in 1937 by Elmer Rice among others, faced the possibility of financial ruin from the outset. Every company and every playwright had one thing in mind: a hit.

As international unrest continued to grow in Spain, Eastern Eurcpe, Africa, and Asia, Americans became increasingly suspicious of what Alan McClean called "political patent medicine" in *Both Your Houses* in 1933. The "hard-line" communist argument, while still present in the work of John Howard Lawson and other writers of the Theatre Union, Mercury Theatre, and other leftist companies, was beginning to lose its impact in the face of stepped-up Popular Front ideology and growing concern about war and continued economic chaos. While the two longest running plays of the decade, *Tobacco Road* (2,611 performances) and *Pins and Needles* (934 performances) continued throughout the thirties, the proclivity for social drama based on angry protest and didactic exhortation declined. In spite of the continued box office success of such plays as well as the strident *Waiting For Lefty* which continued to run into the forties, and other plays of the "drama as weapon" synthesis, there was a marked decline in the number and visibility of "hard-line" radical writers. Sam Smiley notes that only a minority of American writers ever joined the Communist Party in the first place, and many of those soon renounced their decision when faced with restrictions and political rigidity: "The events of the times, not the politics of parties, set off the forces that transformed liberals into radicals."[3]

Many playwrights in the latter half of the decade realized that the direction of their dramatic theses had to be shifted from the working class to the middle class. *Waiting For Lefty* and *Dead End* had won sufficient acclaim, but the audiences who were most supportive were middle-income people, sympathetic with the workers and underprivileged in their struggle against the monied classes, but essentially concerned with problems and social issues of their own. Clurman's "new audience," for all its enthusiasm in response to Odets' "STRIKE!" scene or to the call for better housing in *One-Third of a Nation*, was middle class, on its way up perhaps, but still nostalgic about its antecedents among the lower echelons of society.

Writing *New Theatre* in January, 1936, Clurman summed up the problem:

> The world of the ruling class is real
> in the sense that the rulers know where their interests

lie, work hard and fight systematically to protect them against every possible enemy; the world of the working class is real because its struggle is so primitive and plain that there is no mistaking or avoiding it. But the middle class carries out the orders of the ruling class with the illusion of complete freedom, and it is sufficiently protected from the terror of material nakedness to believe in transcendental explanations of human woe that keep it "calm" without really satisfying it. There is no enemy in the middle class world except with one's own contradictions—and real life (the life that both the upper and lower classes know in their opposite ways) enters upon the scene like a fierce, unexplained intruder.[4]

The discovery and exposure of this "enemy," this "intruder," became a primary theme of the plays of the second half of the decade. The goal was to create a medium, both entertaining and informing, which would treat the fears and emotions of the American people—but this time the "people" were middle class, not working class. This was a task which could not be accomplished from a strident Marxist position, and it would involve more abstract social issues than working conditions or political corruption; it would have to address the forces of the "intangible fate," the forces of injustice, intolerance, and ambition. Furthermore, it would have to build whatever thesis it stated, whatever polemic it offered, on the values of the American middle class. In this sense it would move directly toward what Joseph Wood Krutch called "revolutionary" drama in that it would go beyond the "classical" formula of Sophocles, Shakespeare, and Moliere, a formula which produced a play that argumentatively defended "a set of moral assumptions." Instead, in the second half of the thirties, playwrights began to produce drama which "showed a tendency to be more interested in displaying human life against a certain background of moral assumptions."[5] And by doing so, Krutch points out, "the playwrights were attempting radically to alter the intellectual concepts of the audience."[6] One of the first playwrights to attempt to discover a new mode was Clifford Odets.

In the summer of 1935 a weary Clifford Odets returned

from an ill-fated trip to Cuba on behalf of the American Com-
mission to Investigate Labor and Social Conditions in Cuba.
The entire "investigatory trip," Odets felt, had been a frightening
and embarrassing sham. He and the other members of the com-
mission were described in the press as a "squad of east-side Communists." They were travelling to Cuba ostensibly to investigate
the new regime of Fulgencio Batista and his president, Carlos
Mendieta, which had overthrown Ramon Grace San Martin's
government in 1934 and which reportedly was violently suppres-
sing labor protests and viciously exploiting workers. Odets'
party arrived in Havana, were marched to a detention camp for
the night, and were shipped back to New York early the next
day. The incident achieved wide publicity for American Communists and Popular Front organizations, and since there was
much brandishing of machine guns, Odets' adventure created
quite a sensation. Although he spoke of his experience several
times in public forums and wrote a play, *Cuba,* based on it,
he seemed to chafe under the feeling that he had been used
by the Party to obtain sensational press coverage.

Whether the feeling of being an unwitting tool of the Party
adversely affected Odets' regard for his communist associations
or whether his failure to find anyone interested in producing
Cuba made his reassess his political ties is unclear. Michael Mendelsohn notes that Odets felt his creative energy "was being
inhibited by attempts to pressure him into writing only party
line plays";[7] in any case, he resigned from the Party that same
summer.[8] He was never a committed communist in any case; his
first two productions, for all their revolutionary zeal, look to
communist upheaval only as a last resort; and even then, the
characters seem more liberal than radical. As he continued to
produce plays, he moved away from the synthesis represented
by *Lefty* toward a new thesis that was no less socially critical but
lacked the exhortative force of his first plays.

The year 1935 was an important one for Odets. He produced five plays: *Waiting For Lefty, Till the Day I Die, Awake
and Sing!, Paradise Lost,* and a one-act, *I Can't Sleep,* staged
for a union benefit. Four of these five were enjoying commercial
success on Broadway, and Odets suddenly found himself the
"darling" of American drama. "In less than ninety days," one

writer proclaimed from the pages of *Literary Digest,* "toiling with the unrest of his times as a central theme, a young actor in the New York theatre . . . has become the most exciting spokesman the world of workers yet has produced, and he has become perhaps the most articulate dramatist available in the theatre."[9] But his fame was not just theatrical. Clurman notes that his plays were also having a literary impact: "The book reviewers devoted columns to him: he was being read in the same spirit as were the novels of Dos Passos, James Farrell, Erskine Caldwell, John Steinbeck, Robert Cantwell, and Thomas Wolfe."[10] He was also being compared to O'Neill, silent since 1932, and many felt Odets would replace O'Neill as "the great American playwright" of the twentieth century.[11] Odets' rise was meteoric in its suddenness and brilliance; and from such a seminal year as 1935, it appeared that he was indeed, as many critics proclaimed him to be, the "great white hope" of the American drama.[12]

Almost every critic who has written on Odets has pointed out that his spiraling and rapid success was based on social commitment as demonstrated in his plays. Gerald Rabkin speaks for many when he states:

> The importance of Odets' political commitment from a dramatic point of view resided in its affording him an intellectual substructure upon which to construct his several dramas. Since Odets' virtues were never primarily intellectual, his social orientation enabled him to relate his characters and themes to a coherent world-view. Either explicit or implicit in all his dramas of the thirties is the metaphor born of Marxist commitment.[13]

But Odets recognized that his commitment was not enough to sustain a whole career. The world was changing, attitudes were shifting, and he needed to respond to those shifts as accurately as he had to the social situation in the winter of 1935.

Still, the conflict between Odets the social dramatist and Odets the artist continued. He was "no ivory tower writer," Mendelsohn points out: "He was too deeply committed to the people and their problems to create art for art's sake."[14] But

Clurman notes: "He did not want to remain a Left playwright. He wanted to be at the very center of standard playwrights of quality."[15]   Odets had the start many writers dream of, four Broadway shows in his first year; but to sustain his fame, he realized that he must continue to find Clurman's "new audience" and address their concerns. Edward Murray writes:

> If significant achievement in literature on the thematic level is the result of the writer's ability to "hold in balance," as Fitzgerald put it, "the sense of the futility of effort and the sense of necessity to struggle, the conviction of the inevitability of failure and still the determination to succeed—and, more than these, the contradictions between the dead hand of the past and the high intentions of the future" then one might argue that in his best work Odets manages to project both the horror and the faith that characterized the "vision" of the thirties.[16]

Significantly, Odets understood that the role of the worker was not one an audience, especially a middle class audience, could continue to identify with. But the contradictions and conflicts he perceived in the working class situation also existed in the lives of middle class people from whom Odets himself had emerged. "The source of much of Odets' strength as a 'proletarian' playwright," writes Rabkin, "lay precisely in the fact that he did not force himself to write about the proletariat. Unlike other middle-class writers of Marxist persuasion, he had the esthetic sense to write about areas of his direct experience."[17] With the exception of his first sensational and influential play, *Waiting For Lefty,* virtually all of the rest of Odets' plays deal with the fears and contradictions of the middle class as critics such as Murray and Clurman have pointed out. From *Awake and Sing!* to *Clash By Night,* produced in December, 1941, Odets would pose a new point of view of social issues—a mode of drama Mendelsohn, among others, calls "urban middle class naturalism."[18]

"The trouble with literary terms," writes Eric Bently, "is that in proportion as they become impressive they become useless, in proportion as they become exact, they become inapplicable."[19]   No term is more often applied with less precision to American drama in the thirties than is "naturalism." R. H. Gardner writes: "Naturalism—whose influence, despite its obsolescence, has probably done more to shape the popular concept of theatre in this country than any other—attempts to produce on stage the illustration of life exactly as it is lived off stage."[20]   While this definition seems to apply to a large portion of thirties' drama, it does not take all of it into account by any means, nor does it consider the elements of scientific determinism, authorial objectivity, and the sense of determinism that characterizes either Zola's manifesto published in 1873 with his play, *Therese Raquin*—named the "first consciously conceived naturalistic drama" by the *Oxford Companion to the Theatre*[21]—or the peculiarly American brand of naturalism fostered by Stephen Crane, Frank Norris, and Theodore Dreiser in the turn-of-the-century novel.[22]

"The naturalistic character," writes Warren French, "lives in a dream-world of intense but vaguely formulated desires."[23] In the plays which followed *Lefty*, Odets attempted to identify those desires more concretely, to state them as common goals for what Mendelsohn calls a "middle class consciousness," to argue for an optimistic resolution to the social ills which concerned the class he knew best, and finally, to transform his synthesis into a new thesis which would entertain and inform an audience, and which would respond to questions about the plight of the middle class in the United States. His stock in trade would be dreamers, but the "intruders" he saw as chiefly responsible for the concerns of his characters were ambition and an inability to define concretely what it is they aspire to. Odets had already taken the first step in this direction even before *Waiting For Lefty* was produced.

Awake and Sing!, which surprisingly antedates *Lefty* by two years, shows patterns and tendencies Odets would return to after his success with *Waiting For Lefty*. In a sense, *Lefty* opened the doors to success for the young playwright, and Odets used his advantage to stage a kind of drama that would concern itself with the social problems of the middle class. The original version of *Awake*, entitled *I've Got the Blues*, was rejected by the Group when Odets first submitted it because of what Clurman called "some rather gross Jewish humor and a kind of messy kitchen realism," and also because the ending of the play was "masochistically pessimistic."[24]   But in the wake of the sensation caused by *Waiting For Lefty*, the Group quickly stepped up the pace on its production of Odets' revised version and opened February 19, 1935, at the Belasco Theatre in New York.

Unlike *Waiting For Lefty*, *Awake and Sing!* is not, as Krutch points out, about "one specific protest and rebellion but the persistent and many-sided rebellion of human nature against everything which thwarts it."   The play makes the statement that "the real secret of mankind's success, the real hope for its future . . . lies in the persistence of its passion, its unwillingness to accept defeat for its desires."[25]   But the optimism of a "hope for a brighter future" comes only after intensely brutal interplay between characters and after unselfish human sacrifice.

Set in the Bronx, *Awake* dramatizes the plight of a working class family struggling to seize and hold onto newly discovered middle class position and values.   The Bergers, Bessie and Myron, and their children, Ralph and Hennie, are people "who never had any money but who love it and live for the love of it," Odets writes.[26]   Bessie, the "Jewish Matriarch," rules over the household as "tyrannical mother," "overpowering wife," and "scornful daughter"; she has tried to indoctrinate her children with ideals of middle class respectability and intends for them to succeed in life even if it means perverting their own ambitions and driving them away from her.   But none of the family seems to be able to live up to her expectations: Myron is a hopeless dreamer who dwells on the past; Uncle Morty, Bessie's brother, is a "successful American businessman . . . a 32-degree Mason," who lords his money and material wealth over his sister and brother-in-law; and Bessie's father, Jacob, a retired barber, constantly seeks to alter Bessie's push of the children so that it assumes "the right path" (p. 38).

Jacob is an avowed Marxist.   His exhortations to Ralph have no greater success than Bessie's constant preachments about hard work and respectability, for the grandson is more interested in someday having "a pair of black and white shoes" (p. 42) and marrying a girl with whom he has fallen in love.   For once Jacob and Bessie are in agreement: marriage for Ralph is out of the question. However, Bessie's objections are to the girl's lack of family and, importantly, family money; Jacob objects because he fears marriage will deter Ralph from awakening to the need for social change. He tells him: "Remember, a woman insults a man's soul like no other thing in the whole world!" And he admonishes him to wait until he has done something significant with his life before tying himself down with a wife and family:

> Boychick, wake up! Be something! Make your life something good. For the love of an old man who sees in your young days his new life, for such love take the world in your two hands and make it like new. Go out and fight so life shouldn't be printed on dollar bills. A woman waits. (p. 28)

But Jacob fails to convince Ralph, or anyone else, of his socialist programs, and herein lies a second major contrast between *Awake* and Odets' earlier plays.

In *Waiting For Lefty* striking cabbies turn to communism only when all other alternatives fail, and even in doing so, they couch their sentiments in the idea that they are only "red" because others say so. In *Awake*, Odets presents leftist ideas through an ineffective old man. Unlike Agate's impassioned call for "STRIKE!" Jacob's speeches fall on deaf ears, a point Odets emphasizes when Jacob argues with Morty about the moral implications of his son's capitalistic enterprises:

> So you believe in God...you get something for it? You! You worked for all the capitalists. You harvested the fruit from your labor? You got God! But the past comforts you! The present smiles on you, yes? It promises you the future something? Did you found a piece of earth where you could live like a human being and die with the sun on your face? Tell me, yes, tell me. I would like to know myself. But on these questions, on this theme—the struggle for existence—you can't make an answer. The answer I see in your face...the answer is your mouth can't talk. In this dark corner you sit and

you die. But abolish private property! (pp. 72-73)

Morty is not moved by his father's tirade: "Don't go in the park, Pop—" he laughs at him, "the squirrels'll get you. Ha, ha, ha..." (p. 73).

The major theme of *Awake and Sing!* is rebellion. Not only does Jacob preach that all men should abandon their selfish ambitions and work for a better world, but also that Ralph's decision to go ahead and court his girl constitutes a rebellion against Bessie's ideas of his future. Hennie also rebels; in direct defiance of Bessie's strict sense of morality she becomes pregnant by a man she does not know and will never see again. Although Hennie's condition incenses her mother, Bessie reacts swiftly, marrying Hennie off to Sam Feinschreiber, a newly arrived immigrant with wage-earning potential. Jacob objects to the duping of Sam, and his prediction of disaster is borne out when the marriage soon breaks up with Hennie leaving both her husband and baby and fleeing with Moe Axelrod, a racketeer, who, it turns out, was her first love after all. The conflicts of the play finally come to a climax when Myron unwittingly reveals to Ralph that Sam is not the father of Hennie's baby, and the boy turns away from his family entirely, bitterly telling Jacob and Myron when they try to explain the situation to him, "You never in your life had a thing to tell me" (p. 84). Ralph's rejection of both his grandfather's visions and his mother's codes of conduct drive both Jacob and Bessie over the edge. She races into the old man's room and in a burst of frustration breaks all his Caruso records, his one pleasure in life. And Jacob, having lost any chance of every reaching Ralph, elects to make a supreme sacrifice. He goes up to the roof, flings himself off, and thereby provides his grandson with his insurance money with which to make a decent start in life.

The most frequently heard complaint about *Awake and Sing!* concerned the play's ending, which many critics felt offered flabby Marxism and a tepid commitment to bourgeois values, two antithetical ideas in themselves. Malcolm Goldstein offers the strongest complaint when he writes that Odets "sentimentalizes" Bessie in the end, placing the play "between melodrama and agit-prop."[27] Goldstein is referring to Bessie's final speech in which she defends her moral codes and dedication to making her children's future. In the final act she opens up to Ralph and Hennie, and for the first time in the play, her complaining words ring true:

> Ralphie, I worked too hard all my years to be treated like dirt. It's no law we should be stuck together like Siamese twins. Summer shoes you didn't have, skates you never had, but I bought a new dress every week. A lover I kept—Mr. Gigolo! Did I ever play a game of cards like Mrs. Marcus? Or was Bessie Berger's children always the cleanest on the block! Here I'm not only the mother but also the father. The first two years I worked in a stocking factory for six dollars while Myron Berger went to law school. If I didn't worry about the family who would? On the calendar it's a different place, but here without a dollar you don't look the world in the eye. Talk from now to next year—this is life in America.
>
> (p. 95)

Bessie's final speech is a plea for understanding from her much abused son. Odets' middle class heroine is the way she is because she has no choice, and Ralph suddenly understands her: "I'm not blaming you, Mom," he tells her. "Sink or swim—I see it. But it can't stay like this." Suddenly he recalls Jacob's words and shouts to her: "We don't want life printed on dollar bills, Mom!" (p. 95); but Bessie is unmoved by her father's rhetoric, and she leaves Ralph to ponder his new insight.

Leftist critics disliked the tone of *Awake;* they found it far too mild after the bombastic *Lefty.* And the right, also expecting another Marxist tract, indicted its "ardor," while generally praising it as quality drama.[28] Weales defends Odets' ending, however, when he writes that "the last act is really so effective theatrically."[29] But Brooks Atkinson sums up the general critical reaction to the play's final lines by pointing to Ralph's final speech and calling it more "elegy" than "song": "But there is no doubt," he concludes, "that the characters are awake."[30]

Ralph's curtain speech signals that he has taken hold of Jacob's arguments. He realizes that he cannot accept the in-

surance money, first of all because it is tainted (Jacob's suicide
might prohibit the company from paying), and secondly because he has not earned it himself: "No girl means anything
to me until..." he gropes for words, "Till I can take care of her"
(p. 96). Rushing into Jacob's room he gathers up the old man's
books, vows to read them and to learn. "Maybe we'll fix it so
life won't be printed on dollar bills," he declares to Moe and
Hennie, who are about to depart for Cuba (p. 97).

Ralph encourages his sister to go ahead in her adulterous
flight, thereby rejecting all his mother's fake respectability and
embracing Jacob's philosophy, a legacy the old man would have
far more willingly bequeathed him than money. Fully understanding the meaning of his grandfather's death, Ralph issues
his final statement; fully "awake," he "sings":

> I'm twenty-two and kickin'! I'll get along. Did Jake
> die for us to fight about nickels? No! "Awake and Sing,"
> he said. Right here he stood and said it. The night he died
> I saw it like a thunderbolt. I saw he was dead and I was
> born! I swear to God, I'm one week old! I want the
> whole city to hear it–fresh blood, arms. We got 'em.
> We're glad we're living. (pp. 100-101)

In Ralph's closing lines, Odets uses the device he found so effective in *Lefty,* the "call to action." But wary of attempting
to imbue Ralph's speech with Marxist concretes, Odets creates
a call for a better future based on abstract optimism and the hope
for a better world through the cooperative effort of the young.
Weales points out: "It is not what Ralph is going to do, but
that he has decided to do something . . . that the audience must
accept if he is to be the 'affirmative voice' Odets once called
him."[31] Unlike Agate's demand for "STRIKE!" at the end
of *Lefty* or even Jacob's tirade earlier in *Awake,* Ralph's "call
to action" is not specifically Marxist or political in any way;
but it is an unmistakable move from a lack of direction toward
a positive goal.

Hennie's decision to escape Bessie's clutches with the gangster and Ralph's sudden awakening pose the major critical problems in the play. Admittedly it is difficult for even the most

amoral audience to accept Hennie's abandonment of a devoted husband, Sam, and their child for the questionable love of the crude Moe Axelrod: "You won't forget me to your dying' day—" Moe tells her at one point; "I was the first guy. Part of your insides. . . I wrote my name on you—indelible ink!" And she acknowledges: "One thing I won't forget—how you left me crying on the bed like I was two for a cent" (p. 97). In spite of the fact that Moe's love of the girl came before Sam's—or the child for that matter—Hennie's escape with such a villainous figure strains the audience's sympathy for her.

But it is Ralph's complete reversal which threatens the play's credibility. Not only does he change his mind about Hennie and Bessie's duping of Sam, but he also encourages his sister to leave with Moe. After withstanding years of Jacob's passionate rhetorical exhortations for him to renounce his selfish ambitions and fight for a better world, he experiences a Marxist epiphany during Bessie's self-pity speech and not only abandons his intentions to marry his girl but also dedicates himself to the very cause Jacob had pleaded for so long. Weales points out that the play's ending incorporates two stock romantic devices: "the traditional happy ending for the lovers beset by barriers" and "the speech to which one responds not because the way has been laid dramatically, not even because one believes what is being said, but because the spiritual content . . . is so commanding."[32] But Ralph's recognition and Hennie's adultery are respectively believable and justifiable anyway, because they are the routes the characters would have taken in the first place had Bessie not blocked their way in the name of middle class respectability. "Indeed," writes Murray, "few works in American drama reveal so well what happens to a family when natural relations are perverted."[33] Mendelsohn points out that however incredible Hennie's abandonment of her husband and child may be, Odets would have made a major error in providing such a dreary play with a happy ending.[34] Weales notes that while many critics complained that the play's resolution is too weak—"that the Moe-Hennie thing will not last a month, that that sniveling boy will crawl back into his mother's womb"—these events do not take place within the play itself.[35] In developing his new thesis, Odets merely suggests that the solutions to the middle class dilemma can be found through acts of individual heroism; whether the answers will work for the characters (or, by extension, the audience) or not is dependent upon a collective resolution to accept them rather than on the strength or weakness of the individuals who discover them.   In this area, he had not moved that far away from the synthesis of collective "call to action" he demonstrated in *Lefty*.

Awake and Sing! earned critical praise chiefly for its characterization and language.   Eleanor Flexner, speaking for the left, finds the play lacking in continuity, but she admits that "such characterization and dialogue are not to be found previously in our drama."[36]   And John Howard Lawson concedes that "Odets has found the gaiety and warmth and singing beauty in American speech."[37]   Edith Isaacs writes that Odets' characters have a "double set of nerves," but not "a grain of common sense. . .all have the large chips on their shoulders, moving blindly through an upset world, all suffering from different personal disharmonies, but all basically alike, and all bewildered."[38] Lawson and others see this "bewilderment" as representing Odets' attempt to inject the theory of literary naturalism into his early play; but, as Lawson points out, Odets himself is not yet certain of his ground: "Odets fails to think out the full casual relationships between the social forces as they exist in the environment and the decision of individuals as they come in conflict with these social forces," he writes.[39]   But Lawson— whose *Marching Song* illustrates his thesis that the result of a "full thinking out" is open and complete revolution—misses Odets' key point.   A commitment to full literary naturalism would mean that his hero, in this case either Ralph or Hennie, must be utterly defeated by the forces against which he struggles. On the contrary, both emerge victorious from their ordeal "awake" and "singing."

While the naturalistic generation of writers has "demonstrated to its own satisfaction that there is nothing to admire or hope for in the nature of man," Krutch points out that Odets "comes along and does both."[40]   But setting the individual heroes aside for a moment, Odets' primary point comes into focus: what is defeated in *Awake and Sing!* is not any single individual but a whole family.   The economic and social forces have combined to make Bessie a tyrannical master of the family. And in her fanatical desire to struggle against these forces, to protect her children not only from an immediate threat but from future threats, she makes the lives of all around her miserable; ironically, her zeal to protect those she loves drives them away from her, and the lasting impression of the end of the play is that the Bergers can never exist again as a family unit.

Awake and Sing! represents patterns and themes which would become the basis of the remainder of Odets' drama. Not only does he modify the Marxist thrust of his first produced play, but he also shifts his emphasis from the working class, which wishes dynamically to improve its lot in life but never wishes to abandon its identity, to an upwardly motivated middle class, which seeks always to improve both the status quo and the prospects for the future. Instead of a clamour for "STRIKE!" the social message in *Awake,* as Mendelsohn points out, is to raise middle class consciousness so its members can learn "to tell the difference between dollar bills and life."[41] Furthermore, the revised version of *Awake* indicates a shift in emphasis from the collective action of workers to the integral middle class unit, the family. The Bergers are hardly a model, even after the children rebel; however, the goal of both rebellions seems to be familial harmony: Hennie seeks a permanent relationship with a man she loves—"Till the day she dies she will be faithful to a loved man," Odets writes (p. 33)—and Ralph's rebellion is founded on his being able to support a girl on his own—when "we can take the world in two hands and polish it off," he says (p. 96). But true to his stance in *Lefty,* Odets demonstrates that there is often a discrepancy between the ideal and the actual. "With bitter irony," Goldstein writes, "Odets points out the disparity between the myth and the reality of the American middle class."[42] And, like Ralph and Hennie, Odets himself seemed to be searching through his subsequent plays and through the theme of personal rebellion for, as Mendelsohn puts it, "something to call a family."[43] This search soon led him to his fourth Broadway play of the year, *Paradise Lost.*

Although *Paradise Lost* ran for seventy-three performances after its opening December 9, 1935 (a respectable showing for that depression year), Odets was disappointed in its reception. After the tidal wave of success started by *Lefty* and carried along by *Awake,* he had begun, as Goldstein points out, to regard himself as "a major social force." He had another play,

Remember, in production at the Negro People's Theatre; he had advertised his services as a director free of charge for "any valuable play," and he had been offered $3,000 a week by Metro-Goldwin-Mayer as a screenwriter. He declined MGM's offer, but when the studio came forward with $17,000 ready to back his new play, *Paradise Lost,* he accepted on behalf of the Group Theatre.[44]

There are several important differences between *Paradise Lost* and Odets' earlier plays. First of all, it moves even further away from the exhortative format of *Waiting For Lefty* and parts of *Awake and Sing!* to the extent that the Marxist message is muted and shifted to the lines of a minor character. The structure also becomes more reliant on traditional theatrical elements such as discovery and melodramatic contests between good and evil. Also, the Gordons, unlike the Bergers who actively attempt to rise from their working class origins to middle class respectability, have already arrived. Hence, in the order his plays were produced on stage, Odets' emphasis changes from addressing the problems of an oppressed proletariat (*Lefty*) to threats of concern to a lower middle class family which aspires to a better life (*Awake*) to threats of concern to a bourgeois family which only wishes to maintain its present status (*Paradise Lost*). Ironically, however, the nature of all these threats is the same: capitalist greed, political corruption, and the continuing effects of the depression. But to the Gordons the danger manifests itself in a different manner. Sam Smiley sums up the play's theme: "Each individual must struggle to achieve a full life amidst the dire conditions brought on by the social dislocation of the time, and the struggle for betterment is hopeless unless individuals awaken to reality and join all other workers to arrange life so that dollar bills do not have such almighty importance."[45] The Gordons are placed in a position of defending what they have rather than struggling, as do the Bergers, to attain it. But they are by no means wealthy; there is always the promise of a "big deal" which will come through in time to save them from destruction and permanently elevate their social position and preserve it. Finally, *Paradise Lost* is different from *Awake and Sing!* because Odets moves closer toward a pure demonstration of naturalism. Several characters are destroyed; but Odets still clings to the idea of the family unit as a hero. Leo Gordon is saved to deliver a "call to action" as the play closes, thus ending the chain of defeats on an optimistic note and recalling the ending of such naturalistic novels as John Steinbeck's *The Grapes of Wrath*, wherein the remnants of the Joad family find the courage for hope even in the face of what appears to be total disaster, or Zola's *Germinal*, where the struggle goes on.

The Gordon household is not an affluent home, but it is considerably nicer than the Bronx apartment of the Bergers. Leo, the head of the family, is a liberal, middle-class business-man who owns half of a handbag factory with his neighbor, Sam Katz, a greedy, corrupt capitalist. Sam is apparently responsible for whatever success the business has had in the past, since Leo is content to handle the designs for their bags while Sam runs the front office. The difference between the two men is em-phasized when "a shop delegation" comes to the Gordon home to lodge complaints against Sam. Not only are they making too little to live on, but Sam has also asked them to work longer hours than their present contract calls for; additionally, he has been demanding that they sign pay vouchers for more money than they are making. Leo is shocked, especially when Sam boldly admits that their charges are accurate and tells them to go ahead and strike, warning them: "when a strike comes, I'll hire scabs so quick—."[46] But Sam does not appear as brave after Leo opposes this threat, and he whines: "You hear her? They'll walk out in the middle of the season—the only time in the year we can make a little profit. They'll make a revolution!" But Sam is not so easily swayed: "Leave the business in my hands . . . Go on designing pocket books and don't bother your head," he pleads with Leo. Leo is moved by the workers' plea, however; he promises them: "No one will be exploited in the Cameo shop"; and although he knows it will bankrupt the business to give the workers their raise, he tells Sam: "I don't want my life built on the misery of these people" (p. 187).

Therefore, Leo emerges early in the play as the moral spokes-man; he senses the injustice in society; but, like Myron Berger in *Awake*, he also possesses a sweet naivete. Clara, his wife, regards him as a frequently foolish man; but she tolerates his whims even when they are blatantly illogical, such as his demand that a pet bird be disposed of because he does not "want any-thing German in the house" (p. 160), or when they demonstrate a lack of common sense, such as his mortgaging the house and furniture to keep the business going (p. 162). But while he resembles Myron in his foolishness and lack of foresight, Leo is different from Myron in that he is the undisputed head of his household; there is no Bessie Berger to take the reins and drive everyone along the road she chooses until they rebel. Although Leo lacks judgment in concrete, practical matters, he differs from Myron and the Bergers in that he never allows his dreams to turn him away from the realities of the present for the nostalgia of the past or for the musings of how things might be.

The Gordons, like the Bergers, have high hopes for their children; and as in the case of the Bergers, those hopes are thwarted. Ben, the eldest, has accomplished only one thing in life, an impressive track record as an athlete; he winds up a wasted adult who is good for practically nothing, who consorts with gansters, and who lives on the fame of his athletic laurels. Pearl, a promising musician, has shut out the world and retreats to her room to practice for the concert debut she will never have because the family loses whatever money it possesses and can never sponsor her talent; her music provides a counterpoint to the play's action until it is removed when the piano is repossessed. Julie, the younger Gordon son, is like Ben in that he also dreams of a "big deal" which will make his and his family's fortune. He worships his older brother, but he is different from him because he possesses a genuine talent for business even though he lacks the capital to invest in and exploit his frequent insights. Julie is dying from narcolepsy, and having lived literally in the shadow of his brother's fame (there is a statue of the triumphant Ben in the living room), Julie's plight is made more pathetic by his unbridled worship of his older brother's overbearing, self-confident personality.

All of the Gordon children, like the Berger children, are dreamers. They are separated from Ralph and Hennie and, incidentally, from doomed naturalistic dreamers in American fiction such as Studs Lonigan, only by their awareness that their dreams are futile escapes from reality. They are complemented by Gus, a family friend, who also dreams: "The way I see it there's two kind of men—" he says to Leo; "there is the true man and the dream. We're only the dream yes...the dream. That don't make much sense don't it?" (p. 190). Like Jacob in *Awake*, Gus lives in the past and searches for answers through humanistic philosophy to the problems of this family he has come to love. Gus' greatest pleasure in life is his stamp collection; and, again, he recalls Jacob when he sells the stamps to help the Gordons. Gus sees this sacrifice, as Jacob views his suicide, as a chance to save a basically good man and good family.

The voice of specific social criticism in the play is given to Mr. Pike, the furnace man, whose chief function in the play seems to be to dispense Marxian philosophy in an intelligent, articulate manner. When a local politician, Foley, accuses Pike of being a "red" because the worker will not vote for the Democratic ticket, he explodes:

> For one generation of Irish you're talking pretty big. I'm what they call one hundred per cent American. My ancestors didn't come over on the Mayflower. They missed that one, but they came over on the next ferry. I come stock, lock and barrel out of the Parson family. We fought all your wars, from 1776 up to 1918. Two of my boys...my only two (*Shows pictures in watch*) .... (pp. 167-168)

But as with Jacob in *Awake and Sing!* and Agate in *Waiting For Lefty,* Odets pulls his social critic away from the brink of declaring himself a communist: "you call me a Red and I'll break your goddamn neck!" he yells at Foley (p. 169).

Odets' disassociation of his character with "hard-line" communist commitment is even more pronounced in *Paradise Lost* than in his plays of the previous spring perhaps because his own break with the party had occurred in the meantime or perhaps because he realized that a militant Marxist position would be less and less acceptable to a middle class audience as Popular Front ideals were increasingly disseminated. But Odets' softening of the Marxist thrust of his message does not extend to a softening of his strong pacifism. Pike is also the spokesman for this ideal. Calling the patriotic speech of a "mother of America" "Monkey dust! Gibberish!", the old furnace man flings his glass at the radio and declaims:

> Who are we, Mr. Gordon? If we remain silent while they make the next war—who then are we with our silence? Accomplices, Citizen! Let me talk out my heart! Don't stop me! Citizens, they have taken our sons and mangled them to death! They have left us lonely in our old age. The bully robbers have taken clothes from our backs. We slept in subway toilets here. In Arkansas we picked fruit. I followed the crops north and dreamed of a warmer

sun. We lived and hoped. We lived on garbage dumps.
Two of us found canned prunes, ate them and were poi-
soned for weeks. One died. Now I can't die. But we
gave up to despair and life took quiet years. We worked
a little. Nights I drank myself insensible. Punched my
own mouth. Yes, first American ancestors and me. The
circle's complete. Running away, stealing away to stick
the ostrich head in the sand. Living on a boat as night
watchman, tied to shore, not here or there! The American
jitters! (*Punches himself violently*) There's for idealism!
For those blue-gutted Yankee Doodle bastards are making
other wars while we sleep. And if we remain silent while
they make this war, we are the guilty ones. For we are
the people, and the people is the government, and tear
down from their high places if they dast do what they
did in 1914 to '18 (*Slowly sits trembling*). (pp. 190-191)

Odets' character offers here what is possibly the most convincing
and most poetic of the playwright's speeches of social commitment in the entire decade. It works better than the standard
agit-prop "call to action" first of all because it is completely
integrated into the character of Pike, who is particularly impassioned because he has lost two sons to war, and secondly
because it sounds more like Jeffersonian idealism than Marxist
rhetoric. Also, the speech works better as a theatrical device
because it is not a final curtain line (Leo will provide *Paradise
Lost* with a version of that device); it occurs early in the play,
thus setting up Leo as a foil for the capitalistic, war-mongering
characters as well as a spokesman for liberal, pacifistic, Popular
Front ideas. Finally, the speech stands out because it not only
echoes the words and sentiments of previous speeches of the
same ilk, such as Alan McClean's exit lines at the close of *Both
Your Houses* and Agate's "Stormbirds of the working class"
lines at the end of *Waiting For Lefty,* but also recalls passages
from American naturalistic fiction in the thirties, especially
from John Steinbeck's *The Grapes of Wrath* and the opening
and closing scenes of John Dos Passos' trilogy, U.S.A.[47] "All
these years," Pike concludes, "one thing kept me sane: I looked
at the telegraph poles. 'All those wires are going the same place,'
I told myself" (p. 191). But the old furnace man's answers are
inadequate. Leo softly asks him: "But what is to be done?"
In Pike's response, Odets demonstrates how far he has come

from the confident solutions offered in *Lefty* or even *Awake*:
"I don't know...I mean I don't know..." (p. 191).

Pike is also the character who identifies the enemy, the
"intruder" into the lives of the middle class family. His morose
philosophy seems constantly to be present when one of the
dreamers complains. When Pearl, for example, cynically declares, "For my part I discovered long ago the comic aspects
of this so-called class-war," and states, "I'm interested in myself!", Pike accuses her of pushing aside reality in favor of her
dreams: "You liar and traitor to your own heart's story!" he
yells at her. "You! lay awake dreaming at night. Don't you
know it ain't comin', that land of your dreams, unless you work
for it?" (p. 199). And when Leo asks Pike if he ever "met a
happy man" in all his travels, Pike defines the nature of the
middle class enemy: "The *system*. Breeds wars like a bitch
breeding pups! Breeds poverty, degrades men to sentimental
gibbering idiots, . . . There's your children, you, Sam Katz—a big
hand got itself around you, squeezin' like all hell gone on!"
(p. 206). Pike identifies the forces at work against the hopes
and dreams of people like the Gordons; and although he posits
no concrete solutions, knowing who or what the enemy is seems
to give the simple and gentle Leo insight and courage in the same
way Jacob's words inspire Ralph in *Awake and Sing!*

As the play closes, Leo and Clara and the near-comatose
Julie huddle together in the bare livingroom and stare at the
statue of Ben. The house and furniture have gone to pay the
mortgage since the handbag business is now bankrupt. Ben is
dead, killed in a shootout with police. In the words of one of
the company workers, Leo has "lost the paradise he had" (p. 227)
and all seems to be lost. Suddenly, however, as Clara breaks
into tears and Julie mutters incoherently, Leo comes awake
and delivers a spontaneous "call to action." "There is more to
life than this!" he tells his remaining family. "Everywhere now
men are rising from their sleep. Men, men are understanding
the bitter black total of their lives." Slowly Clara stops crying
and begins to listen to him as his voice builds in volume and
his rhetoric becomes more poetic: "Oh, yes, I tell you the whole
world is for men to possess. Heartbreak and terror are not the
heritage of mankind! The world is beautiful. No tree wears a
lock and key . . . " Ultimately he pronounces his final hope
for the future of society: "Men will sing at their work, men will
love. Ohhh, darling, the world is in its morning...and *no man*

fights alone!"   (pp. 229-230).   Leo's "call to action" is a synthesis of the strident emotion of Agate's "STRIKE!" call and
the vague vision of a better world and promising future of Ralph's
closing lines in *Awake and Sing!*   Although he offers no concrete solutions any more than Pike does in his Marxist tirades,
Leo is convinced that merely being aware of his place in a brother-
hood of man which transcends class distinctions is reason enough
to fight for a better life, a better world.

Reactions to *Paradise Lost* varied widely: it was called
"honest" and "naive," "thoughtful" and "shortsighted," "moving" and "wooden."   Krutch writes that the play was "exag-
gerated almost to the point of burlesque," that it suggested
that Odets "had completely lost his grip on reality."[49]   But
Rabkin defends the play's departure from credibility in its piling
of disaster upon disaster: "The characters in the play are all
condemned," he writes, "—but they are all presented as denizens
of a world made unreal by false hope and futile illusion."[50]
Clurman agrees with this point of view in his introduction to
the published play: "It is a play removed from both petty realism
and from 'leftist' phrase-mongering.   It is a play that attempts
to be true in the naturalistic sense, and visionary in the naturalistic sense."[51]   Whether critics approved or disapproved of Odets'
fourth Broadway production, however, they almost all agreed
that the play's chief flaw was Leo's closing speech.

Calling the ending of the play "a prologue," even Clurman
confesses that he finds the final speech a "weakness," and other
critics have joined him in complaining that Leo's sudden insight
and zealous commitment to join the "fight" for a new world
for the future are unprepared for and unbelievable.[52]   Admittedly, for a man who has failed so completely at everything
from promoting an already heroic son and talented daughter
to saving a small business to believe that he can somehow bring
about a change in the social order of a world does tend to stretch
credibility.   However, Leo's speech and its commitment possibly
only appear to be weak because the social message seems flaccid,
abstract, and vague compared to the poetic and forthright cer-
tainty of Pike's outburst earlier in the play.   Furthermore, Odets'
inclusion of a "call to action" may have been an automatic response to what he considered a necessary ingredient for a socially

significant drama. Certainly he had reason to believe in the use of such an inspirational curtain speech after the results it brought at the end of *Waiting For Lefty*.

But *Paradise Lost*'s structure bears almost no resemblance to *Lefty* or any of its antecedents, agit-prop or otherwise, which depended on such devices. *Paradise Lost* is virtually melodrama, dependent upon stock devices; and it is closer to the "well-made" play of the decade than to any didactic or protest drama written by anyone at any time. But regardless of the structural success of Leo's "call to action," it is consistent with Odets' social philosophy; it illustrates Odets' fundamental belief in an optimistic, affirmative rejection of both naturalistic determinism and of what Clurman calls the "nihilism of the cynical hobo" by a man who now sees "that his own position among the homeless may be the beginning of a new self-realization in terms of the millions of dispossessed who constitute the outstanding fact in this period of our history."[53] Thus, Leo is an ideal hero in Odets' dramatic vision; although Leo is not destroyed in spite of his terrible and inevitable defeats, Leo's experience illustrates Odets' commitment to the concept of literary naturalism—through his character, Odets affirms the validity of the struggle of an individual or a family against overwhelming forces. His result, however, is optimistic and positive: the alternative to destruction is social realization.

As one of the few critics who contends that Odets' perception of the middle class character was jaundiced, Edith Isaacs writes: "There is nothing in their [the Gordons'] thinking or acting to indicate that they are liberal. They are the dregs of the social system, money-loving, money-starved capitalists who have gone rotten through spinelessness and the frustration of their own golden longings. No revolution would help them."[54] But Isaacs may be missing an important point in the development of Odets' drama. Like Lawson and the leftist critics, she seems to expect Odets to stick to his theme of proletarian revolution and Marxist didacticism. Odets' plays in 1935 indicate a progression in his philosophy as well as his style. "He quickly outgrew the tendency to preach and to intrude forced themes," Mendelsohn writes. He wanted to achieve a "superior craftsmanship."[55] Odets was attempting, Clurman and others contend, to live up to the reputation he had been awarded after the spring of 1935, and to do this he realized that his plays had to entertain as well as inform.   Also, Clurman points out, Odets' understanding of the middle-class family was a full one; he had grown up in one, and ever since his professional association with the Group Theatre, one of the most middle-class companies extant in New York during the thirties, he had regarded it as his home and its members as his adult family.

Clurman also notes that Odets' depiction of the dilemma of the middle class is accurate because, as he states, the average middle-class person perceives, as Leo Gordon does, that "something is wrong," but he can neither define it nor discover what to do about it until he had lost virtually everything.   The upper class "perpetrates the general fraud," and the lower or working class struggles against it, correctly perceiving its chief enemy to be an exploiting economic system.   "The kind of middle class depicted in *Paradise Lost* dwells between the upper and lower classes, fooled by one, ignorant of the other, removed from the plain facts of both--naive, puzzled, frustrated . . . it lacks an enemy it can recognize and attack."   Lacking concrete weapons , Clurman concludes, it despairs, grows cynical, vindictive, "or it dreams of shadowy satisfactions from the past or in the distant or unattainable future."[56]   Odets' depiction of a middle class family's plight was not yet an "interpretation of life." It was still too mechanical, too reliant upon the analysis of the social forces themselves rather than upon the effects such forces had on the lives of individuals.   *Paradise Lost* does combine much of the anger of *Awake and Sing!* with a heightened sense of the naturalistic hero's struggle.   It is still a call for collective action and response in the manner of *Waiting For Lefty*, but it is indicative of a new direction for Odets; for the struggles in both *Awake* and *Paradise Lost* are increasingly defined in personal terms.   Leo's closing "call to action," for all its possible defects, speaks more eloquently and more credibly to the hope for a better future than any speech Odets had yet written.   In *Paradise Lost* Odets moved his dramatic themes into the realm of the middle class family for good, and he himself succumbed to the lure of upward motivation.   The following year he left Broadway for Hollywood.

"The greater the imagination of a writer," writes Krutch, "the less the validity of his work depends upon the validity of his formal creed."[57]   Once he was established in Hollywood,

Odets realized the security and success so many of his middle class characters dream of. What he lacked, however, was the sense of family the Group Theatre had provided, for it was that company more than anything else which had nurtured and sustained him. Also, most dramatists were highly suspicious of Hollywood's influence on the ability of an artist to produce "legitimate" drama. The movies were considered to be "lowbrow" entertainment, and the high salaries paid to writers and actors in motion pictures were looked upon as a perversion of professionalism.[58] "The two greatest threats to modern drama" are defined by Eric Bentley as being "cinema" and "the incandescent lamp."[59] In the late thirties, many theatrical writers, producers, and directors had good reason to regard the rapidly developing movie industry with a suspicious eye. A studio could take a moderately successful Broadway play, which had been painstakingly produced and which might have netted its writer and cast a few thousands of dollars, and cut it, alter its dialogue, mute its explicitness in violence or sex, change or sometimes even reverse its political or social message, or entirely rewrite the play, adding or deleting whole scenes to please the censors, the movie-going public, or to fit a particular matinee idol, and then make millions with it. Some playwrights regarded cinema as the best available example of capitalist exploitation of art in the United States. Plays such as Kingsley's *Dead End,* Jack Kirkland's adaptation of *Tobacco Road,* Thornton Wilder's *Our Town,* most of Maxwell Anderson's historical plays, and Lillian Hellman's *The Children's Hour* and *The Little Foxes* were filmed in Hollywood after they had been "cleaned up" by either the playwrights themselves or by a studio staff writer; and in several cases such as *Dead End, Tobacco Road, Our Town,* and *The Children's Hour,* the result was often that the movie versions bore little resemblence to the original scripts. Odets went to Hollywood in any case; however, when the Group Theatre called on him for a new play to save them from financial ruin, he responded with what is possibly his finest drama of the decade, *Golden Boy.*

"I wrote this play to be a hit, to keep the Group Theatre going," Odets said of *Golden Boy;* and a hit it was.[60] Running for two hundred fifty performances after its opening at the Belasco Theatre, November 4, 1937, it also enjoyed a long and successful run on the West Coast under Stella Adler's direction; it was taken on tour by both Group-sponsored and non-Group troupes; after the New York closing, it opened in London and subsequently in Paris for long runs in both cities. A movie was made of the play in 1939, and it happily kept most of Odets' script in tact except for the addition of a happy ending. Reviews of the play were mixed, concentrating on the play's entertainment value, but as Weales and Clurman point out, even those reviews not favorable to the play spawned audience curiosity and filled the orchestra seats night after night. "By money standards," Clurman wrote shortly after the play closed in New York, it was "the greatest success in the Group's history."[61] Only the "hard-line" communist critics seemed to understand Odets' social message, and they generally pointed it out by complaining that it was so obscure that it was almost non-existent. John Gassner, commenting on the reaction of leftist critics, states that Odets "drew in his horns of prophecy or, shall we say, his pseudophedia of social idealism."[62] But Eleanor Flexner recognized the significance of what Odets was trying to do: *Golden Boy*, she notes, is an attempt to reconcile "controversial ideas with the requisite entertainment content" that would at once garner profits and yield substance.[63] *Golden Boy* was written both to entertain and to inform, and it represents the closest synthesis of those two characteristics he would ever achieve.

Today *Golden Boy* seems clichéd and dated; however, complications, climax, and its characterizations set a pattern for later screenplays and television dramas: *Kid Galahad*, adapted by Seaton I. Miller from a novel by Francis Wallace (1937); *Body and Soul*, by Abraham Polansky (1947); *Champion*, adapted by Carl Foreman from a story by Ring Lardner (1949); *Somebody Up There Likes Me* (the Rocky Marciano biography), by Ernest Lehman (1956); *Requiem for a Heavyweight*, by Rod Serling (1956); *Rocky*, by Sylvester Stallone (1976); and the most recent version, *Raging Bull* by Mardik Martin and Paul Schrader (1981). Joe Bonaparte, the gentle but athletic son of Italian immigrant, dreams of becoming "somebody," of having fame and fortune– "You could build a city with his ambition to be somebody," one character says.[64] In spite of considerable talent as a violinist, Joe lacks faith in his musical ability as an avenue to success. Like Pearl in *Paradise Lost*, he recognizes that musicians are not much in demand in a depression-wracked society, and he searches for a quicker way to the top. As an athlete with some pugilistic talent, Joe hangs around the gymnasiums of New York, sparring with small-time contenders for extra money; he knocks one out on the eve of a big fight, takes his place in spite of the skepticism of the manager, Moody, and wins the match to everyone's surprise and delight.

Joe's boxing talent does not come so much from physical strength as from intellectual analysis of his opponents' weaknesses. He studies his foes' techniques, figures out his flaws, and exploits them. Moody quickly recognizes that if Joe combined hard-hitting punches with his thinking technique, he could be a real champion, and soon the boy's career is launched toward the Title. As Joe continues to win fight after fight, he becomes more and more conceited and anxious to reach the pinnacle of success. He also draws further and further away from his violin until he finally severs his tie with music completely by hitting too hard and breaking his hands. Ultimately, he manages to combine his intellectual and physical abilities but exploits his advantage too much by killing the Chocolate Drop in the ring. The realization of what he has become drives him to a suicidal death in an automobile crash.

Odets combines many of the ideals and dreams of previous young characters in Joe Bonaparte. Like Ben in *Paradise Lost*, he has physical strength, and like Ben, he finally becomes involved with a gangster, Eddie Fuseli, who points him in the way of immoral behavior and death. Like Julie and Pearl, he has intellectual and artistic gifts, but he knows the social situation of the times will not permit him to exploit them, and like them he is doomed. But he especially resembles Ralph in *Awake and Sing!*, because he seems to lack maturity and to grasp for vague ideas of success rather than concrete goals. He justifies his decision to "take a vacation" from his music in much the same way Ralph speaks of his lingering melancholia:

> Every birthday I had I sat around. Now'sa time for standing. Poppa, I have to tell you—I don't like myself, past, present and future. Do you know there are men who have wonderful things from life? Do you think they're better than me? Do you think I like this feeling of no possessions, of learning about the world from Carp's encyclopedia? Frank don't know what it means—he travels around, sees the world! (*Turning to* FRANK.) You don't know what it means to sit around here and watch the months go ticking by! Do you think that's a life for a boy my age? Tomorrow's my birthday! I change my life! (p. 252)

But Joe's decision to become a prize fighter has deeper motivations than Ralph's desire for "black and white shoes" or even life "that isn't printed on dollar bills." He tells Lorna, Moody's mistress, that he wants "to get even with people" and he cannot do that "by playing the fiddle. . . . If music shot bullets I'd like it better"; he goes on: "Artists and people like that are freaks today. The world moves fast and they sit around like forgotten dopes" (p. 264). Ralph, Ben, Julie, Pearl, or any of Odets' characters who dream of success and triumph over their origins are reflected in Joe's character; but Joe also searches for a concrete object to symbolize his attainment. He finally decides on an automobile, a Dusenberg, a "fancy speed wagon" as Moody calls it (p. 276), which can provide him with an escape from the reality of what he is and where he came from: "Cars are poison in my blood," he tells Lorna. "When you sit in a car and speed you're looking down at the world. Speed, speed, everything is speed—nobody gets me" (p. 266); and ironically, the car, a symbol of both his success and his desire to succeed, is the physical object which destroys him.

One major difference between *Golden Boy* and Odets' earlier plays dealing with the plight of the middle class family is that Joe, the child-dreamer, is the central figure. In *Awake*, Bessie dominates every scene (even those she is not present in); in *Paradise Lost*, Leo is the main character who suffers from the disintegration of his family and of his life's work; Joe's father, like Bessie and Leo, clashes with his children and watches his dreams for at least one of them end tragically, but he neither accepts the tragedy stoically as Leo does, nor does he attempt to alter by force the course of events. At the outset, in fact, Mr. Bonaparte accepts Joe's decision to fight and tries to understand it: "I don't say prize fight'sa no good for Joe," he tells Moody. "Joe like-a to be fame, not feel asham" (p. 256). But as Joe's career advances and he ceases to "pull his punches" to save his musician's hands, the old man becomes more and more reluctant to accept Joe's choice of careers. Finally, Joe demands that his father "give him the word" to go on fighting, but the old man refuses: *"No! No word!"* he cries out at him. "You gonna fight? All right! Okay! But I don't gonna give no word! No!" (p. 272). Still the love between the father and son provides a touching counterpoint to the play, and when Joe breaks his hands, the audience is almost required to have more sympathy for Mr. Bonaparte's shattered dreams than for Joe's loss of musical capability.

Other characters in the play recall Odets' previous casts, but changes have occurred here as well. The poet-philosopher-dreamer (Jacob in *Awake* and Gus in *Paradise Lost*) has become Carp in *Golden Boy,* still a "friend of the family" role, but reduced through Odets' change in emphasis to an almost foolish stance. The would-be capitalist who has yet to make it is represented by Siggie, Joe's brother-in-law, who wants nothing more in the world but enough money to buy his own cab; but Joe's father, who has the money to buy his boxer-son a twelve-hundred dollar violin, refuses to finance his daughter's husband's venture. Siggie looks upon Joe's growing success as his ticket to success as well: "It looks like the gold bug has visited our house," he slyly suggests when news of Joe's first victory comes to him (p. 253). Later he echoes sentiments heard often before in Odets' plays as he drunkenly tells Joe of his expectations:

> My god is success. Need I say more? I'm prouda you Joe. Come home a champ. Make enough dough to buy your sister's boyfriend a new cab. Yes, boys and girls, I'm looking into that crystal ball and I see strange and wonderful events! Yazoo! (p. 270)

But Siggie is disappointed, for not only does Joe refuse to give him any money, but what cash Joe does send home is promptly returned by his father who decides he wants nothing to do with his son's prize fighting.

Lorna is possibly the most pathetic figure in the play. Used by Moody to woo Joe into using his hands with more force in the ring, she soon begins to fall in love with him as hard as the young boxer falls for her. Even though she truly loves the incorrigible Moody, she stays with the manager only because she senses that she is not good enough for Joe. She tries to be "hard-boiled" and unfeeling; but in spite of her assurances to Moody that she is only "a tramp from Newark" and knows "a dozen ways" to handle the young fighter (p. 262), she softens in her attempts to control him and sympathizes with the distress of his father. Although Moody finally divorces his wife and sets the date for his and Lorna's long-awaited marriage, she is destroyed along with Joe in the fateful auto crash.

Many critics view *Golden Boy* as a modern allegory, and Clurman agrees: "What the golden boy of this allegory is fighting for a place in the world as an individual; what he wants is to free his ego from the scorn that attaches to 'nobodies' in a society in which every activity is viewed in the light of competition." Clurman goes on to point out that the chief symbol in the allegorical plot, naturally, is boxing—representing life's struggle, the attempt of a frustrated artist to "punch" his way into a world and find acceptance by it, "peace with it, safety from becoming the victim that it makes of the poor, the alien, the unnoticed minorities." To achieve such success, Clurman concludes, the allegorical hero is forced "to exploit an accidental attribute of his make up, a mere skill, and abandon the development of his real self."[65] Other critics have discovered other symbols in their interpretations of Odets' play as allegory: Murray, for example, points out the two park-bench scenes where Joe and Lorna meet to explore their feelings for each other and Joe's motivations for wanting to box. During these scenes a traffic light flashes, alternating between the red (stop) and green (go) as if in comment on both the lovers' desire for each other and Joe's indecision about whether to begin using his hands without worrying about damaging them.[66] Murray also points out that Joe's name, Bonaparte, recalls Napolean I, who ruthlessly abandoned caution in a desire to "conquer the world," but who was ultimately defeated by his own overriding ambition.[67]

Gerald Weales states that the play takes a further allegorical step that audiences are reluctant to accept: "the analogy between boxing and capitalism." Joe, Weales contends, "is regularly an instrument, a machine or a commodity, a possession." His "marketability" is discussed throughout the play, but Weales notes that in the end there are "two worlds" gathered to mourn Joe's death: "one to mourn the loss of a property, the other the loss of a man."[68] Clurman agrees. The irony of the last scene, he says, is "that he who begins by trying to beat the competitive world becomes himself a thing possessed."[69] In addition to these symbols and allegorical interpretations which seem to reinforce the play's bent toward a naturalistic hero's defeat, there are other symbols which seem to emphasize other significant social points.

Moody, the manager, is a clear-cut symbol of capitalist greed in one of its ugliest forms, as critics indicate; however, Moody has Joe's interests—as a boxer—at heart, and regardless of his insensitivity to the boy's musical ambitions, he exploits Joe only as much as one might expect an investor to exploit his investments. He wants the maximum potential from his business—thus he encourages Joe to hit harder—but he does not wish to push Joe too far too fast and risk losing his investment altogether. Joe's fatal bout with the Chocolate Drop is arranged against Moody's will. Joe wants it, but it is the pressure exerted by Eddie Fuseli which forces Moody to schedule the fight.

Fuseli is the opposite of Moody. First of all, his interest in Joe stems from a desire for a source of income from illegal gambling. Secondly, Fuseli cares little for Joe's physical welfare; he encourages him to fight more and more difficult bouts possibly before he is ready to. Also, Joe's interest in cars, fancy clothes, and a better life is fueled by Fuseli. However, the gangster is unhappy over Joe's growing love for Lorna, partly because of the myth that women are bad for an athlete's health, partly because be recognizes that she is the chief obstacle in Joe's total commitment to fighting, and partly because he is jealous. Fuseli is a homosexual.

But Fuseli stands for something more sinister in American society than organized crime or hoodlumism. Since the earliest years of the decade and even in the twenties, the gangster figure symbolized the force and oppression of the capitalistic system. Traditionally gunman and racketeer figures in drama were always acting at the instructions of corrupt capitalists and politicians and were financed by monies gained from exploiting the workers they helped to oppress. Odets had typified the role of the "muscle" in *Waiting For Lefty* through his use of a gangster character who was bodyguarding Harry Fatt. But in *Awake and Sing!* the gangster character, Moe, is not threatening as a tough, physical man but as a friend to the capitalists in the play, Morty and Myron, and as a threat to familial unity. In *Paradise Lost* the gangster, Kewpie, also threatens the Gordon family and succeeds in destroying one of its members, but his motivations are more sinister than Moe's. Moe is apparently motivated by love, but Kewpie is jealous of Ben's success with women and of the fame of the young, middle class athlete. In *Golden Boy*, Fuseli is defined clearly as an enemy both of the capitalist, Moody, and of the lower middle class boy trying to make good. A gunman who "walks like a cat," Fuseli, like Moe, apparently learned his "trade" in the army. Roxy, Moody's friend, tells him: "I remember this Eddie Fuseli when he came back from the war with a gun. He's still got the gun and he still gives me goose pimples!" And Moody responds: "That Fuseli's a black mark on my book.

Every once in a while he shoots across my existence like a roman
candle" (p. 275). Fuseli wants a "piece" of Joe, and Moody
is bullied into selling it to him, recognizing that in the face of
such brutal criminality, he has no choice; but implications that
Fuseli represents a more sinister evil than the threat of physical
violence emerge almost immediately.

The use of a gangster to symbolize a fascist began about
the same time as the Popular Front movement in the United
States. With Hitler's Nazi Party and its reported hoodlum-like
tactics in Germany as well as the Third Reich's territorial ambitions in Europe, the analogy of a gangster as a threat to capitalists
and as the encroachment of fascism on the free peoples of Austria
and Eastern Europe was a popular one. The militant role of
German and Italian troops in Spain during its Civil War also
encouraged the idea of linking fascists and gangsters, and the term
"gestapo tactics" had become a cliché long before World War II.
In plays such as Lawson's *Marching Song,* Hellman's *Days to
Come,* and dozens of motion pictures (many of which had nothing
to do with social issues), the gangster or "heavy" was frequently
seen as a "pistol-packing" "muscleman" who stupidly repeated
patriotic-like platitudes learned from his superiors in a usually
ill-fated attempt to pervert the original meanings of such phrases
to hs own evil ends. Fuseli is an exception to this motif only in
that he succeeds in pushing Joe too far, and the fighter's death
is a disappointment to him chiefly because he has lost a "sure
thing."

The gangster's allegorical relationship to Nazism is established
quickly: "Give a rat like that a finger and you lose a hand before
you know it," Moody tells Roxy (p. 276). Like the people
of Germany who appeared to be somewhat apathetic about
Hitler's methods, Joe accepts Fuseli's partnership with Moody
with only one condition, that the gangster not interfere with
the boxer's private life. Other than that he seems not to care:
"cut it up any way you like," he tells Moody. But Eddie begins
meddling in Joe's personal affairs right away. He resents Moody's
insolence: "the only reason I take your slop," the hood tells
the manager, is that Moody is "clever" and good for the boxer
(p. 292). Later, Fuseli indicates his bitter resentment over the
way Lorna treats the young fighter; he yells at her:

> Get outta my sight! You turned down the sweetest boy
> who ever walked in shoes! You turned him down, the

golden boy, that king among the juveniles! He gave you
his hand–you spit in his face! You led him on like Ger-
tie's whore! You sold him down the river! And now you
get the nerve to stand here, to wait and see him bleeding
from the mouth–(p. 311)

Fuseli's attention to Joe's personal life increases throughout
the play until it becomes almost an obsession for the gangster.
He comes to feel that he totally owns the fighter.

In allegorical form Odets shifts the social struggle away
from working class against capitalist and even away from middle
class against undefined economic forces; in *Golden Boy* capitalism,
though still not presented in a favorable light, struggles with
fascism for the control of a middle class boy who looks to both
as the way to success.

Hence, two struggles actually go on in the play: a middle
class hero struggles against the frustration of trying to improve
his life, and a capitalist struggles against encroaching fascism
which attempts to force him to abuse his position and exploit
the hero even more than he ordinarily does. Odets recognized
both these struggles as significant social concerns. He also saw
the necessity of subordinating the play's Marxist thrust by allowing the spokesman for the left to be a character who is rarely
on stage and who fulfills a minor part in the play's action. Frank,
Joe's brother, is an organizer for the C.I.O.; Frank is a mildly
disapproving older brother who is frequently away from home
"fighting" in his own way against the forces which oppress mankind. He believes in all the old Marxist causes—higher wages,
decent working conditions—but these never obtrude onto *Golden
Boy*'s major themes. After the exhortative "call to action"
of *Lefty*, the rambling ideology of Jacob *cum* Ralph in *Awake*,
and the poetic, impassioned pacificism of Pike and the visionary
optimism of Leo in *Paradise Lost*, Frank's simple statement
of ideals reflects the degree of change Odets had gone through
in his attitudes by late 1937: "I don't get autos and custom
made suits," Frank tells the assembled characters who wait for
word of Joe's death; "But I get what Joe don't. . . . The pleasure
of acting as you think! The satisfaction of staying where you
belong, being what you are . . . at harmony with millions of
othes" (p. 318). Odets is clearly offering the play's major message
in Frank's speech, but it is so closely integrated with the themes
of the play, boxer versus musician, middle class boy who is over-

come with ambition, that it loses whatever leftist punch it has.
The "call to action" which had characterized all of Odets' earlier
plays had evaporated.

Odets had so skillfully concealed his social concern in the
play that Krutch wrote in 1939 that *Golden Boy* was "capable
of engaging the interest of a spectator little concerned with either
political agitation or the attempt to interpret human nature in
Marxian terms."[70] Goldstein complains that the play is "sturdily
constructed, but the structure rests on a week foundation." But
he writes that "Odets shows himself in possession of a newly
heightened curiosity about the problems of the individual," in
spite of his intention "to expose the flaws in American
society."[71] Odets departed from the family-unit-as-hero theme in
Golden Boy (there is no *Mrs.* Bonaparte, Frank lives all over the
country, Siggie and Joe's sister are apparently unwanted tenants in
Mr. Bonaparte's flat, and Joe himself moves out early in the play)
and concentrates on the role of the individual. Krutch, who
identifies the play's major theme as "the lonely agony of souls
imprisoned in private hells of frustrated desire and inarticulate
hate," notes that Odets "keeps his political theories in the background" and explores the action of his characters as they struggle
with the forces of life: "The agonies of his characters are real
and affecting, whatever one may think of the reasons for their
existence."[72] And most critics agree that Odets' play can, as
Edward Murray puts it, "survive a rigorous study of its form
and content *as literature*";[73] but not all are agreed on exactly
what kind of play it is.

Sam Smiley writes that "the dichotomy between materialism and human values remains too strict for *Golden Boy* to be a
tragedy, and the action is too closely under the control of thought
for it to be mimetic melodrama. Structurally, it is a serious,
persuasive play."[74] But it is Gerald Rabkin who pins down the
chief literary value of the drama: "If Joe was destroyed by his
false image of success," he writes, "he was not entirely culpable;
this image was created by a society in which man's basest instincts
are glorified."[75] Joe's rise from an unknown musician who
sparred with small-time contenders to a champion who loses
control of his fists at the same time that he loses everything he
dreams of symbolizes his struggle with overwhelming social forces.
He is doomed from the outset, for he is a tool to be used, broken,
and discarded by society. He is not a bad man; but, on the contrary, he is a victim who cannot distinguish between symbols of

success and the real thing, who cannot be satisfied, in Frank's words, with "being where he belongs" but is ever climbing, and who is eventually destroyed by the very thing he regards as the epitome of his accomplishments. Like Charlie Anderson at the end of Dos Passos' naturalistic novel *The Big Money,* Joe dies in an automobile crash, destroyed in an attempt to "speed" away from who he is and what he has become in his struggle to succeed.

Golden Boy represents a "triumph of dramatic technique and artistry," writes Murray.[76] Although Odets disliked the play after he wrote it and disparaged the script "he had written for money,"[77] this 1937 effort represents an apex, a height he never quite achieved again. Edith Isaacs wrote of Clifford Odets: "Few authors have opened the door to fame so easily."[78] But the door seemed to close as far as Broadway was concerned after *Golden Boy*'s run was over. He produced three more major scripts before the United States entered World War II: *Rocket to the Moon* (1938), *Night Music* (1939), and *Clash By Night* (1941); and although one of them, *Night Music,* was possibly a "better made" play than any of his previous works and another, *Clash By Night,* was made into a film a decade later, none of these brought him nearly the success and recognition *Lefty* and *Golden Boy* had.

In his later plays Odets continued to explore the themes of homelessness and middle class frustration; he continued to work within the framework of naturalism and economic determinism, but he never again rose to the theatrical or literary heights he had achieved between 1935 and 1937. Morris Freedman suggests that Odets' success was an "accident" in the first place: "He happened onto the scene and came to maturity at a moment in American drama when certain audiences and critics demanded messages with their plays, significance with their literature."[79] But John Gassner believes that Odets' career began to decline because his drama lost its social significance rather than because audiences lost their appetite for it: "Many a playwright used social faith as a crutch," he points out; "even Odets' considerable dramatic talent could not consistently sustain him."[80] Clurman agrees with Gassner's statement: "Odets wanted to run with the hares and hunt with the hounds . . . he wanted to be the great revolutionary playwright and the white-haired boy of Broadway. . . . He wanted the praise of the philosophers and the votes of *Variety*'s box score."[81] Odets' transformation of *Lefty*'s synthesis from working class protest drama to a new thesis of middle class, naturalistic, and literary drama cost him the defense of the left and put him in the line of fire of the right. Mendelsohn points out that the critics "continued to hunt for propaganda and radicalism even when it was no longer there; they refused to accept what Odets was writing on its own merits and, instead, compared everything he wrote to his first few plays."[82] After *Golden Boy*, Odets lost his force as a maker of social drama. "He became," Weales concludes, "the revolutionary playwright who quit making revolutions, the promising playwright who never kept his promises."[83] In spite of his attempt to, in Krutch's words, "radically alter the intellectual concepts of his audience," Odets' slipped into melodramatic stasis; he was unable to balance his social concerns with his dramatic medium; he was still writing "classical" drama, as Krutch defines it, drama which imitates life rather than interprets it.

Still, Odets' work in the theatre during the last half of the thirties brought entertainment and informative drama another step toward Krutch's idea of "revolutionary" drama, which concentrates on the machinations of the characters' lives as they are played out against a background of moral assumptions. His increasing use of both allegory and naturalism to portray the hero struggling against society also gave a literary cast to his plays which the social drama had not enjoyed before. But Odets' new thesis, represented best perhaps by *Golden Boy*, was not sufficient. What he had gained in developing the literary aspects of his writing he had lost in its social commitment. "With the absence of the substructure of social protest, the drama flounders in a sea of hysteria," writes Rabkin; "I am not implying the *necessity* of social metaphor in drama, but merely pointing out the crucial role it played in Odets' career as dramatist."[84] When Odets softened his social exhortation and political didacticism in favor of dramatic or literary style, many in his audience missed his point. He attempted to solidify his plays' meanings, but the result was often a rigidity of theme which put off critics and audiences alike. His plays continued to "work" theatrically, but the verve and drive which had moved the audience at the end of *Lefty* or brought them to see *Golden Boy* and applaud its artistry were gone, and Odets' plays became melancholy and flat without the tonic of commitment he gave them between 1935 and 1937.

NOTES

[1] Malcolm Goldstein, *The Political Stage: American Drama and Theatre of the Great Depression* (New York: Oxford University Press, 1974), p. 365.

[2] *Ibid.*, p. 366; these figures do not include productions of the Federal Theatre Project.

[3] Sam Smiley, *The Drama of Attack: Didactic Plays of the American Depression* (Columbia, Mo.: University of Missouri Press, 1972), p. 59.

[4] Harold Clurman, "Interpretation and Characterization," *New Theatre* (January 1936) p. 21.

[5] Joseph Wood Krutch, *"Modernism" in Modern Drama: A Definition and an Estimate* (New York: Russell & Russell, Inc., 1953), p. 112.

[6] *Ibid.*, p. 108.

[7] Michael J. Mendlesohn, *Clifford Odets: Humane Dramatist*, with an introduction by Morris Freedman (Deland, Fla.: Everett Edwards, 1969), p. 13.

[8] Gerald Weales, *Clifford Odets: Playwright* (New York: Pegasus, 1971), pp. 101-102. Reprinted with permission of the author. Odets' associations with and activities as a member of the Communist Party are discussed by Mendlesohn as well; further discussions may be found in Harold Clurman's *The Fervent Years* [cited below] and Edward Murray's critical biography, *Clifford Odets: The Thirties and After* [cited below] ; virtually all critics agree that Odets' ties with the Party were limited and short-lived.

[9] Quoted in Gerald Rabkin, *Drama and Commitment: Politics in the American Theatre of the Thirties* (Bloomington: Indiana University Press, 1964), p. 170. Reprinted with permission of the publisher.

[10] Harold Clurman, *The Fervent Years: A Story of the Group Theatre and the Thirties* (New York: Alfred A. Knopf, 1945; rpt; New York: Harcourt Brace Jovanovich, 1975), p. 157. Reprinted by permission of Alfred A. Knopf.

[11] Mendelsohn, p. 19.

[12] John Gassner, *The Theatre in Our Times: A Survey of the Men, Materials, and Movements in the Modern Theatre* (New York: Crown Publishers, 1954), p. 310.

[13] Rabkin, p. 199.

[14] Mendelsohn, p. 19.

[15]Edward Murray, *Clifford Odets: The Thirties and After* (New York: Frederick Ungar Publishing Co., 1968), Clurman cited, p. 28. Reprinted with permission of Frederick Ungar Publishing Co., Inc.

[16]Murray, p. 22.

[17]Rabkin, p. 182.

[18]Mendelsohn, p. 100; here Mendelsohn appears to be making two distinctions in literary naturalism: first of all he separates Odets' settings from the rural settings used by such playwrights as Kirkland in *Tobacco Road* and the "Living Newspaper" playwrights in such plays as *Triple-A Ploughed Under* as well as such novelists as John Steinbeck and Erskine Caldwell; second, he is distinguishing between the characters of such plays as Kingsley's *Dead End* and Lawson's *Marching Song*, most all of whom are lower and working class, and Odets' characters, most all of whom belong to either lower or upper middle class either due to their incomes, attitudes, or self-identities.

[19]Eric Bentley, *The Playwright As Thinker: A Study of Drama in Modern Times* (New York: Harcourt, Brace & Co., 1946), p. 23.

[20]R. H. Gardner, *The Splintered Stage: The Decline of the American Theatre* (New York: The Macmillan Company, 1965), p. 17. Reprinted with permission of the publisher.

[21]Phyllis Hartnoll, ed., *The Oxford Companion to the Theatre*, 3rd ed. (London: Oxford University Press, 1967), p. 671.

[22]See Bentley's discussion of Zola's naturalism in *The Playwright as Thinker*, pp. 5-6, 211-212, et passim.

[23]Warren G. French, *John Steinbeck*, 2nd ed. (Boston: Twayne Publishers, 1975), p. 44.

[24]*The Fervent Years*, p. 127.

[25]Joseph Wood Krutch, *The American Drama Since 1918* (New York: Random House, 1939), p. 269.

[26]Clifford Odets, *Six Plays of Clifford Odets: Awake and Sing!* (New York: The Modern Library, 1939), p. 255; subsequent citations from this play will be made parenthetically in the text. Reprinted with permission of Grove Press, Inc.

[27]Goldstein, p. 96.

[28]*Ibid.*

[29]Weales, p. 74.

[30]Brooks Atkinson and Albert Hirschfield, *The Lively Years: 1920-1973* (New York: Association Press, 1973), p. 103.

[31]Weales, p. 73.

[32]*Ibid*, pp. 74-75.

[33]Murray, p. 43.

³⁴Mendelsohn, p. 29.

³⁵Weales, p. 74.

³⁶Eleanor Flexner, *American Playwrights: 1918-1938: The Theatre Retreats From Reality,* with a Preface by John Gassner (New York: Simon & Schuster, 1938), p. 299.

³⁷John Howard Lawson, *Theory and Technique of Playwriting* (New York: Hill & Wang, 1960), p. 249.

³⁸Edith J. R. Isaacs, "Clifford Odets: First Chapters," *Theatre Arts Monthly* 4 (April 1939): 257-258.

³⁹Lawson, p. 249.

⁴⁰Krutch, p. 270.

⁴¹Mendelsohn, p. 121.

⁴²Goldstein, p. 304.

⁴³Mendelsohn, p. 117.

⁴⁴Goldstein, pp. 301-302.

⁴⁵Smiley, p. 172.

⁴⁶Clifford Odets, *Six Plays: Paradise Lost* (New York: The Modern Library, 1939), p. 188; subsequent citations from this play appear parenthetically in the text.

⁴⁷The sense of despair Pike echoes in his speech especially resembles this passage from Dos Passos' work:

> Head swims, hunger has twisted the belly tight, ache in the broken shoes, under the threadbare suit carefully brushed off with the hand, the torn drawers have a crummy feel, the feel of having slept in your clothes; in the nostrils lingers the staleness of discouraged carcasses crowded into a transient camp, the carbolic stench of the jail, on the taut cheeks the shamed flush from the boring eyes of cops and deputies, railroadbulls (they eat three squares a day, they are buttoned into wellmade clothes, they have wives to sleep with, kids to play with after supper, they work for the big men who buy their way, they stick their chests out with the sureness of power behind their backs). Git the hell out, scram. Know what's good for you, you'll make yourself scarce. Gettin' tough, eh? Think you kin take it, eh?
>
> The punch in the jaw, the slam on the head with the nightstick, the wrist grabbed and twisted behind the back, the big knee brought up sharp into the crotch, the walk out of town with sore feet to stand and wait at the edge of the hissing speeding string of cars where the reek of ether and

lead and gas melts into the silent grassy smell of the earth.

Eyes black with want seek out the eyes of the drivers, a hitch, a hundred miles down the road." (John Dos Passos, "Vag," *U.S.A.* [New York: The Modern Library, 1937], p. 559). Reprinted with permission of Elizabeth H. Dos Passos.

[48] Goldstein, p. 308.

[49] Krutch, p. 271.

[50] Rabkin, p. 427.

[51] Clurman, "Paradise Lost," *Six Plays*, p. 427.

[52] *Ibid.*, p. 426.

[53] *Ibid.*

[54] Edith J. R. Isaacs, "At Its Best: Broadway in Review," *Theatre Arts Monthly* 20 (February 1936): 95.

[55] Mendelsohn, p. 113.

[56] Clurman, "Paradise Lost," p. 423.

[57] Krutch, p. 274.

[58] Clurman, *The Fervent Years*, p. 170, et passim.

[59] Bentley, p. 7.

[60] Odets quoted in Weales, p. 123.

[61] Harold Clurman quoted in Weales, p. 125.

[62] Gassner, p. 433.

[63] Flexner, p. 314.

[64] Clifford Odets, *Six Plays: Golden Boy* (New York: The Modern Library, 1939), p. 276; subsequent citations from this play will appear parenthetically in the text.

[65] Clurman, "Golden Boy," *Six Plays*, p. 430.

[66] Murray, p. 69.

[67] *Ibid.*, p. 58.

[68] Weales, p. 129.

[69] Clurman, "Golden Boy," p. 430.

[70] Krutch, p. 273.

[71] Goldstein, p. 318.

[72] Krutch, pp. 272-273.

[73] Murray, p. 71.

[74] Smiley, p. 106.

[75] Rabkin, p. 195.

[76] Murray, p. 71.

[77] *Ibid.*

[78] Isaacs, "First Chapters," p. 258.

79 Morris Freedman, "Introduction," in Mendelsohn, *Clifford Odets*, p. x.

80 John Gassner, *Dramatic Soundings: Evaluations and Retractions Culled from 30 Years of Dramatic Criticism* (New York: Crown Publishers, 1968), p. 391.

81 *The Fervent Years*, p. 266.

82 Mendelsohn, p. 108.

83 Weales, p. 14.

84 Rabkin, p. 199.

LILLIAN HELLMAN: THE WELL-MADE MELODRAMA

It would take a "strong mind and will," to use John Gassner's phrase,[1] to create a play that could combine social statement with entertaining drama. As Odets' plays slipped increasingly into melancholy themes and Lawson and other leftists continued to exhort Marxist philosophy through loosely constructed melodramas, audiences and critics began to look for fresher themes and newer approaches to social problems. In 1934 another new playwright had entered Broadway's professional ranks; and many expected her to fulfill that bill. Her name was Lillian Hellman.

Lillian Hellman's first Broadway production opened two months before *Waiting For Lefty*'s triumphant off-Broadway premiere.[2] Like Clifford Odets, she was an unknown quantity to both Broadway audiences and producers; also like the Group Theatre's newly discovered talent, she managed to astound with her innovative style. But Hellman was different both in her techniques and in her interpretations of social problems. Unlike Odets, she was not a "theatre person," an actor who desperately wished to write plays. Her desire to write drama is a curious one which is not fully explained either by her biographers, Richard Moody and Doris Falk, nor by her own revelations in her autobiographical works, *An Unfinished Woman, Pentimento,* and *Scoundrel Time.* She worked under the tutelage of Dashiell Hammett, who apparently shaped her writing through often caustic and unappreciative criticism. He also seemed to give direction to her social ideas and leftist sentiments.[3] Hammett, whose novels, *The Maltese Falcon* and *The Thin Man,* had been successfully filmed by Hollywood, had little patience with the didactic, "hardline," protest drama of the left, and he frequently looked with disdain upon efforts of such writers as Odets to combine social protest and well-constructed drama; he walked out of *Awake and Sing!*, telling Hellman that he found Odets' characters more self-pitying than revolutionary: "I don't think writers who cry about not having had a bicycle when they were kiddies are ever going to amount to much."[4]

Hellman's approach to her writing was careful and professional. Her notebooks are testimony that her plays were not
ground out hurriedly as Odets' *Waiting For Lefty* had been.[5]
Never lacking in detail, these notes reveal serious consideration
of everything from characters' names to technical data concerning
industry, economics, and politics to a voluminous collection of
facts, statistics, and folklore, detailing cultural attitudes of the
people from whom she would draw her characters and plots.
For each of her plays there is an indication that, if she did not
know the subject well, she found out; she was never afraid of
research. Also, she demanded credit for herself as author of her
plays. "She cannot abide," Harold Clurman wrote of her, "the
truth of what Pirandello once set down in a paradoxical apo-
thegm: 'In the theatre the work of the author does not exist any
longer.'" Unlike Odets, who responded to the "ensemble philosophy" of the Group Theatre, often allowing the director
and actors to shape the final product in a collaborative effort,
Hellman insisted on total control of her own plays from inception
to production; "Miss Hellman has no talent for collaboration,"
concludes Clurman.[6]

Hellman was introduced into the literary world by Hammett;
however, her association with writers of the left was limited. She
was never a member of the Communist Party. Her mid-thirties
trip to Moscow via Nazi Berlin and war-torn Spain was filled with
frightening intrigue which possibly contributed to a vehement
anti-fascist stance that many interpret as being pro-left; however,
she undoubtedly knew many "hardline" leftists and avowed
Communists, for it would have been almost impossible to have
been associated with the American theatre in the mid-thirties
and not have had many acquaintances in the Party. There is some
evidence that she attended Party meetings; however, these so-
called "meetings" were often social affairs, sometimes designed
to raise money for pro-left organizations and publications. They
were usually attended by professional theatre people who engaged
mostly in "shop talk."[7] Hellman's association with Odets, for
example, made much of during the House UnAmerican Affairs
Committee investigations of the late forties and early fifties,
was limited: "We had met possibly four or five times," she
recalls in her account of the HUAC hearings, "but I never saw
him after he moved to Hollywood."[8] There are no overt, prop-

agandistic statements in any of Hellman's pre-war plays; her interest in being successful as a writer superseded her political philosophy which might be best described as "Popular Front Liberalism."

Even so, Hellman was a significant contributor to the development of the social drama in the thirties. Her plays, Sam Smiley states, while not purely Marxist, represent "the highest achievements" of the leftist writers "in their organization, communication of social awareness, and intensive employment of thought."[9]   Gerald Rabkin points out that her themes were founded on an "implied hope that the young could have their chance without interference from the obstructive oldsters"; in fact, comparisons with the author of *Awake and Sing!, Paradise Lost,* and *Golden Boy* ran throughout the bulk of critical response to the social drama in the thirties. However, in spite of such claims as Clurman's that Hellman and Odets represent the most "outstanding playwrights" of the decade,[10] their significant differences in their social-critical stance and techniques of writing set them far apart.

Hellman's three pre-war plays, *The Children's Hour, Days to Come,* and *The Little Foxes,* are almost completely antithetical to Odets' middle class social drama even though they share some similarities in use of device and characterization. In the course of the two playwrights' development, they wrote two plays which were almost parallel in their scripts, *Days to Come* and *Paradise Lost.* But Hellman's play failed miserably; and Odets' script, while not a wild success, enjoyed a healthy run. But even in these stories of a frustrated and sympathetic middle class beset with labor problems and social conflicts that it cannot overcome, there are important differences in points of view and handling of subject matter. Like Odets, Hellman employed melodramatic devices in her construction of rising and falling action; both playwrights freely used allegory to depict the struggle between good and evil, capital and labor, socialist and fascist; and both playwrights wrote with a conscious eye toward injustice, corruption, the elusiveness of material success, and man's capacity for sadism and cruelty to his fellow man. But it is in these similarities that the major distinctions exist between Odets' and Hellman's plays.

Hellman's concern with middle class problems began with her first play in 1934; Odets, while including middle class characters in *Waiting For Lefty,* only gradually increased the social position of his families in the plays which followed. From the near working-class Bergers, Odets moved to the limited affluence of the Gordons and ultimately retreated to the Bonapartes' tentative monetary security. Hellman's families are usually quite well off, and while money and materialism are their main concerns, they want more because they are greedy, not because they have not yet arrived. Moreover, Hellman's characters do not define their desires in concrete items such as "black and white shoes" or "fancy speed wagons"; they desire power and real wealth. Both writers employ characterizations which reflect "types," but while Odets' "types" are easily identifiable as "worker," "capitalist," or "gangster-fascist," Hellman's "types" are more oblique; the "capitalist" might be a benevolent grandmother, or the "gangster-fascist" might be a teenage girl. Another important difference is the Marxist theme of class struggle which appears in various proportions in virtually all of Odets' work. Hellman's class struggle loses much of its Marxist flavor as she emphasizes social injustice rather than class exploitation, personal rather than political or economic corruption, and a desire for understanding rather than revolution. The theme which dominates her first play, for example, is a plea for tolerance of people who appear to be different.

Finally, Hellman never used a "call to action" or any such device reminiscent of agit-prop drama, and her heroes and heroines are invariably defeated by their own personal frailty or their own internal corruption rather than by social forces of economic determinism which gradually come to dominate Odets' drama. Hellman used economics and other social elements to create an abstract set of what Joseph Wood Krutch calls "moral assumptions," and she attempted to dramatize the lives of human beings as they are played out against the backdrop of those assumptions. Her drama, therefore, became less dependent upon economic determinism and more reliant upon the "intangible fate" Clurman spoke of in 1936.

Gerald Rabkin writes that Hellman "commanded a technique which could survive abrupt changes in the winds of doctrine."[11] Odets' plays could not do this. His decline in the late thirties and eventual complete move to Hollywood as a screen-writer are noted by Alan S. Downer when he comments that, after the decade closed, Odets "continued to write the best American plays of the thirties and nothing else."[12] But Hellman's career continued to grow. She carried her talent to Hollywood early,

not only adapting both *The Children's Hour (These Three)* in
1935, but also writing the screenplay for Kingsley's *Dead End.*
The move west apparently did not affect her ability to produce
timely and meaningful plays; she managed seven successful plays
and adaptations after 1940 and established herself as a director,
teacher, memoirist, and distinguished and still productive screen-
writer. But her ability to adapt her technique to fit Clurman's
ever changing "new audience" in the changing social climate
of the late thirties placed her squarely opposite those who continued to call for radical social change and a better world through
vagaries and Marxist platitudes.

The Children's Hour was Hellman's first and most successful play of the decade. Based on the narrative account of an
1810 Scottish trial,[13] it is set in and around a country boarding
school for girls run by two friends, Karen Wright and Martha
Dobie, who, after years of hard work and sacrifice, have managed
to bring the school to a sound financial footing. One of the stu-
dents, Mary Tilford, in reaction to what she thinks is unfair
punishment and in an attempt to attract attention, convinces
her grandmother, Mrs. Tilford, the main financial backer of the
school, that the two teachers, Martha and Karen, are lovers; and
she coerces her classmate, Rosalie, to back up her accusation.
Mary's chief evidence rests on an overheard conversation between
Martha and her aunt, Lily Mortar, during which the pending
marriage between Karen and Joe Cardin, Mrs. Tilford's nephew,
is discussed. By taking phrases such as "unnatural as it can be,"
and "You don't like their being together," and "you'd better
get a beau of your own now—a woman of your age" out of con-
text,[14] Mary persuades her grandmother not only to remove
her from the school, but also to withdraw her financial support,
thus bankrupting and closing it.

When the two women appear before Mrs. Tilford and Mary,
the older woman faces them down and continues to believe
Mary's story even when the teachers bring suit to attempt to
clear themselves. Unfortunately, the only one who can explain
the overheard conversation is Mrs. Mortar, who has been fired
from the school and refuses to return to testify in the women's
behalf. They lose their suit, and the school remains closed.

Every character in *The Children's Hour* is defeated either
physically or metaphorically: Martha commits suicide; Karen
becomes a wasted person who will always live with the suspicion
that others will have for her; Joe loses Karen's love and trust;

Mrs. Tilford loses self-respect; Mary will grow up into an adult who can never be trusted; and Mrs. Mortar, who returns just in time for Martha's suicide, loses her single opportunity to prove herself worthy of trust and affection by refusing to testify. Even the minor characters lose significantly: Agatha, Mrs. Tilford's maid and a surrogate mother for Mary, cannot ever again love or trust the child; and Mary's classmates lose the school where they were happy in their studies.

"Hellman," writes Doris Falk, "never claimed to be writing classic tragedy but she *was* writing more than is usually meant by melodrama. Her serious plays are always about good and evil, and evil may seem to prosper unjustly, but the actions and the strivings of the characters have meaning and consequence."[15] The moral assumptions against which Martha and Karen fruitlessly struggle manifest themselves as one single abstraction, the "big lie." And the characters' ultimate defeat after hurling themselves against it, with each attempt seemingly increasing the strength of the force, casts them clearly in the roles of tragic heroines of what Krutch calls "modern" drama: that is, protagonists who are defeated by the moral assumptions of society.

The "big lie" of *The Children's Hour,* homosexuality, especially in female school teachers, was strong stuff even for Broadway in the liberal days of the thirties. Plays on general homosexual themes such as Edouard Bourdets' *The Captive* had been closed by police in previous years,[16] and when Hellman's script became a movie, the conflict was changed from an accusation of Lesbianism to a love triangle between the two teachers and Joe. But Hellman's particular version of the "big lie" has its chief value in an allegorical application, for the injustice and unfairness of the charges of Lesbianism between the two women are mitigated when Martha admits that even though she never revealed her feelings to Karen or anyone else, the charges are true. The significant question raised by the play, therefore, is not whether the two women are lovers, but whether it makes any difference. Several critics objected to Hellman's making one of the falsely accused guilty. Richard Moody sees Martha's confession as well as other elements in the last act— "Why didn't Cardin shake the truth out of Mary, out of Rosalie? Why didn't he testify at the trial?"—as upsetting to the audience. He writes that "our sympathies are invested with two heterosexual teachers falsely accused of Lesbianism, who are being punished by a society that can be perverted by lies and can tol-

erate the punishment of the innocent"; but then, he concludes,
Hellman shifts her position: "Another play is beginning about
Lesbians who live in a society that punishes Lesbians."[17]   Doris
Falk counters such criticism by pointing out the use of the Les-
bian charge as metaphor: "What if, after all, one—or even both—
women had such feelings, consciously or unconsciously? Would
the 'guilty' deserve destruction at the hands of society?"[18]
But both these critical biographers of Hellman miss an important
point: the issue in *The Children's Hour* is not Lesbianism, nor is
it even homosexuality among school teachers or even in the abstract; the issue is the "big lie." For the mere accusation that a
person *is* something or believes in something by even an irresponsible source does as much damage as the proof or even the revela-
tion that the charge is true. Martha and Karen are doomed from
the time Mary utters the damning words to her grandmother,
for everyone who then hears the lie—believing it or not—will
suspect that it is true. When the "big lie" is involved, even proving
innocence cannot completely erase the smear that remains from
the accusation.

      In 1934 the issue most clearly at hand was anti-semitism,
evident not only abroad in Nazi Germany but even at home
in the United States. In Hitler's Reich the mere accusation that
a person had "Jewish blood" could be enough to bring about
harrassment, arrest, and even death. But, as Odets illustrates
in "Interne Episode" of *Waiting For Lefty,* the Germans had no
monopoly on bigotry. Similar allegorical applications might be
made to social issues of the thirties, but the fact that Hellman
recognized the versatility of the "big lie" is evident from her
1952 revival of the play during the McCarthy "witchhunts"
for Communists in every strata of American society.[19]   Hence,
the message of the play is not only a warning against blind acceptance of the "big lie," proven or not, but it is an indictment
against a society which allows such issues to be raised at all.

      The Children's Hour is a very tightly constructed drama
moving from rising action at the opening curtain to the climax
of Martha's suicide in what seems to be a very short time. Many
critics felt the play should have ended with the gunshot and that
all which follows it ruins the effect of Hellman's social statement.
Hellman agrees. She writes:

> The play probably should have ended with Martha's sui-
> cide, the last scene is tense and overburdened. I knew

> this at the time but I could not help myself. I am a moral writer, often too moral a writer, and I cannot avoid, it seems, the last summing up. I think that is only a mistake when it fails to achieve its purpose, and I would rather make the attempt, and fail than fail to make the attempt.[20]

But to have left the audience unaware of Mrs. Tilford's discovery of Mary's treachery might not have achieved the complete despair which marks of the last act. Regardless of her feelings about what critics write, she did not rewrite the last act for either the 1952 or the 1962 revivals. Falk also points out that in the final scene the meaning of the opening lines, "It is twice blest; it blesseth him that gives and him that takes . . ." (p. 5), quoted from *The Merchant of Venice*, is revealed: "The reference is to mercy," she explains, "singularly lacking in those who implement the destruction of others."[21] By forgiving Mrs. Tilford, Karen demonstrates that even in her defeat she is superior to those who blindly persecute others because of such things as the "big lie."

Mary, the character who is chiefly responsible for the "big lie" is also an allegorical character. On one level she is a child who imitates the wrong role model in her elders, but she carries that imitation so far as to come to represent pure evil. Mrs. Mortar is a consummate liar and fake. She tells the girls long fabrications about her successful theatrical career. She also feels unwanted and out of place in the school, knowing that she lives off of Martha's largesse, and knowing that she really cannot make her own way in the theatre or elsewhere. She exhibits her unhappiness through malicious accusations, eliciting a reply from Martha at one point: "Aunt Lily, the amount of disconnected unpleasantness that goes on in your head could keep a psychologist busy for years" (p. 17). Another time her niece tells her: "When you're at your best, you're not for tender ears" (p. 19). In following Mrs. Mortar's example, Mary becomes a pathological liar and complete fake; she manufactures excuses, pretends illness, and physically and mentally abuses her classmates.

At first the two women and Joe regard Mary's behavior as childish capriciousness and petulance, but they are unaware of the fear which Mary inspires in the other girls. By the time they realize how dangerous and disturbed the child is, it is too late for anyone to believe them. Later, however, when Mrs. Tilford realizes how evil Mary really is, Karen repeats that something is "wrong" with the girl and that she should be sent away; but for Mrs. Tilford, the presence of her granddaughter will serve to remind her of her guilt: "NO. I could never do that," she tells Karen, "Whatever she does, it must be to me and no one else. She's—she's—." "Yes. Your very own to live with the rest of your life," Karen finishes for her (p. 68).

But on another level, Mary symbolizes something more than simply a particularly evil child who uses violence and threats to get her way; she also stands for something pernicious in society, an element which is innocently disguised as "right" but in reality is utterly destructive. It can spread suspicion and destroy anyone or anything it wants to in the name of morality. In later years plays such as *Watch on the Rhine* would expose this villain as fascism. But just as Odets and others used the gangster or racketeer to represent this element of evil which often forces its way into positions of trust among the conservative stratum of the social order and perverts whatever good it finds there, Hellman's Mary points out a particularly sinister aspect of "the enemy within"—its childlike quality—which evokes trust and even pity from those who are duped by it. The question which remains in both symbolic figures, however, is whether the gangster—or child—is more culpable for the result of such encroachment than the passive society which permits it to take control. In the final scene of *The Children's Hour,* Hellman defiantly points the finger of guilt at society as a whole.

Critical reaction to Hellman's first play was overwhelmingly positive. Expressions such as "terrifying and ennobling experience," "it shines with integrity," "the work of a courageous dramatist," and "a stinging tragedy" filled the reviews, drowning out the few negative comments from a handful of critics.[22] The successful response was best measured, perhaps, by George Jean Nathan who not only remained until the final curtain but joined in the applause.[23] *The Children's Hour* was nominated for the Pulitzer Prize, but, as several critics pointed out, the subject matter probably prevented its winning. It was a phenomenal success, not only for a first play but for any play during the time; none of her subsequent plays would garner such favorable notices or financial success.

The chief significance of *The Children's Hour* lies in its social statement. It is more subtle than the didactic preachments contemporary with it in the social drama; it demonstrates, as Goldstein notes, "the playwright's ability to weave tough-minded expressions of liberal social attitudes into a suspenseful plot."[24] In spite of the complaints of leftist critics such as Lawson that the climax of the play was weak because the analogy between Mary and a consciously motivated evil force is obscured by her childlike attitude,[25] many critics and audiences recognized that Hellman's point, as Doris Falk notes, is "ethical, moral, Christian . . . not political."[26] and hailed the play as an ingenious combination of entertainment and significant social instruction.

Hellman's combination of ethical and moral tolerance with concrete labor issues and political reform in her next play led her to disaster; her second play had the dubious distinction of being possibly the shortest-lived play on social themes to open on Broadway during the entire decade. Even Lawson's *Marching Song* and Rice's *We, The People* enjoyed more success; *1931*—ran for nine nights; *Days to Come* closed in seven. Opening night, December 14, 1936, was filled with evil omens. Kaufman and Hart's wildly acclaimed *You Can't Take It With You* was scheduled for the following evening; Hellman, to calm her jangling nerves, unwittingly drank ninety-four cent brandy and became violently ill during the performance; Hammett walked out of the opening night party, telling her that he had "changed his mind" and it was a "terrible play"; and William Randolph Hearst and his entire party stalked out before the first act was over. Although no critics suggested that she give up writing, almost all were hard pressed to find anything positive to say about the play. Hellman's second effort was a complete and unmitigated failure.

The main significance of *Days to Come* lies in its largest defect. Although Hellman lacked the knowledge and social awareness required to write a protest drama of the working class pitted against its decadent and corrupt oppressors, the play does, especially in the last act, begin to indicate her understanding of the personal conflicts of the middle class family as they deal with their own set of oppressive forces. Noting the "burning intensity" in the lines exchanged between the family characters, Moody cites Krutch's initial reaction to the play: "Miss Hellman is not a specialist in abnormal psychology or in Marxian interpretation of society. She is a specialist in hate, frustration, a student of helplessness rage, an articulator of inarticulate loathings."[27] Her attempt to combine these themes with Odets' middle class social concerns had failed principally because she did not fully understand the issues or the kinds of people involved. From the anger and hatred she exhibited in *The Children's Hour* against the Tilfords, and the furious, underlying evil she shows to be present in the Rodman family in *Days to Come,* she would mold another attempt to bring the form of social drama to bear on the plight of the middle class.

Opening in Baltimore on February 2, 1939, *The Little Foxes* was moved, after some minor rewriting, to New York on February 15, with Tallulah Bankhead in the lead. It ran for four hundred ten nights and represented a triumph for Hellman, who was now proclaimed to be the source of powerful drama. The play offers a scathing criticism of a class of people who manipulate society and the lives within it with a ruthless eye toward greater personal wealth and power.

Set in the home of Regina and Horace Giddens in a small, Southern town in 1900, the play concerns the conflicts which grow out of a business deal between a Chicago industrialist and Ben and Oscar Hubbard and their sister, Regina Giddens. The two brothers have inherited their father's wealth and are anxious to conclude the deal—the building of a cotton mill nearby which can exploit the region's poor as a cheap labor force—but Horace Giddens, Regina's husband--whom she married for his money since she was excluded from the Hubbard fortune--is away in Baltimore recovering from a heart ailment and has not come up with his one-third of the money necessary to consummate the transaction.

The first major conflict involves a struggle between Ben, the bachelor brother who is clearly the most powerful of the three children, and Regina, who counters his forceful personality with cunning and deceit. Because Horace has not agreed to the deal, she tells Ben that her husband is reluctant because he wants a bigger cut of the profits. Ben agrees to her terms, taking the extra money from Oscar's share. Although he is not happy with the arrangement, Oscar finally agrees to go along with the reduction in his cut because Ben tells him that Regina agrees that Leo, Oscar's son, will marry Alexandra, Horace and Regina's daughter, thus keeping all the profits in the family. In the first act, therefore, Hellman draws a picture of greed and corruption among middle class characters whose only thoughts are of profits and personal gain.

The only character in the play who readily elicits audience sympathy is Birdie, Oscar's wife. Although she is former-ly a member of Southern aristocracy, Birdie is not as despicable as her husband and his family because she is so weak and pathetic and completely at their mercy. "Audiences suffered with Birdie when they saw her treatment at the hands of Oscar," Doris Falk writes, "and pitied her even more when she confessed that she drank in private."[28]   But it is Birdie who counsels Alexandra to beware of the evil motives and methods of Oscar, Ben, and Regina. She admonishes her: "Don't love me. Because in twenty years you'll be just like me. They'll do all the same things to you. . . . You know what? In twenty-two years I haven't had a whole day of happiness."[29]   Oscar has used her as an avenue to more wealth and more power, for he has control of the wealth her father left her; and now that her usefulness is done, he and the others abuse her, vaguely resentful of her heritage and specifically bitter of her weakness.

There really are no heroes in *The Little Foxes.*   In this allegory of a contest between good and evil, good is hardly given equal time. The second conflict in the play occurs when Regina, worried about Horace's continued silence regarding the business deal, sends Alexandra to bring him home in spite of his illness. But Horace, now close to death, has no interest in joining Regina and her brothers in exploiting the town's cheap labor force. He rails at her:

> I'm sick of you, sick of this house, sick of my life here.
> I'm sick of your brothers and their dirty tricks to make
> a dime. Why should I give you the money? . . . To pound
> the bones of this town to make dividends for you to
> spend?   You wreck the town, you and your brothers.
> (p. 176)

And when he learns that the two brothers have stolen money from his safety-deposit box to finance his share of the deal, he strikes back through Regina, telling her that he will disinherit her, leaving all to Alexandra so she can escape the town, the family, and especially a forced marriage with Leo. But Regina manages to defeat him in the end, for in the ensuing argument he has a heart attack. After her refusal to help him find his medicine, he dies. Thus Horace's conversion to good comes too late to save either his town or his daughter. Regina has triumphed as a force of evil, and whatever intentions Horace had to thwart her and her brothers' plans die along with him.

Even though Horace is dead and Alexandra will not receive his money to aid her in an escape, this "princess" in Hellman's middle class court resolves to flee the evil represented by the family with or without her father's legacy. She reveals her understanding of the malevolence of such people when she calls them "the little foxes that spoil the vines." Only instead of grapes, these foxes "eat the earth"; she tells Regina:

> Mama, because I want to leave here. As I've never wanted anything in my life before. Because now I understand what Papa was trying to tell me. All in one day: Addie said there were people who ate the earth and other people who stood around and watched them do it. And just now Uncle Ben said the same thing. Really, he said the same thing. . . . Well, tell him for me, Mama, I'm not going to stand around and watch you do it. I'll be fighting as hard as he'll be fighting . . . someplace else. (p. 199)

Although it is by no means a "call to action" in the manner of Odets' closing speeches, Alexandra's escape from her mother and the reasons she gives for wanting to escape represent the hope for a better world, the hope for the future.

But while the optimism expressed in these lines climaxes the final conflict in the play—the conflict between Alexandra and a future champion of evil—it is cautiously tempered; rather the final conflict in the play—the conflict between Alexandra she is escaping them and the social malevolence they represent. The point of the play, therefore, is that the battle between those who are evil is possibly more significant than the possibility of the triumph of good over them. Neither Horace nor Alexandra is victorious as a force of good, for his struggle has killed him, and she lacks a full understanding of how ruthless the forces of evil can be.

The other characters are defeated by their own greed and ambition. Ben and Regina's conflict will continue: they hold each other at bay through mutual blackmail (She knows he engineered the theft of Horace's money; he knows she stood by and let Horace die without his medicine). Oscar's fate is totally wrapped up with theirs, as is the fate of Leo who actually committed the larceny. The attempt to gain greater wealth and more power has brought all of them down, including Birdie, who is a hopeless alcoholic; ironically, however, the cotton mill will be built in any case, and the town's labor will be subjugated by these capitalists even in their defeat.

The only criticism of the play which was less than favorable dealt with the acting. Hellman managed to please most all the critics, even the left, with the result that she was branded or hailed (dependent upon who was writing) as a "fellow traveller," and a "distinctive social voice."[30] "The sheer raw emotion of the play, especially the second act," in Moody's words, is "unsurpassed in the modern theatre."[31] No other social playwright had so successfully combined the powers of dramatic entertainment and social concern into a play which so completely captivated its audience and so decisively made its point. It is an "object lesson in evil," writes Smiley, "in which the villain triumphs but has an uncertain future."[32] *The Little Foxes* reflects almost all of the anger and frustration the social playwrights of the thirties felt toward the corrupt forces of the power-conscious and exploitative middle class, and it does so as an explosive and dynamic work of dramatic art.

When compared to Odets' versions of the middle class, *The Little Foxes* represents an antithesis. Whereas Odets used melodramatic scenes through which he could state social polemics, Hellman used social problems as background for what most critics finally agree is extremely well-executed melodrama. The play "remains," Smiley continues, "unfinished," because Hellman's mode does not move completely into art which interprets life but remains art which imitates life, translated through the "drama as weapon" mood of the thirties.[33] There are devices throughout the play which are melodramatic: secret strongboxes, death on the stairs, the thwarting of the villain's plan to marry the girl and obtain the money. But what chiefly separates Odets' and Hellman's drama is the direction of their social polemics. Odets indicts a social order which calls for "life printed on dollar bills." His characters are not guilty for trying to aspire to a better life or a better world; they are culpable of trying to make their ascent blindly, without clearly defining what it is they want, and ultimately of settling for material possessions or money instead. Hellman's characters know what they want or they have already acquired it. They are guilty of abusing their position, their power, and they fail to recognize evil either in others or in themselves. Odets' characters are never as wealthy as Hellman's; even her workers seem more prosperious than the Bergers or the Bonapartes; however, they all share a mistrust of other classes that often builds to a frenzied hatred and violent response. The main struggle in both playwrights' work is against ignorance, which comes from a failure to understand what other people in other classes are like as well as what they themselves are good for. But while Odets dealt with economic and political issues in his plays, and his characters are destroyed by forces of economic determinism and blind struggles with social oppression, Hellman concentrated on moral and ethical themes, and her characters are defeated by what Clurman called "intangible fate" and their own human weakness. The result in virtually all the plays of both writers is the same, however: Those who reach too far, either for good or evil, are defeated, left homeless and divorced from identity with any class.

NOTES

[1] John Gassner, *Dramatic Soundings: Evaluations and Retractions Culled from 30 Years of Dramatic Criticism* (New York: Crown Publisher, 1968), p. 391.

[2] Doris Falk, *Lillian Hellman* (New York: Frederick Ungar Publishing Company, 1978), p. vii. Reprinted with permission of Frederick Ungar Publishing Company, Inc. Falk lists in her chronology that *The Children's Hour* opened in May, 1934; however, almost every other source confirms the New York opening as November 21, 1934; Richard Moody [cited below] indicates that the play was accepted for production in May; thus Ms. Falk may have confused the dates.

[3] In 1951 Dashiell Hammett was cited for contempt of Congress for refusing to answer questions or name names for the House UnAmerican Affairs Committee investigations; the exact nature or extent of his leftist sentiments and involvements during the thirties or at any other time are not known; in her memoirs of the period surrounding the HUAC investigations, Ms. Hellman discusses her impressions of Hammett's politics in both time frames; see Lillian Hellman, *Scoundrel Time*, with an introduction by Gary Wills (Boston: Little, Brown and Company, 1976), passim.

[4] *Scoundrel Time*, p. 68.

[5] The collection at the Humanities Research Center at the University of Texas at Austin contains notes, journals, and correspondence relative to Hellman's early plays as well as first draft typescripts of several plays. A full

catalogue with annotation has been published and is available; see Manfred Triesch, comp., *The Lillian Hellman Collection at the University of Texas, Austin* (Austin: The Humanities Research Center, the University of Texas, 1968); as of May, 1978, no significant additions had been made to the collection since Triesch's catalogue was published.

⁶Harold Clurman, "Introduction," *Lillian Hellman: Playwright*, by Richard Moody (New York: The Bobbs-Merrill Company, Inc., 1972), p. xiv. Reprinted with permission of the author.

⁷Garry Wills, "Introduction," in *Scoundrel Times;* Wills offers a full discussion of both the HUAC hearings and their relationship to actual activities of the parties being interviewed by the Committee, pp. 3-35.

⁸*Scoundrel Time*, p. 66.

⁹Sam Smiley, *The Drama of Attack: Didactic Plays of the American Depression* (Columbia: University of Missouri Press, 1972), p. 59.

¹⁰Harold Clurman, *The Fervent Years: A Story of the Group Theatre and the Thirties* (New York: Harcourt Brace Jovanovich, 1975), p. 157.

¹¹Gerald Rabkin, *Drama and Commitment: Politics in the American Theatre of the Thirties* (Bloomington: Indiana University Press, 1964), quoted on p. 170.

¹²Alan S. Downer, *American Drama and Its Critics: A Collection of Critical Essays* (Chicago: The University of Chicago Press, 1965), p. 134.

¹³Falk, p. 105.

¹⁴Lillian Hellman, *The Collected Plays: The Children's Hour,* (Boston: Little Brown and Company, 1971), p. 86; subsequent citations from this play will be made parenthetically in the text.

¹⁵Falk, p. 44.

¹⁶Malcolm Goldstein, *The Political Stage: American Drama and Theatre of the Great Depression* (New York: Oxford University Press, 1974), p. 149.

¹⁷Moody, p. 55.

¹⁸Falk, p. 41.

¹⁹In 1953 Arthur Miller produced *The Crucible* which metaphorically treated the same theme by dramatizing the 1692 Salem witch trials. Miller joined Hellman and Elia Kazan, Lee J. Cobb and Will Geer among other actors, directors, writers and technicians of the thirties in feeling the pressure of HUAC and the Senate hearings led by Senator Joseph McCarthy. Moody and others have noted the fear of the so-called "black-list" which ran through the entertainment industry and ultimately prevented many talented artists from working.

²⁰Hellman quoted in Moody, p. 55.

²¹Falk, p. 45.

²²Moody, p. 57; one of the dissenting comments came from Joseph

Wood Krutch; Moody quotes him as saying that he was "amazed that 'any-thing so inept was ever allowed to reach production,'" p. 57.

[23]*Ibid.*, p. 57.

[24]Goldstein, p. 149.

[25]John Howard Lawson, *Theory and Technique of Playwriting* (New York: Hill and Wang, 1960), p. 249.

[26]Falk, p. 46.

[27]Joseph Wood Krutch quoted in Moody, p. 69.

[28]Falk, p. 54.

[29]Lillian Hellman, *The Collected Plays: The Little Foxes* (Boston: Little Brown, 1971), p. 183; subsequent citations from this play will be made parenthetically in the text. Reprinted with permission of Random House, Inc.

[30]Moody, pp. 84-85.

[31]*Ibid.*, p. 98.

[32]Smiley, p. 100.

[33]*Ibid.*, p. 102.

THE SOCIAL COMEDY: DRAMA WHICH INTERPRETS LIFE

"The gift that playwrights of this generation made to the theatre," writes Malcolm Goldstein, "lay in their ability to discuss all sides of serious issues in dialogue that argued rather than exhorted."[1] Before presenting such a "gift," however, American dramatists went through a process of education and development that sought to discover what would satisfy the "new audience" Clurman had sensed that night in the balcony during *1931—*. It is ironic, but perhaps fitting, that one of the best examples of synthesis of the modes, movements, and methods of drama that characterized the social theatre during the thirties should be the social comedy, for that vehicle, more than any other, has represented the social critics in drama in virtually all eras in virtually all nations. From the satiric *Lysistrata* to *Volpone* to Moliere's several farces to *The Rivals* to the unblushing comedy as a basis for attack on social ills, the history of social comedy is a rich one. In a sense, it is greater than tragedy's when used in a socially significant way; for tragedy inevitably turns on individual fortunes, not the fate of society.

Philip Barry had spent the bulk of the depression years writing morose plays dealing philosophically with the disillusionment of a depressed and chaotic world. There is no clear indication that he was influenced at all by any playwright or dramatic movement during the decade; however, in 1939 he produced a play that seemed to take up all the strands left trailing by writers of social drama in their attempt to find the formula which would both entertain and inform, which would instruct without offense, and which would criticize without castigation, a formula, in other words, which would interpret life instead of merely imitating it.

Opening on March 28, 1939, at the Shubert Theatre in New York, *The Philadelphia Story* commenced a run of ninety-six performances before being taken on tour; it propelled its star, Katherine Hepburn, to an astoundingly successful career, and it saved a faltering Theatre Guild from bankruptcy by providing it with its first successful show in several seasons.[2] It became one of the best loved and most often revived plays of the period, and this distinction is only made more remarkable because Barry had not had a single successful show in the entire decade.

Significantly, the play is not a protest or didactic drama; it does not exhort its audience at all. It is high comedy of the "well-made" variety which had boosted Barry's career in the twenties. The play is not about class struggle in the Marxist sense; it depicts class conflict in the old style of Barry's comedies: the rich are contrasted with the poor. But following his traditional approach to the conflict, the wealthy characters in Barry's new comedy are not fat, greedy capitalists who grow more and more despicable as they continue to exploit the oppressed working class; and the working class characters are not downtrodden proletarians who shout angry Marxist slogans and call for bloody revolution. Instead, Barry's analysis of class differences winds up being a call for understanding between the "haves" and the "have nots," a call for tolerance on the part of both camps, and a use of morality and ethics as the common ground.

The play is set at the Lord estate where Tracy, who has just divorced one husband, C. K. Dexter Haven, is preparing for her second marriage to George Kittredge, General Manager of Quaker State Coal, the company belonging to her father, Seth Lord. Departing from the metaphysical and melancholy moods of his other thirties plays, Barry returns to the quick-paced, witty dialogue for which he had been famous in the twenties. No one is particularly fond of George, except Tracy, but the marriage is proceeding as scheduled. All appears to be going well until the family learns that a magazine, *Destiny*, has discovered a scandal involving Seth Lord and will publish it unless a reporter and a photographer are permitted to cover the private ceremony, an arrangement worked out by Tracy's brother, Sandy. Tracy is openly outraged over Sandy's trade-off, and she reacts defensively to the intrusion of such proletarians at a society gathering: "Who the hell do they think they are, barging in on peaceful people—watching every little mannerism—jotting down notes on how we sit, and stand, and talk, and eat and move—"[3] But the reporters arrive anyway, and one of them, Mike Connor, is as hostile toward Tracy's wealth and social position as she is toward his "working class" origins: "I have to tell you in all honesty," he tells Sandy, "that I'm opposed to everything you represent" (p. 505).

Eventually Mike and Tracy clash, and in the ensuing exchanges Barry illustrates the fine points of class conflict as the reporter and the debutant trade verbal blows. Mike tries to score points by reminding Tracy of her "general uselessness" (p. 522), and Tracy returns fire by calling him an "intellectual snob." As their debate heats up and they become more and more intoxicated, however, they eventually put aside their differences, admitting that beneath the surface, each is a warm, attractive human being. Thus reconciled, they go for a moonlight swim, and when the "debauchery" is discovered by George, the wedding is off.

Joseph Wood Krutch identifies two themes in *The Philadelphia Story:* one is that spiritual pride can prevent personal relationships and the second is that there is "no monopoly on hearts that are pure and fair." But the major issue of the play, he continues, is a definition of "integrity" and "decency" which transcends social class.[4] Tracy, for all her sense of propriety, is an unmitigated snob at the beginning of the play. Dexter, who blames that attitude for breaking up their marriage, calls her a "mood goddess" who does not want a "loving husband and companion" but a "high priest" (p. 524). He tells her: ". . . you'll never be a first-class woman or a first-class human being, till you have learned to have some regard for human frailty. It's a pity your own foot can't slip a little sometime—but no, your sense of inner divinity won't allow it. The goddess must and shall remain intact" (p. 526). And Seth, whose philandering has earned him Tracy's scorn but not cost him his wife's love, tells her that she is "a prig—and a perennial spinster, however many marriages" (p. 531).

George, on the other hand, reveals that his "love" for Tracy is more inclined toward "worship" than romance: "That's the wonderful thing about you, Tray," he tells her. "You're like some marvelous, distant. . . . Oh queen, I guess. You're so cool and fine and—and always so much your own. . . . It's—it's a kind of beautiful purity, Tracy, that's the only word for it. . . . It's what I first worshipped you for, Tracy, from afar." But when she tells him she does not wish to be "worshipped," but loved, he fails to convince her that he is capable of such an emotion (p. 528). Hence it is Mike, the "lower-class" working stiff writer, who reveals to Tracy the difference between priggishness and decency. He not only refuses to take advantage of her when she is amorously inclined due to the drink and the nude swim—"You are extremely attractive—and as for distant and forbidding, on the contrary," he explains. "But you were somewhat the worse—

or the better—for wine, and there are rules about that, damn it"
(p. 565)—but he also recognizes the humanity in her and accepts
her as a woman first and as a socialite only secondly if at all.

Through Mike and Tracy and their initial conflict as it gives
way to a mutual understanding, Barry epitomizes the clash between social classes and points out the danger which exists when
there is no attempt on the part of either party to reach tolerance
and understanding. Although Mike and his fellow reporter, Liz,
come from a lower stratum of society, they are not really "lower-
class" individuals. If anything they share the same middle-class
values that Bessie Berger and Leo Gordon possess, for they combine ambition and aspiration in an attempt to have a better life.
If they are frustrated in their attempt, that frustration is manifest as contempt for and envy of those who have more. In their
experience with the Lords, however, they gain a special insight
into the class for whom they have such antipathy, and their hate
begins to dissipate: "I've just got so damn tolerant all at once,
I doubt if I'll ever be able to write another line," Mike tells Tracy
after their "affair" (p. 557). And Tracy, who decides that she
really wants someone to love her rather than worship her, elects
to remarry Dexter instead of trying to live out her life as a "virgin
goddess" with a man such as George, who is trying to use her to
change his identity and forget his origins. The Lords and Dexter
follow Tracy to the understanding that, indeed, "there are no
rules about human beings" (p. 541). By the same token that Mike
and Liz are more representative of a less affluent section of the
middle class than of the working class, the Lords are not really
as aristocratic as they first appear to be. Like the Tilfords and
the Hubbard-Giddens in Hellman's plays, they have inherited
wealth; but especially like the characters in *The Little Foxes*,
they rely upon capitalism to sustain their wealth: Seth owns a
coal mining company. The Lords share many of the same moral
standards and values as Mike and Liz; only their interpretations
seem less effectual because of their social rank and their accu-
mulated wealth. But Barry's central point is, as Joseph Roppolo
points out, that "social position and wealth have no monopoly
on virtue, there is such a thing as inverted snobbery, and a warm
human being has distinct advantages in life over either a plaster
saint or a virginal moon goddess."[5] Hence, in Barry's play, the
two visions of middle class life shown by Odets and Hellman
come together in a mutual understanding and friendship that
transcends economic class and social position.

The single character who does not awaken to a greater understanding is George, and his outrage over Tracy's indiscreet swim is actually a manifestation of another "type" in the modes of Hellman and Odets. Like Johnny Case in *Holiday*, George is a "self-made man." Beginning as a coal miner in Lord's company, he has risen to management through labor relations and some shrewd anticipation of congressional moves. He plans to consummate his success by marrying the boss' daughter. Anxious to lose sight of his working-class origins, George has adopted an affected manner of priggishness and snobbery which are repulsive even to the Lords whom he tries to imitate. Dexter characterizes him as "no great tower of strength . . . just a tower" and tells Tracy that he is "beneath her" in "mind and imagination" (p. 525). No one has much respect for George except as a hard worker who is sober and honest.

When George discovers Tracy's "affair" with Mike, however, he begins to show a truer nature. As Mike carries the naked Tracy upstairs, Dexter tries to console her husband-to-be by explaining: "But we're all only human, you know"; however, George explodes: "you—all of you—with your damned sophisticated ideas!" (p. 548). His demand for a "full explanation" seems the "proper thing" to do; however, his imitation of what he senses as propriety costs him the marriage and reveals not only that he probably never loved Tracy at all, but also that he never really felt comfortable among the Lord family and friends: "You and your whole rotten class," he says in disgust as he begins his final exit; "Listen, you're all on your way out—the lot of you—and don't think you aren't—and good riddance" (p. 567). George's primary mistake has been that he has attempted only to imitate the people he thinks he wants to be like; at no time does he try to understand their values and interpret the meaning of their lives.

George's rise from miner to manager may parallel Johnny's career in *Holiday*, but unlike Barry's earlier character, George acquires no depth of character as a result of the experience. Like Joe Bonaparte, he defines success in material terms—he even regards Tracy as an object to be possessed rather than a woman to be loved. Whereas Johnny remains proud of his simple integrity, George is anxious to trade his blue collar for a white tie; and when thwarted, he can only make a pernicious threat.

But George's character can be evaluated on another level. The only praise offered in the play for Tracy's choice of a second husband comes as a compliment on his sobriety, except when Tracy offers a visual image of him addressing the men at the mines:

> TRACY: You ought to see him with the men—they simply adore him.
> GEORGE: Oh—come on Tracy!
> TRACY *[Backing a few steps to Left]*: Oh, but they do! Never in my life will I forget that first night I saw you, all those wonderful faces, and the torchlights, and the way his voice boomed.
> GEORGE: You see, I'm really a spellbinder—that's the way I got her. (p. 512-513)

To an American audience in 1939 the parallel with Hitler's "Cathedral of Ice" rallies at Nuremberg that they saw in newsreels might not go unnoticed.[6] Brooks Atkinson characterizes George as a "fascist prig," and further references to George's right-wing tendencies tend to reinforce Atkinson's conclusion.[7] Mike, for example, initially likes George and feels sorry for him because Dexter clearly outclasses him in every way; but after George reveals his lack of tolerance, Mike changes his mind: "I've made a funny discovery," he tells Tracy, "that in spite of the fact that someone's up from the bottom, he may be quite a heel. And even though someone else's born to the purple, he still may be quite a guy" (p. 558). And Dexter's assessment of George's declaration of Tracy's "guilt" before he hears her out is that he is "unAmerican" (p. 566). Hence, Barry takes the fascist figure and synthesizes him from two elements: from Odets' gangster-fascist, he eliminates the gunman aspect but retains the idea that such a character could be encroaching upon honest people and perverting what power he finds there to his own evil ends; from Hellman's idea of a "masked" figure, he takes the idea that even though a fascist may appear to be one of the kinds of people he works against, he is really an "enemy within." George represents a threat to both strata of society which clash in *Philadelphia Story*: he apparently placates the workers by convincing them that he is acting in their interests (like Fatt in *Lefty* or Fuseli in *Golden Boy*); and he puts the capitalists off the defensive by pretending to be one of them (like Mary in *The Children's Hour* or the gangster-leader and strike breaker, Wilkie, in *Days to Come*). He is revealed in Barry's play because he never comes to an understanding of either class. Like a true villain, he is exposed by his own evil excesses.

The "major premise" of all high comedy, writes John Mason Brown, is its "equality": "It takes for granted not only that the author and his audience are equals socially and intellectually, but, what is far more important, that they also share that greatest test as well as that most ultimate privilege of equality—the capacity for laughing at the same thing, at the same time and in the same way."[8]   While noting that *The Philadelphia Story* is "a plea for tolerance of the rich on the part of those who have less," Goldstein concurs: "In truth, the piece is no more than a story of love in idleness with an undercurrent of sensuality and an overlay of democratic mottoes, the whole calculated to please a comfortable audience. But to say so much (or so little) is not to deny its charm or the value of works of its kind in a well-balanced theatre."[9]   By charming and pleasing the audience, however, Barry's play effectively combines the principles of entertainment and information so many playwrights of the period had sought.   Although he offers no didactic social programs, exhorts no fundamental political or philosophical principles for social change, he manages to fulfill Krutch's dictum for "revolutionary" drama by attempting "radically to alter the intellectual concepts of the audience," in this case, concepts concerning the nature of class distinctions.

The Philadelphia Story is not iconoclastic in its form. It uses essentially the same structure as *Holiday*, Barry's last successful play (boy meets girl, boy loses girl, boy gets girl); but a span of ten years separates the two scripts. The political and social upheaval which had affected the entire nation as well as the drama is evident in a comparison which offers a unique contrast in values between two times separated by a depression and ten years of economic turmoil. Audiences had changed in their regard for the elements of society represented in the 1939 play. Johnny Case, for example, is seen as a confident rebel, accomplished in his work, but defiant in his right to be his "own man." Transformed into George Kittredge, whom Goldstein calls a "latent fascist," the "up and coming" young man is no longer admirable but is contemptible and foolish. Julia Seton, whose snobbery contrasts with the openness of her sister, Linda, is transformed into Tracy Lord. She is just as spoiled and strong-headed as Julia, but Tracy has the capacity for change, for developing an understanding of "human frailty" both in herself and in others.

Barry's view of the very rich has also changed over the years.
In The Modern Temper Krutch comments on the nature of the
shifting attitudes toward the middle class who arrive at success:

> When the American individual has built his house, made
> his machines, encircled himself with every comfort and
> finery that he could bear, he found himself more nervous
> than proud, more wistful than mature. He did not wholly
> understand the things he had wrought, which saddened
> and frightened him somewhat, even as he boasted of them.
> He did not know his fellowman. . . . He is no longer
> sure that his isolation spells strength or that his power
> means security.[10]

In this regard Edward Seton's sense of propriety and social behavior has given way to Seth Lord's disregard for such matters;
and the carefree abandonment of responsibility of the Potters
in *Holiday* has yielded to Dexter's sense of a personal need for
fulfillment that transcends wealth and class. But the most significant change in Barry's social comedy is his replacement of
the snobbish and obnoxious Crams in *Holiday* with the leftist
and hostile Mike and Liz who undergo the greatest change in the
play by learning what Roppolo calls "a highly moral lesson involving tolerance, understanding and love."[11]

In an allegorical sense, *The Philadelphia Story* shows the
meeting of two polarized elements of society, both of which
had been the subject of all social drama in the thirties. As in
other plays, they clash bitterly, but instead of ending in a revolutionary call for action or a philosophical call for a better
world or ending in a violent upheaval signifying the triumph
of one over the other, Barry's play successfully combines them
in a synthesis of mutual respect and appreciation of each other's
point of view and values. In spite of the sinister threat from
George as he exits the Lord home, there is a feeling of solidarity
among the two classes remaining on stage that had not been seen
before in the American social theatre.

The Philadelphia Story was not simply a return to the social
satire either, even though it is satiric and even though it is a social
drama. The play concentrates on the personal involvements of its
characters, but those machinations are revealed as the characters
respond to a set of stimuli connected to a backdrop of moral
assumptions. It is not "drama as weapon," but it is drama as

gentle persuasion. Its arguments do not exhort or declaim; they present two sides of a thorny question, class relationships, in hopes of arriving at an equitable and mutually satisfying conclusion. In short, Barry's synthesis, representing the last combination of dramatic modes in the social drama during the decade, fulfills Krutch's requirements for "revolutionary" drama in the modern theater: It was drama that did not imitate life but interpreted it.

As he had done a decade before, Barry unified his theme and his form into what became an ironically prophetic drama; for within months Europe would be plunged into war, and all the classes and political divisions in the United States would soon join in one unified effort, synthesizing their philosophies and politics in a common cause against a common foe.

NOTES

[1] Malcolm Goldstein, *The Political Stage : American Drama and Theatre of the Great Depression* (New York: Oxford University Press, 1974), p. 124. Reprinted with permission of Oxford University Press.

[2] Joseph Patrick Roppolo, *Philip Barry* (New York: Twayne Publishers, Inc., 1965), p. 91. Reprinted with permission of Twayne Publishers, a Division of G. R. Hall and Co., Boston.

[3] Philip Barry, *The Philadelphia Story* in *States of Grace: Eight Plays by Philip Barry,* ed. and with a biographical essay by Brendan Gill (New York: Harcourt Brace Jovanovich, 1975), p. 502; subsequent citations from this play will be made parenthetically in the text.

[4] Joseph Wood Krutch, *The American Drama Since 1918* (New York: Random House, 1939), p. 269.

[5] Roppolo, p. 92.

[6] Albert Speer, *Inside the Third Reich,* trans. Richard and Clara Winston (New York: The Macmillan Company, 1970), especially pp. 65-83; the sensational films made of these rallies by Lini Riefenstahl were widely distributed to newsreel compilers and were frequently used as "stock footage" whenever any story broke concerning Hitler's party or military action. As the designer of the Nuremberg rally "set" used spotlights and flags not

only to give the impression that more people were present than actually were there but also to focus the attention of the massed party members toward a single speaker, Himmler, Goebbles or Hitler himself, the overall effect was memorable even to film audiences.

[7]Brooks Atkinson and Albert Hirschfeld, *The Lively Years: 1920-1973* (New York: Association Press, 1973), p. 144.

[8]John Mason Brown, *Upstage: The American Theatre in Performance* (Port Washington, New York: Kerrnikat Press, 1930), p. 20.

[9]Goldstein, pp. 354-355.

[10]Joseph Wood Krutch, *The Modern Temper: A Study and a Confession* (New York: Harcourt, Brace and World, 1929), p. 288.

[11]Roppolo, p. 111.

CONCLUSION:
THE CONTRIBUTION OF THE SOCIAL DRAMATISTS

On the evening of May 10, 1849, the New York militia was called out to quell a riot which had erupted in front of the Astor Palace Opera House in Manhattan. During the ensuing street battle, twenty people were either killed outright or fatally wounded, and thirty were injured. The reason for the riot was William C. Macready's performance of William Shakespeare's *Macbeth*. Macready, a celebrated English actor, had been forced to cut the previous night's performance short due to hecklers who disrupted the play with cat calls and yells and threw eggs, apples, pennies, and even chairs at the stage, thus endangering the actors and those patrons seated in the orchestra. The "audience's" antipathy to the famous Macready's production was a reaction both to the cool response the American actor Edwin Forrest had received during a recent tour of England and to the tendency of American theatre managers to book British plays with British actors instead of native scripts with native talent playing the leading roles. When the crowds found the doors to the Astor Palace shut against them on the performance's second night, they rioted.[1]

Since Thomas Godfrey produced the first American play to be professionally staged, *The Prince of Parthia*, on April 24, 1767,[2] Americans have taken their drama very seriously. Throughout the nineteenth century, the "state of the art" was never particularly exact, and those who looked to the theatre in the United States for development and improvement chafed under the constant presence of the better drama which came from England and Europe. Americans tried their hands at virtually every form of dramatic entertainment, but most of the successful efforts of the century were imitations of plays which had already enjoyed fame abroad. As early as 1845 Edgar Allen Poe spoke through the lines of his theatrical reviews to the problem of developing a distinctively American drama which would be more realistic in its portrayal of life and more meaningful in its message than the entertaining but ephemeral plays which dominated the contemporary stage. He wrote:

> Dramatic art is, or should be, a concentralization of all that which is entitled to the appellation of art. When sculpture shall fail, and painting shall fail, and poetry and music;—when men shall no longer take pleasure in eloquence, and in grace of motion, and in the beauty of women, and in truthful representation of character, and in the consciousness of sympathy in their enjoyment of each and all, then and not till then, may we look for *that* to sink into insignificance, which, and which alone, affords opportunity for the conglomerations of these infinite and imperishable sources of delight.
>
> The next step may be the electrification of all mankind by the representation of *a play* that may be neither tragedy, comedy, farce, opera, pantomime, melodrama or spectacle, as we now comprehend these terms, but which may retain some portion of the idiosyncratic excellence as yet unnamed because as yet undreamed of in the world.[3]

Almost a century after Poe penned these lines, during the Great Depression, his prophecy came very close to being fulfilled. Not only was the American drama exploring all of the areas and forms he mentioned, it was also exploring ideas and themes which had never been the province of drama before. Furthermore, this period of exploration and experimentation gave a basis for further development in American dramatic art which is still going on.

The development of the American drama during the nineteenth and twentieth centuries was often the result of a conflict between the theatre and the art it produced. Quality playwriting was always subordinated to quality production, and even production was often sacrificed if a famous actor could be engaged to play a leading role. Even though the theatre of the nineteenth century was never a literary theatre, men such as Poe, William Cullen Bryant, Mark Twain, Henry James, William Dean Howells, Bret Harte, and Hamlin Garland actively supported it both through critical writing and through their own plays. They often called for a more artistic theatre, one which would synthesize the necessary elements of entertainment with a higher level of writing which would have an intellectual as well as an aesthetic appeal. It was not until World War I, however, that such groups as the

Provincetown Players and the Washington Square Players opened new vistas for the American drama by combining the theatrical company with the theatrical writer to produce a series of plays which both attracted audiences and approached literary ideals. In this combination, "modern" drama was born in the United States, and throughout the decade which followed, it continued to mature until it was a rebellious adolescent which would try any device, any form, any idea in an effort to entertain and inform its audience.

The influence of foreign writers was, of course, still important; but unlike the "modern" American novel which can easily trace antecedents to Zola, Flaubert, or Proust, the literary influence of European playwrights on American dramatists became increasingly indirect. It would be an error to imagine that the Americans ignored the work of Ibsen, Shaw, or Chekhov, but it would also be an error to look upon the development of American drama in the twentieth century as a direct outgrowth of such foreign writers or as an attempt to specifically imitate their master works. Eugene O'Neill, Maxwell Anderson, Elmer Rice, Philip Barry, and others demonstrated in the formative decades of the twenties and thirties that, of all the influences which shaped the American drama, none was stronger than the influence of the American experience. And during the thirties, this experience, pronounced and emphasized by the Great Depression, became both the central theme and major concern of all American playwrights, even those who did not address the problems directly.

"The modern drama," John Gassner writes, "was born in rebellion and cradled in criticism."[4] Always sensitive to audience response during a period when money for tickets as well as production was scarce, playwrights understood the necessity of pleasing those who came to criticize as well as those who came to be entertained. Francis Ferguson states: "The art of the theatre . . . seems to be as close to the art of politics as it is to poetry, painting or music. The theatre artist . . . depends upon his constituency."[5] During the thirties writers of the social drama explored the cares and concerns of their audience, presenting alternatives and answers in the same way candidates for public office present platforms. They were not always successful (neither are politicians), but they always kept a close eye on the changing times, and when the polemics they offered went awry, when the methods they used to offer them failed to work, they shifted, refined, changed, and combined their modes in an ever constant attempt both to entertain and inform.

If any common element can be identified in all the social plays of the 1930's, it is an attempt on the part of the playwrights to raise the consciousness of their audience, to educate it, to bring it to action, or to make it aware of the problems the writers perceived in society. In his study, *The Radical Novel in the United States*, Walter Rideout identifies four "types" of "proletarian" novels: those centered upon a strike; those concerned with an individual's conversion to communism; those dealing with the lowest layers of the social order; and those describing the decay of the middle class.[6] The social drama of the thirties also touched on all these themes: Clifford Odets' *Waiting For Lefty* and its agit-prop antecedents deal with strikes and conversions to leftist, usually communist, alternatives; Sidney Kingsley's *Dead End,* Jack Kirkland's *Tobacco Road,* and other plays deal with the bottom tiers of the social order; the later plays of Odets and all of Lillian Hellman's drama focused on the decay of the middle class. Frequently combinations of these four types may be seen, such as in Clair and Paul Sifton's *1931—,* John Howard Lawson's *Marching Song,* and Hellman's *Days to Come.* Other areas of inquiry such as pacificism, anti-fascism, and exposure of anti-semitism and political corruption also invaded the subject matter of the social dramatists. Like the radical novel, the social drama succeeded in achieving a synthesis of political and economic concerns with moral and ethical issues. The social drama actively sought a balance between the polarized segments of society; and ultimately, it called for understanding among all peoples from all classes of life. Instead of merely imitating life or using the stage as a political platform from which to render preachment and exhortation, the social dramatists sought to understand life, and they wanted to use their drama to interpret it. By doing so, the social playwrights of the thirties became as representative of their age through their drama as John Dos Passos, Theodore Dreiser, James T. Farrell, Erskine Caldwell, and John Steinbeck were representative of it through their prose.

Douglas McDermott states: "the social drama of the thirties was not an accident but an intention."[7] The writers were engaged in a deliberate attempt to change the status quo in their depression-torn country. If they were sometimes unrealistic or overzealous in their espousal of radical political ideas, they never lost sight of a common belief in the inherent worth of the individual, in their optimistic vision of an awakened and informed society. As Harold Clurman points out, this optimism also separated them from their contemporaries in the novel; they did not share the "sense of fateful doom" the fiction writers seemed to exude; they "thought they saw a way out."[8] And Gassner notes: "Even at the worst, the sense of disaster was apt to be qualified by some stubborn confidence in the human spirit."[9] From the earliest plays of the depression where characters such as Johnny Case in *Holiday* or Adam in *1931*—leave the stage to follow a personally motivated rebellion, to the final acts of the thirties where young women such as Alexandra in *The Little Foxes* or Tracy Lord in *The Philadelphia Story* understand the evil which threatens society and resolve to struggle against it even though it means altering the convictions of a lifetime, playwrights continued to uphold their faith in the individual as he or she worked for a better world. Through their plays, Anderson, Odets, Lawson, and others continued to demonstrate their theme that society could face and conquer any of its problems if only it would learn to bring individuals together to work in a common cause for a common good.

The revolt of the social playwrights against corruption, oppression, injustice, and eventually against family and something they amorphously called the "social order" was not a blind revolt; it was more of an inquiry into old and established institutions and ideas, and a suggestion of alternatives which seemed to be more positive than anything anyone else could name,and an investigation of values and principles of moral and ethical behavior to see if the motivations behind such values were honest. If the result of such inquiry, suggestion, and investigation was that society itself was wicked, they called for change; but it was never a call for fanatical or irrational revolutionary upheaval. They called for careful understanding of the forces—economic, social, political—which oppressed mankind and a discarding of whatever false values—greed, materialism, power—prevented the ultimate triumph of the individual.

In this sense the social playwright attempted to be what Clurman calls the "conscience of his time," and as such he "always appears to be ahead of it, often seems even to himself cut off from the very people whose aspiration he expresses."[10] With the exception of most of the authors of the agit-prop plays, the majority of the playwrights of social drama were of the middle and upper-middle class. It is not surprising, therefore, that after

several explorations of working class dilemmas, they returned
to the people they knew best. The "new audience" Clurman
perceived in the balcony the night *1931*—closed was not made
up of workers or even lower-middle class individuals, and the
positive response of this audience to proletarian-oriented plays
such as *Waiting For Lefty* and *Dead End* was more a reaction
of liberal tendencies and perhaps a sense of democratic responsibility than direct identification with the characters on stage.
The overwhelming response to Odets' "STRIKE!" scene, for
example, is better testimony to his dramaturgical skill than to
any sense of Marxist idealism in the audience; and Odets' realization of this can be seen in the way his characters turn to
radical action only because they have no other way to go. In
fact, the most radical "calls to action" in the thirties' social
drama was more in the way of a call of warning to the middle
class to join with the working class in a struggle for a better
world or face the vengeance of an angry but reluctantly revolutionary majority. "The attributes of a play as entertainment,"
writes Clurman, "make it like any other entertainment. What
makes a play different is that it pretends to affect men's hearts,
to change their very lives in matters of aspiration, sentiment,
conviction."[11] Even in their most didactic moments, even when
their political convictions threatened to entirely overtake their
dramatic form, the social dramatists always kept foremost in
their minds the idea of pleasing the audience. For all the preachments, speeches, and "calls to action" they wrote into their
drama, they never completely lost sight of what makes a play
"well made."

John Gassner writes: "The theatre of the thirties will be
remembered for its playwrights, not because they produced
masterpieces for the ages, but because they responded to the
challenge of their times vigorously and excitingly. They had
the defects of their virtues. . . . But they were faulty *and* alive
instead of perfect and dead or meticulous and tepid."[12] Just
as the social playwrights kept an eye on box office receipts and
reviews and on the political and economic events of their day,
they also watched their techniques and constantly tried to improve them. They borrowed ideas from every possible source,
tried them, and kept or discarded them as they proved effective
or disastrous. It was an exciting era in the development of a genre
if for no other reason than because of the variety of different
forms being tried out on the Broadway stage. On a given evening

agit-prop, high comedy, melodrama, and tragedy might be playing in the various theatres of the Great White Way, and the willingness of playwrights to seek new and innovative forms for their social messages created a versatility and freshness the theatre had never known before. Additionally, the development of technologically improved sets and lighting and sound systems, the use of modern acting techniques adapted from Stanislavski, and the increasing developments of expressionism and cinematic techniques all enhanced the "modernism" of the theatre of the thirties. The experimentation with structural form also helped to bring the American drama to maturity. It had discovered something significant to say when it explored social issues, and in its physical changes and structural experimentation, it discovered a new way to say it.

Between the opening of Philip Barry's *Holiday* in 1928 and the closing of *The Philadelphia Story* a decade later, the development of the drama in the United States revealed a series of tenacious trials and errors. The first synthesis of the social comedy and radical Marxist plays produced the political satire and soon gave way to the combination of political drama and agit-prop protest plays, the proletarian drama. This synthesis also yielded to the combination of plays which examined the decay of the middle class, Odets from the bottom and Hellman from the top of the social order. And from melodramatic thesis and antithesis and synthesis which emerged brought all classes together in an attitude which was no less critical of social ills, but which used the old arguments as ironic counterpoints to a theme which demonstrated the possibility of mutual reliance and mutual understanding of all classes. Along the way, the social drama went through many tumultuous forms: the high comedy of Philip Barry's plays, the well-made political satire of Maxwell Anderson, the unstructured but bombastic didactic agit-prop and proletarian drama of Clifford Odets, and finally, the "middle-class" naturalism and melodramatic plots evidenced in Clifford Odets' post-*Lefty* works and Lillian Hellman's plays. Although each of these is dynamically different and some of them are iconoclastic both in their makeup and in their polemics, all of them, even those which consciously followed the "drama as weapon" philosophy, sought to interpret life. They wanted to produce life on the stage just as it appeared in the streets, homes, and businesses of American society; but they also attempted to penetrate the surface of mere imitation and expose the human relationships which were being played out every day in the streets of the nation. Odets and Hellman's experiments in naturalistic theory and the defeat of the hero maintained an imitative quality as they slipped again and again into stock, melodramatic devices and depicted the forces of society in forms of good and evil locked in combat over the fate of individual fortune. But their attempts to render sound interpretations of life continued. Philip Barry ultimately re-emerged as the master of high comedy and proved that art which could successfully interpret life instead of merely imitating it was possible. In *The Philadelphia Story* Barry illustrated through comedic metaphor the significance of human quality in solving the problems of society through understanding. After all the bombast, polemic, and exhortations of the thirties, Barry illustrated through his interpretations of life that, as Tracy Lord puts it, "there are no rules about human beings."

The Philadelphia Story moved the modern American play into the realm of "revolutionary" drama as Joseph Wood Krutch defines it. None of the other social dramatists had been completely successful in "radically altering the intellectual concepts of the audience," but they never ceased to try. Their efforts to use imitative melodrama and infective caricature to indict a set of social ills cause critics such as Eleanor Flexner to accuse them of "retreating" from reality, from avoiding the necessary commitment for social changes. She finds their attempts at preachment and "calls to action" crude and primitive, but she admits that the work of some of the writers "has enriched the theatre with a vast new field of subject matter, novel and vital forms . . . and above all has brought to the consideration of social problems a positive and dynamic point of view which, when coupled with first-rate craftsmanship, yields superb theatrical results."[13] What Flexner never realizes is that "superb theatrical results" are vitally necessary for any play to succeed, however socially conscious it may be. Barry did understand this concept, however; and by exposing the stereotypes which had become so familiar to the audiences of the thirties to be real people who yielded to capricious whims, unreasonable prejudices, and, most importantly, to the compassion which rises with sympathetic understanding of one's fellow man, Philip Barry demonstrated that effective social drama could also be "superb" theatre. It was less important that the audiences who saw social plays learn a lesson from the experience than that they experience one writer's interpretation of life. And, for that information to be communicated to those who came to see it, Barry and others understood that the play must keep the audience's attention and charm them as well.

In the years which followed the decade, the social drama would be used to propagate anti-fascism to audiences conscious of a very real threat of war. In the fifties, sixties, and seventies, the idea of a play speaking directly to social problems would become more rare on Broadway but would become quite common in the insular fields of motion picture and television drama and comedy.[14] Barry's synthesis, however, would leave a rich legacy for the post-war American dramatists: Tennessee Williams, Arthur Miller, William Inge, Edward Albee, and others would continue to explore human relationships through the themes of personal rebellion and the value of mutual understanding. They would also indict social villains; but as authors of "revolutionary" drama, as Krutch defines it, their emphasis would be on interpreting the lives of the characters they examined so audiences could try to understand human nature better. Without the developments of the social dramatists, such depths of emotion and complexities of life might never have been explored. This is the fundamental importance of the social dramatists.

The most important thing to understand about American drama before World War II is that insofar as the playwrights themselves were concerned, they failed. They set out to create a pure "art theatre" which would not have to bow before the financial pressures of the commercial stage, but they finally came to realize that, without sufficiently good box office, even the most artistic production would close. They set out to create a National Theatre which would draw on the people of the United States for its subject matter, depicting both slum dwellers and farmers in their overall plight, but the efforts of the Federal Theatre Project also came to grief in the light of financial realities. They also set out to create a theatre of social awareness which could function as a sounding board for radical political opinions no matter how unpopular, but Lawson and the Theatre Union also failed to sustain audience support as times changed and political winds shifted. In 1939 Krutch pointed out another failure: "to create a serious American drama which could take its place as American literature."[15] But in the years following the "social decade" the American drama began to take its place as a literary genre; and from the work of the social playwrights, future dramatists would find direction and forms. In this sense, no other period of development of theatre has seen so much success in such a short period of time. Malcolm Goldstein states that "the number of new plays that later generations would find worthy of revival . . . had never been so large."[16] And each time audiences see a restaging of Hellman's *The Children's Hour* or Maxwell Anderson's *Both Your Houses* or Clifford Odets' *Waiting For Lefty* or Philip Barry's *The Philadelphia Story*, they are reminded of a time when "drama was a weapon" and playwrights sought to find a method of writing which would both entertain and inform, which would interpret life rather than merely imitate it.

NOTES

[1]Bernard W. Hewitt, *Theatre U.S.A.: 1665 to 1957* (New York: McGraw-Hill Book Co., 1959), p. 150.

[2]*Ibid.*, p. 28.

[3]Edgar Allen Poe quoted in Hewitt, pp. 139-140.

[4]John Gassner, *Dramatic Soundings: Evaluations and Retractions Culled from 30 Years of Dramatic Criticism* (New York: Crown Publisher, 1968), p. 337.

[5]Francis Fergusson, *The Human Image in Dramatic Literature* (New York: Doubleday & Co., Inc., 1957), p. 20. Reprinted with permission of the author.

[6]Walter Rideout, *The Radical Novel in the United States* (New York: Cambridge University, 1956), p. 256.

[7]Douglas McDermott, "Propaganda and Art: Dramatic Theory and the American Depression," *Modern Drama*, 11 (May 1968): 73-81.

[8]Harold Clurman, *The Fervent Years: A Story of the Group Theatre and the Thirties* (New York: Harcourt Brace Jovanovich, 1975), p. 81.

[9]Gassner, p. 388.

[10]Clurman, p. 181.

[11]*Ibid.*, p. 12.

[12]Gassner, p. 387.

[13]Eleanor Flexner, *American Playwrights: 1918-1938: The Theatre*

Retreats from Reality, with an introduction by John Gassner (1938, rpt; New York: Simon and Schuster, 1966), p. 290.

[14]The most notable exceptions of recent years have been *Hair* and *Oh Calcutta!,* both musical revue-type plays which have been critical of the established social order; women's theatre and ethnic theatre, especially Black and Chicano theatre, have also made much of the protest drama in the past twenty years; however, Broadway fare has been substantially more tame since World War II than it was in the hey-day of the social drama of the thirties.

[15]Joseph Wood Krutch, *The American Drama Since 1918* (New York: Random House, 1939), p. 11.

[16]Malcolm Goldstein, *The Political Stage: American Drama and Theatre of the Great Depression* (New York: Oxford University Press, 1974), p. 366.

SOURCES CONSULTED

Aaron, Daniel, and Robert Bendiner, eds. *The Strenuous Decade: A Social and Intellectual Record of the Nineteen Thirties.* Documents in American Civilization Series. New York: Anchor Books, 1970.

Aaron, Daniel. *Writers on the Left.* Oxford: Oxford University Press, 1977.

Annebrink, Lars. *The Beginnings of Naturalism in American Fiction: A Study of the Works of Hamlin Garland, Stephen Crane, and Frank Norris with Special References to Some European Influences, 1889-1903.* New York: Russell & Russell, Inc., 1961.

Anderson, Maxwell. *The Basis of Artistic Creation.* New Brunswick: Rutgers University Press, 1942.

—. *Both Your Houses.* New York: Samuel French, 1933.

—. *Dramatist in America: Letters of Maxwell Anderson, 1912-1958.* Edited by Laurence Avery. Chapel Hill: University of North Carolina Press, 1977.

—. *Elizabeth The Queen: A Play in Three Acts.* New York: Longman's, Green & Co., 1934.

—. and Harold Hickerson. *Gods of the Lightning and Outside Looking In.* New York: Longman's, Green & Co., 1928.

—. *Key Largo: A Play in a Prologue and Two Acts.* Washington, D. C.: Anderson House, 1939.

—. *Mary of Scotland: A Play in Three Acts.* Garden City, NY: Doubleday Doran & Co., 1934.

—. *The Masque of Kings.* Washington, D. C.: Anderson House, 1937.

—. *Night Over Taos.* New York: Samuel French, 1932.

—. *Off Broadway: Essays About the Theatre.* New York: William Sloan, Associates, Inc., 1947.

—. *Saturday's Children.* New York: Longman's, Green & Co., 1927.

—. and Laurence Stallings. *Three American Plays by Maxwell Anderson and Laurence Stallings.* New York: Harcourt,

Brace & Co., 1926.

—. *The Wingless Victory: A Play in Three Acts.* Washington, D. C.: Anderson House, 1936.

—. *Winterset.* Introduction "A Prelude to Poetry in the Theatre" by the author. Washington, D. C.: Anderson House, 1935.

Archer, William. "The Development of American Drama." *Harper's Magazine,* December 1920, pp. 75-86.

Atkinson, Brooks, and Albert Hirschfeld. *The Lively Years: 1920-1973.* New York: Association Press, 1973.

Avery, Laurence, comp. *A Catalogue of the Maxwell Anderson Collection at the University of Texas.* Austin: The Humanities Research Center, the University of Texas, 1968.

Bailey, Mabel Driscoll. *Maxwell Anderson: The Playwright as Prophet.* New York: Abelard-Schuman, 1957.

Baritz, Loren, ed. *The Culture of the Twenties.* Indianapolis: Bobbs-Merrill Co., Inc., 1970.

Barry, Philip. *Here Come the Clowns: A Play in Three Acts.* New York: Coward-McCann, Inc., 1939.

—. *Holiday: A Comedy in Three Acts.* New York: Samuel French, 1928.

—. *Hotel Universe: A Play.* New York: Samuel French, 1930.

—. *In a Garden: A Comedy in Three Acts.* New York: Samuel French, 1929.

—. *The Joyous Season: A Play.* New York: Samuel French, 1934.

—. *Paris Bound: A Play in Three Acts.* New York: Samuel French, 1929.

—. *Spring Dance: A Comedy in Three Acts.* New York: Samuel French, 1936.

—. *States of Grace: Eight Plays by Philip Barry.* Edited with a biographical essay by Brendan Gill. New York: Harcourt Brace Jovanovich, 1975.

—. *You and I: A Comedy in Three Acts.* New York: Brentano's Publishers, 1923.

—. *White Wings: A Comedy in Three Acts.* New York: Samuel French, 1929.

Behrman, S. N. *4 Plays by S. N. Behrman.* New York: Random House, 1952.

—. *No Time for Comedy.* New York: Random House, 1939.

Belasco, David. *The Heart of Maryland and Other Plays by David Belasco.* Ed. Glenn Hughes and George Savage. Princeton: Princeton University Press, 1941.

Bentley, Eric. *The Life of the Drama.* London: Methuen & Co., Ltd., 1966.

—. *The Playwright as Thinker: A Study of Drama in Modern Times.* New York: Harcourt, Brace & Co., 1946.

—. *What is Theatre?* New York: Antheneum, 1968.

Blankfort, Michael. *The Crime.* New York: New Theatre League, 1936.

Bogard, Travis. *Contour in Time: The Plays of Eugene O'Neill.* New York: Oxford University Press, 1972.

Broussard, Louis. *American Drama: Contemporary Allegory from Eugene O'Neill to Tennessee Williams.* Norman: University of Oklahoma Press, 1962.

Brown, John Mason. *Upstage: The American Theatre in Performance.* Port Washington, N. Y.: Kerrnikat Press, 1930.

Brown, John Russell, and Bernard, Harris, eds. *American Theatre.* New York: St. Martin's Press, 1967.

Clark, Barrett H. "American Drama In Its Second Decade." *The English Journal* 21 (January 1932): 1-11.

—. and George Freedly. *A History of Modern Drama.* New York: Appleton-Century Co., 1947.

Clurman, Harold. *The Fervent Years: A Story of the Group Theatre and the Thirties.* New York: Alfred A. Knopf, 1945; rpt. Harcourt Brace Jovanovich, 1975.

—. "Interpretation and Characterization." *New Theatre*, January 1936, p. 21. Corrigan, Robert W., ed. *The Theatre in Search of a Fix.* New York: Dell Publishing Co., 1973.

—. *Theatre in the Twentieth Century: Playwright, Actor and Critic on the Modern Theatre.* New York: Grove Press, 1963.

Cowley, Malcolm. "While They Waited For Lefty." *Saturday Review,* 6 (June 1964), 16-19, 61.

Daly, Augustin. *Man and Wife and Other Plays.* Edited by Catherine Sturtevant. Princeton: Princeton University Press, 1942.

Dawson, S. W. *Drama and the Dramatic.* The Critical Idiom Series, General Editor, John J. Jump. London: Metheun & Co., Ltd., 1970.

De Rohan, Pierre, ed. *Federal Theatre Plays: Prologue to Glory, by E. P. Conkle, One-Third of a Nation, Edited by Arthur Arent, and Haiti, by William Dubois.* Introduction by Hallie Flanagan. New York: Random House, 1938.

Dos Passos, John. *Airways, Inc.* New York: The Macauley Co.,

1928.

—. *U. S. A.* New York: The Modern Library, 1937.

Downer, Alan S., ed. *American Drama and Its Critics: A Collection of Critical Essays.* Chicago: University of Chicago Press, 1965.

—. *Fifty Years of American Drama: 1900-1950.* Chicago: Henry Regnery Co., 1951.

Driver, Tom F. *Romantic Quest and Modern Query: A History of the Modern Theatre.* New York: Delacorte Press, 1970.

Dusenburg, Winnifred L. "Myth in American Drama Between the Wars." *Modern Drama* 6 (December 1963): 294-308.

Eaton, Walter Pritchard. "The Dramatist as Man of Letters: The Case of Clyde Fitch." *Scribner's Magazine* 46 (April 1910): 490-497.

Engel, Lehman, ed. *The Critics.* New York: Macmillan Co., Inc., 1976.

Falk, Doris V. *Lillian Hellman.* New York: Frederick Ungar Publishing Co., 1978.

Fergusson, Francis. *The Human Image in Dramatic Literature.* New York: Doubleday & Co., Inc., 1957.

Flexner, Eleanor. *American Playwrights: 1918-1938: The Theatre Retreats From Reality.* Preface by John Gassner. 1930; rpt. New York: Simon & Schuster, 1938.

French, Warren G. *John Steinbeck.* 2nd ed. Boston: Twayne Publishers, Inc., 1975.

Frenz, Horst, ed. *American Playwrights on Drama.* New York: Hill & Wang, 1965.

Gardner, R. H. *The Splintered Stage: The Decline of the American Theatre.* New York: The MacMillan Co., 1965.

Gerstenberger, Donna. "Verse Drama In America: 1916-1939." *Modern Drama* 6 (December 1963): 309-322.

Gassner, John. *Dramatic Soundings: Evaluations and Retractions Culled from 30 Years of Dramatic Criticism.* New York: Crown Publishers, 1968.

—. *The Theatre In Our Times: A Survey of the Men, Materials and Movements In the Modern Theatre.* New York: Crown Publishers, 1954.

Goldstein, Malcolm. *The Political Stage: American Drama and Theatre of the Great Depression.* New York: Oxford University Press, 1974.

Green, Paul. *The House of Connelly and Other Plays.* New York: Samuel French, 1931.

Halliwell, Leslie. *The Filmgoer's Companion.* 6th ed. New York: Avon, 1977.

Hartnoll, Phyllis. *The Oxford Companion to the Theatre.* 3rd ed. New York: Oxford University Press, 1967.

Hect, Ben, and Charles MacArthur. *The Front Page.* New York: Covici-Friede, 1928.

Heffner, Hubert C. *The Nature of Drama.* Boston: Houghton-Mifflin Co., 1959.

Hellman, Lillian. *The Collected Plays.* Boston: Little, Brown & Co., 1971.

—. *Pentimento: A Book of Portraits.* New York: New American Library, 1973.

—. *Scoundrel Time.* Introduction by Gary Wills. Boston: Little, Brown & Co., 1976.

—. *An Unfinished Woman: A Memoir.* Boston: Little, Brown & Co., 1969.

Hennequin, Alfred. "The Drama of the Future." *Arena* 3 (March 1891): 385-393.

Hewitt, Bernard W. *Theatre U.S.A.: 1665-1957.* New York: McGraw-Hill, 1959.

Hoffman, Frederick J. *The 20's: American Writing in the Post-War Decade.* New York: The Macmillan Co., 1965.

Howells, William Dean. *The Complete Plays of W. D. Howells.* Edited with an Introduction by Walter J. Meserve. New York: New York University Press, 1960.

—. "The Recent Dramatic Season." *North American Review,* March 1909, pp. 462-480.

Isaacs, Edith J. R. "At Its Best." *Theatre Arts Monthly,* February 1936, pp. 94-97.

—. "Clifford Odets: First Chapters." *Theatre Arts Monthly,* April 1939, pp. 257-266.

—. "Going Left With Fortune." *Theatre Arts Monthly,* May 1935, pp. 327-331.

—. "Merry Feast of Playgoing: Broadway in Review." *Theatre Arts Monthly,* April 1935, pp. 254-256.

James, Henry. *The Complete Plays of Henry James.* Edited with an Introduction by Leon Edel. New York: J. B. Lippincott Co., 1949.

Kingsley, Sidney. *Dead End: A Play in Three Acts.* New York: Random House, 1936.

—. *Men in White: A Play in Three Acts.* New York: Covici Friede Publishers, 1933.

Kirkland, Jack. *Tobacco Road: A Play in Three Acts.* New York: Samuel French, 1934.

Kostelantz, Richard. "American Theatre--Performance Not Literature." *Re: Arts and Letters* 5 (Fall 1971), 41-49.

Kozlenko, William, ed. *The Best Short Plays of the Social Theatre.* Introduction by William Kozlenko. New York: Random House, 1939.

Krutch, Joseph Wood. *The American Drama Since 1918.* New York: Random House, 1939.

—. *"Modernism" in Modern Drama: A Definition and an Estimate* Ithaca, New York: Cornell University Press, 1953, rpt. New York: Russell & Russell, Inc., 1962.

—. *The Modern Temper: A Study and a Confession.* New York: Harcourt, Brace and World, 1929.

Lawson, John Howard. *The Hidden Heritage: A Rediscovery of the Ideas and Forces that Link the Thought of Our Time with the Culture of the Past.* New York: The Citadel Press, 1950.

—. *Marching Song.* New York: Dramatists Play Service, 1937.

—. *Roger Bloomer: A Play in Three Acts.* New York: Thomas Seltzer, 1923.

—. *Theory and Technique of Playwriting.* New York: Hill & Wang, 1960.

—. *With a Reckless Preface: The Pure in Heart and Gentlewoman.* New York: Farrar & Rinehart, Inc., 1934.

Lewis, Emory. *Stages: The Fifty-Year Childhood of the American Theatre.* Englewood Cliffs, New Jersey: Prentice Hall, 1969.

Ley-Piscator, Maria. *The Piscator Experiment: The Political Theatre.* Carbondale and Edwardsville: Southern Illinois University Press, 1967.

Lynn, Kenneth S. *The Dream of Success: A Study of the Modern American Imagination.* Boston: Little, Brown & Company, 1955.

Mantle, Burns. *American Playwrights of Today.* New York: Dodd, Mead & Co., 1929.

—. ed. *The Best Plays of 1928-29: and the Yearbook of the Drama in America.* New York: Dodd, Mead & Co., 1929.

—. ed. *The Best Plays of 1929-1930: and The Yearbook of the Drama in America.* New York: Dodd, Mead & Co., 1930.

—. ed. *The Best Plays of 1930-31: and The Yearbook of the Drama in America.* New York: Dodd, Mead & Co., 1931.

—. ed. *The Best Plays of 1931-32: and The Yearbook of the Drama in America*. New York: Dodd, Mead & Co., 1932.

—. ed. *The Best Plays of 1932-33: and The Yearbook of the Drama in America*. New York: Dodd, Mead & Co., 1933.

—. ed. *The Best Plays of 1933-34: and The Yearbook of the Drama in America*. New York: Dodd, Mead & Co., 1934.

—. ed. *The Best Plays of 1934-35: and The Yearbook of the Drama in America*. New York: Dodd, Dead & Co., 1935.

—. ed. *The Best Plays of 1935-36: and The Yearbook of the Drama in America*. New York: Dodd, Mead & Co., 1936.

—. ed. *The Best Plays of 1936-37: and The Yearbook of the Drama in America*. New York: Dodd, Mead & Co., 1937.

—. ed. *The Best Plays of 1937-38: and The Yearbook of the Drama in America*. New York: Dodd, Mead & Co., 1938.

—. ed. *The Best Plays of 1938-39: and the Yearbook of the Drama in America*. New York: Dodd, Mead & Co., 1939.

Marker, Lisa-Lone. *David Belasco: Naturalism in the Theatre*. Princeton: Princeton University Press, 1975.

Mathews, Jane Dehart. *The Federal Theatre: 1935-1939: Plays, Relief, and Politics*. Princeton: Princeton University Press, 1967.

McDermott, Douglas. "Propaganda and Art: Dramatic Theory and the American Depression." *Modern Drama* 11 (May 1968) : 73-81.

Mendelsohn, Michael J., *Clifford Odets: Humane Dramatist*. Deland, FL: Everett Edwards, 1969.

—. "The Social Critics on Stage." *Modern Drama* 6 (December 1963): 277-285.

Moody, Richard. *Dramas from the American Theatre: 1762-1909*. New York: The World Publishing Co., 1966.

—. *Lillian Hellman: Playwright*. Introduction by Harold Clurman. New York: The Bobbs-Merrill Co., Inc., 1972.

Moses, Montrose J., and Joseph Wood Krutch. *Representative American Drama: National and Local*. Revised ed. Boston: Little, Brown & Co., 1941.

Murray, Edward. *Clifford Odets: The Thirties and After*. New York: Frederick Ungar Publishing Co., 1968.

Nannes, Casper Harold. *Politics in the American Drama as Revealed by Plays Produced on the New York Stage 1890-1945*. Philadelphia: University of Pennsylvania Press, 1950.

Nathan, George Jean. *The Entertainment of a Nation: or, Three Sheets in the Wind*. New York: Alfred A. Knoph, 1942.

—. *Testament of a Critic.* New York: Alfred A. Knopf, 1931.

The New York Times Directory of the Film. New York: Arno Press, 1974.

The New York Times Directory of the Theatre. New York: Arno Press, 1974.

Odets, Clifford. *Clash By Night.* New York: Random House, 1942.

—. *Night Music.* Introduction by Harold Clurman. New York: Random House, 1940.

—. *Six Plays of Clifford Odets.* Preface by the author with three introductions by Harold Clurman. New York: The Modern Library, 1939.

O'Neill, Eugene. *Selected Plays of Eugene O'Neill.* New York: Random House, 1938.

Patterson, James T. *America in the Twentieth Century: Part I, A History to 1945.* New York: Harcourt Brace Jovanovich, Inc., 1976.

Piscator, Edwin. *The Political Theatre: A History 1914-1929.* Translated by Hugh Rorrison. New York: Avon Books, 1976.

Poggi, Jack. *Theatre in America: The Impact of Economic Forces: 1870-1967.* Ithaca, N. Y.: Cornell University Press, 1968.

Porter, Thomas E. *Myth and Modern American Drama.* Detroit: Wayne State University Press, 1969.

Quinn, Arthur Hobson. *The History of the American Drama From the Civil War to the Present Day.* 2 vols. New York: F. S. Crofts & Co., 1937.

—. "The Real Hope for the American Theatre." *Scribner's Magazine* 97 (January 1935): 30-35.

—. *Representative American Plays: From 1767 to the Present Day.* 7th ed., revised. New York: Appleton-Century-Crofts, Inc., 1957.

—. "The Significance of Recent American Drama." *Scribner's Magazine* 72 (July 1922): 97-108.

Rabkin, Gerald. *Drama and Commitment: Politics in the American Theatre of the Thirties.* Bloomington: Indiana University Press, 1964.

Raines, Robert A. *Modern Drama and Social Change.* Englewood Cliffs, New Jersey: Prentice-Hall, 1972s

—. "The First Decade." *Theatre Arts Monthly,* May 1949, pp. 53-56.

Rice, Elmer. *Minority Report: An Autobiography.* New York: Simon & Schuster, 1963.

—. *Seven Plays by Elmer Rice.* New York: The Viking Press, 1950.

Rideout, Walter. *The Radical Novel in the United States.* New York: Cambridge University Press, 1956.

Roose-Evans, James. *Experimental Theatre: From Stanislavski to Today.* New York: Avon Books, 1970.

Roppolo, Joseph Patrick. *Philip Barry.* New York: Twayne Publishers, Inc., 1965.

Saroyan, William. *My Heart's In the Highlands.* New York: Samuel French, 1939.

—. *Razzle Dazzle.* New York: Harcourt Brace and Co., 1942.

Scholes, Robert E. and Carl H. Klaus. *Elements of Drama.* New York: Oxford University Press, 1971.

Sherwood, Robert E. *Idiot's Delight.* New York: Charles Scribner's Sons, 1936.

Shivers, Alfred S. *Maxwell Anderson.* Boston: Twayne Publishers, Inc., 1976.

Smiley, Sam. *The Drama of Attack: Didactic Plays of the American Depression.* Columbia: University of Missouri Press, 1972.

Speer, Albert. *Inside the Third Reich.* Translated by Richard and Clara Winston. New York: The MacMillan Company, 1970.

Steinberg, Cobbett. *Reel Facts: The Movie Book of Records.* New York: Vintage Books, 1978.

Szanto, George H. *Theatre & Propaganda.* Austin: University of Texas Press, n.d.

Teichmann, Howard. *George S. Kaufman: An Intimate Portrait.* New York: Atheneum Books, 1972.

Thompson, Alan Reynolds. *The Anatomy of Drama.* 2nd ed. Berkeley and Los Angeles: University of California Press, 1946.

Triesch, Manfred, comp. *The Lillian Hellman Collection at the University of Texas.* Austin: The Humanities Research Center, the University of Texas, 1968.

Valgemae, Mardi. *Accelerated Grimace: Expression in the American Drama of the 1920s.* Carbondale: Southern Illinois University Press, 1972.

Walcutt, Charles Child. *American Literary Naturalism: A Divided Stream.* Minneapolis: The University of Minnesota Press,

1956.

Weales, Gerald. *Clifford Odets: Playwright.* New York: Pegasus, 1971.

Williams, Raymond. *Marxism and Literature.* New York: Oxford University Press, 1977.

—. *Modern Tragedy.* London: Chatto & Windus, 1966.

Wilson, Edmund. *Shores of Light: Literary Chronicle of the Twenties and Thirties.* New York: Farrar, Straus & Giroux, 1952.

Wimsatt, William K., and Cleanth Brooks. *Literary Criticism.* New York: Random House, 1957.